Love and Marriage in the Middle Ages

LOVE AND MARRIAGE IN THE MIDDLE AGES

Georges Duby

Translated by Jane Dunnett

The University of Chicago Press

GEORGES DUBY is professor of history at the College de France. His numerous works include *The Three Orders, The Age of the Cathedrals,* and *The Knight, The Lady and the Priest* all published by the University of Chicago Press.

First published in French as *Mâle moyen age* © Flamarion 1988.

The University of Chicago Press, Chicago 60637
Polity Press, Cambridge, England

Translation © 1994 by Polity Press and the University of Chicago
Chapter 2 © 1983 by Oxford University Press, New York
Chapter 3 © 1983 by Past and Present Society, Oxford
Chapter 12 © 1982 by R. L. Benson and G. Constable

First published by Polity Press and the University of Chicago Press 1994
Published with the assistance of the French Ministry of Culture
University of Chicago Press edition 1994
Printed in Great Britain
03 02 01 00 99 98 97 96 95 94   1 2 3 4 5
ISBN: 0-226-16773-9(cloth)

Library of Congress Cataloging-in-Publication Data
Duby, Georges.
    [Mâle Moyen Age. English]
    Love and marriage in the Middle Ages / Georges Duby : translated
by Jane Dunnett.
        p. cm.
    Translation of: Mâle Moyen Age.
    Reprints of essays first published 1967–1986.
    Includes bibliographical references (p.   ) and index.
    1. Marriage—France—History. 2. Family—France—History.
3. France—Social conditions—987–1615. 4. Marriage customs and
rites, Medieval. 5. Middle Ages.   I. Title.
HQ623.D83613 1994
306.8'0944—dc20   93–8306
                                                                CIP

This book is printed on acid-free paper.

Contents

Part III Cultures, Values and Society

Author's Note

This book contains a collection of essays, and each chapter takes stock, at successive stages, of work in progress. This has to be done from time to time, before venturing further. They are like the pages of a workshop notebook. They were written between 1967 and 1986 in a variety of circumstances: some for pleasure, the majority for those periodic meetings of historians where they confront the outcome of their research and exchange criticism and encouragement. The interest of these notes lies in the tentative but fruitful exploration of a little-known territory.

The Middle Ages were resolutely male. All the opinions that reach and inform me were held by men, convinced of the superiority of their sex. I hear only them. Nevertheless, I listen to them speaking here about desire, and consequently about women. Men were afraid of them and, to reassure themselves, despised them. But I have to make do with evidence such as this, distorted though it is by passion, prejudice and the rules of the game of courtly love. I propose to exploit it. My aim is to reveal the hidden part, the feminine. To find out what women were in those distant times, that is my present endeavour.

Sources and Acknowledgements

1 'Marriage in Early Medieval Society': translated from 'Le Mariage dans la société du haut Moyen Age', inaugural lecture given at the conference organized by the Italian Centre for Studies on the High Middle Ages, Spoleto, 22–8 April 1976 (extract).
2 'What do we Know about Love in Twelfth-Century France?': Zaharoff Lecture for 1982–3 (New York, Oxford University Press).
3 'The Matron and the Mismarried Woman': first published as 'The Matron and the Mis-married Woman: Perceptions of Marriage in Northern France circa 1100', in *Social Relations and Ideas: Essays in Honour of R. H. Hilton*, ed. T. H. Aston, P. R. Coss, Christopher Dyer and Joan Thirsk (Past and Present Publications, Cambridge University Press, 1983), pp. 89–103. World Copyright: The Past and Present Society, 175 Banbury Road, Oxford, England. Published here with the kind permission of the Past and Present Society.
4 'On Courtly Love': translated from 'A propos de l'amour que l'on dit courtois', Académie royale de langue et de littérature française, Brussels, 13 December 1986.
5 *Le Roman de la Rose*: translated from the Preface to *Le Roman de la Rose* (Paris, Club Français du Livre, 1976).
6 'Towards a History of Women in France and Spain': translated from 'Histoire des femmes en France et en Espagne. Conclusions d'un colloque', given at a conference entitled 'La condición de la mujer en la Edad Media' (Madrid, Universidad Complutense, 1986).

7 'Family Structures in the West during the Middle Ages': translated from 'Structures familiales dans le Moyen Age occidental', Twelfth International Conference on the Historical Sciences, Moscow, 16–23 August 1970.

8 'The Relationship between Aristocratic Family and State Structures in Eleventh-Century France': translated from 'Structures familiales aristocratiques en France du XIe siècle en rapport avec les structures de l'Etat', Proceedings of the conference on 'Europe in the Eleventh and Twelfth Centuries', Warsaw and Poznán, 1967.

9 'Philip Augustus's France: Social Changes in Aristocratic Circles': translated from 'La France de Philippe Auguste. Les transformations sociales en milieu aristocratique, 'Proceedings of the conference organized by the CNRS, Paris, 29 September to 4 October 1980 (extract).

10 'Problems and Methods in Cultural History': translated from 'Problèmes et méthodes en histoire culturelle', Proceedings of the Conference 'Objet et méthodes de l'histoire de la culture', Tihany, 10–14 October 1977.

11 'The History of Value Systems': translated from 'L'Histoire des systèmes de valeurs', *Studies in the Philosophy of History*, 11, no. 1 (1972) (Middletown, Conn., Wesleyan University Press).

12 'The Renaissance of the Twelfth Century: Audience and Patronage': first published as 'Audience and Patronage', in *Renaissance and Renewal in the Twelfth Century*, ed. R. L. Benson and G. Constable (Cambridge, Mass, Harvard University Press, 1982). Published here with the kind permission of R. L. Benson and G. Constable.

13 'Observations on Physical Pain in the Middle Ages': translated from 'Réflexions sur la douleur physique au Moyen Age', conference organized by the University of Warsaw, 1986, *Revue des sciences médicales*, 345 (1986).

14 'Memories without Historians': translated from 'Mémoires sans historien', *Nouvelle Revue de psychanalyse*, 15 (Spring 1977).

15 'Heresies and Societies in Preindustrial Europe between the Eleventh and Eighteenth Centuries': translated from 'Hérésies et sociétés dans l'Europe préindustrielle XI–XVIII siècles', Colloque de Royaumont (Paris and The Hague, 1968).

Translator's Acknowledgements

I am grateful to both Karen Fontanive and Professor Peter Newmark for commenting on parts of my translation.

Jane Dunnett

I

LOVE AND MARRIAGE

1

Marriage in Early Medieval Society

Like all living organisms, human societies have a basic impulse which compels them to perpetuate their existence and to reproduce themselves within stable structures. The permanent character of such structures within human societies is instituted jointly by nature and by nurture. For what matters is the reproduction not only of individuals but also of the cultural system which unites them and orders their relationships. To the dictates of the individual genetic code are therefore added the dictates of a collective code of behaviour, of a set of rules which also claim to be inviolable. These rules set out, firstly, to define the respective status of male and female, to distribute power and duties between the two sexes. Next they aim to control the chance events of birth, to replace the maternal line of descent – the only one that is self-evident – by the paternal filiation. Finally, they designate which among possible pairings are legitimate, that is to say those pairings which alone are considered capable of adequately ensuring the reproduction of the group – in short, rules whose object it is, naturally, to establish a couple, to make official the mingling together of the blood of two families, but more importantly to sanction the union not only of two individuals but also the joining of two social units, of two 'houses', so that a similar unit may be created. The cultural system I am describing is the system of kinship, the code I am describing is the code of marriage. Indeed, at the core of these regulating mechanisms which have a fundamental social function, lies marriage.

Regulation, officialization, control, codification: the institution of marriage is, by its very position and by the role which it assumes, enclosed in a rigid framework of rituals and prohibitions – rituals because it involves publishing, that is making public, and thereby socializing and legalizing a private act, and prohibitions because it involves setting boundaries between the norm and the marginal, the licit and the illicit, the pure and the impure. These rituals belong to the sphere of both the secular and the sacred. Through the sexual act or *copulatio*, the door opens on to the shadowy, mysterious and terrifying world of sexuality and pro-creation – in other words, the realm of the sacred. Marriage is therefore situated at the meeting point of two orders, the natural and the supernatural. In many societies, and notably in that of the early Middle Ages, marriage is governed by two distinct powers, partly combined and partly in competition, by two regulat-ory systems not always acting in accord, but both seeking to confine marriage strictly within law and ceremony.

The rigidity of this legal and liturgical exterior, the liveliness of the commentaries which it inspired and the development of ideological reflections justifying its rigours, mean that the insti-tution of marriage lends itself far better than many social facts to study by historians of medieval Christianity. They can understand it from a very early date through texts which are explicit. But this advantage has a drawback. The position of medievalists is far less assured than that of ethnologists analysing exotic societies, and even of writers on ancient history, since the culture which they are studying is to a large extent their own; it is hard for them to distance themselves sufficiently from this culture; despite themselves they remain prisoners of a ritual and of a value system which are not fundamentally different from those which they are studying and would like to demythologize; but they can easily discern only the exterior, its outer, public, formal appearance. Everything, or almost everything contained within this shell, all the private, lived experience, escapes them.

It therefore seems methodologically essential to me to highlight very clearly the two dangers which threaten our attempts at eluci-dation, the two diversions which the nature of the sources may present in the course of our research if we do not proceed cau-tiously. The historian would be making the first of these errors of perspective if he did indeed confine himself to prescriptive statements, the terms of regulations and the formulae of legal documents, if he relied on what the words say and if he believed that they effectively governed people's behaviour. It should always be borne in mind that any prescription of law or morality forms only one element of an ideological construct erected to justify certain actions, and to some extent to disguise them, and that beneath this cover, in the realm of conscience, all rules are to some extent transgressed.

The historian, like the sociologist but with far greater difficulty, must apply himself to marking out the extent of the margin between theory and practice. Moreover, the screen formed by these rules can be more insidiously misleading. Take, for example, those records of gifts or sales where, in the course of the twelfth century, in certain provinces there was increasingly frequent reference to the wife alongside her husband. Should one interpret this as the sign of an actual advance for women, of a loosening of the hold exercised by men in the home – in short, of the gradual triumph of the principle of the equality of husband and wife which the Church, even at that time, was endeavouring to have accepted? Should one not, rather, consider that, since it involved rights over possessions and inheritance, the wife was required to act, not so much because of what she had but because of what she guaranteed and handed down, and that the slow withdrawal of the husband's monopoly increased the rights of the males of his lineage and of his progeny over the fortune of the couple above her own? As regards the second illusion, the historian would succumb to it if he adopted unreservedly the point of view of the clerics who wrote more or less all the accounts which are available to us, if he were involuntarily to share their pessimism or their optimism, to take at face value what these men – the majority of whom were celibate or professed to be – said about the realities of married life.

The two dangers which I have set out are serious. They have slowed down, and still do, the progress of research. This is why I stress the need to cut through the thick, opaque layer of moralizing which completely envelops our evidence. Since marriage is a social act, probably the most important of all social acts, and since it is a part of social history, I believe it would be detrimental to the success of research if a value system and its mode of production, its ideological presentation and underlying material foundations, were not examined in their entirety. The task is certainly a difficult one; however, it is facilitated by at least two circumstances.

In the period which concerns us, we are not limited to prescriptive writings. Marriage is mentioned in other documents which rapidly increased after the year 1000. There were stories and chronicles, countless narratives which, of course, do not say a great deal, but what they do say is at least concrete and not too distorted. In addition, there is the whole literature of court entertainment, even though it is as misleading as ecclesiastical discourse; it, too, is a prisoner of ideology, but of a different ideology, a rival one, and this makes it possible to see things from a different angle and so, at times, to make the necessary corrections.

Our period also saw the development in the West of sometimes bitter phases of a conflict between two powers, a confrontation which is best expressed in Gelasian terms. On one side, there was the secular power supported by the 'laws', the might of those whose task it was to promulgate these laws and to have them obeyed in conventional patterns of behaviour. This power rested also on the relations of production. This means that, in all probability, the history of marriage is not the same at different levels of the social hierarchy, that is to say, at the level of the masters and of those exploited by them. On the other side there was the spiritual power, whose authority was implemented and supported by the tireless endeavours of the priests to place marriage within the framework with which they sought to control all moral behaviour and to locate marriage properly within it. It was precisely this duality, the alternation between rivalry and shared aims, that stimulated the process of reflection and the efforts to regulate. At the same time it gave rise (despite the fact that those who were writing during that period belonged to the Church) to a diversity of insights. Even if one limits oneself to superficial observation, to what is merely a dogmatic, ritualistic, statutory framework, these allow a clearer perception of what constitutes the object of our research.

In this age-long contest, the spiritual power tended to gain the advantage over the secular. It was a period when the institution of marriage gradually became Christianized. Resistance to this acculturation weakened imperceptibly, or rather was compelled to entrench itself in new positions, to establish itself firmly so as to prepare for further counter-offensives. This is the chronological framework. I will merely add, very subjectively, some partial and unconnected observations, some of which may help to focus the debate, but which I regard as no more than signposts.

Let us therefore first set side by side the two framing systems which, because of their aims, were almost entirely alien to one another. There was the lay model which, in this ruralized society, where each unit was rooted in landed inheritance, had the role of preserving through the generations the continuity of a mode of production. In contrast, there was an ecclesiastical model whose timeless aim was to check the impulses of the flesh, that is to say to repress evil by containing sexual excess within strict boundaries.

Maintaining the 'status' of a house from one generation to another was a necessity which determined the entire structure of the first of these two models. In different degrees, according to various regions and ethnic groups, Roman and barbarian traditions together formed the raw materials; at any rate, this model formed the basis for the notion of inheritance. Its role was to ensure that a stock of possessions, reputation and honour was handed down intact, and to guarantee the lineage a position, a 'rank', which was at least equal to that enjoyed by previous generations. Consequently all those responsible for the future of the family, that is to say all the males who had some claim to the inheritance, and at their head, the senior member whom they advised and who spoke in their name, believed that it was their first right and duty to marry off their children, and to marry them off well. This meant giving away their daughters and negotiating as best they could their daughters' reproductive potential and the advantages with which they were supposed to endow their offspring. It also meant helping a son to find a wife – to find her elsewhere, in another family, to bring her into his family, where she would cease to depend on her father, brothers and uncles, and would instead be subject to her husband, whilst condemned always to remain a stranger, always a little under suspicion of secret betrayal in the bed to which she had gained admittance, and where she was to fulfil her primary function, that of providing children to the group of men who received, dominated and kept watch over her.

In these children were united what she brought with her and what they received from their father – the hope of two lines of succession and reverence for these two ancestral lines which provided the names given to each child, according to rules which I am attempting to reformulate. The positions which they would hold in the world, the opportunities which they, in turn, would have to make a good marriage, depended on the clauses of the contract entered into when their parents were married. We can accordingly understand the importance of the agreement and see that it represented the culmination of long and tortuous negotiations, in which all the members of each household were involved. It constituted a long-term and provident strategy, which explains why the arrangement between the two families and the exchange of promises often took place far ahead of the time when the marriage was consummated. It was a strategy which required the greatest circumspection since it aimed to avoid, by means of subsequent compensations, the risk of impoverishment which, in an agrarian society, lineages ran as soon as they became prolific.

There were, it seems, three main attitudes which guided the negotiations which preceded any marriage. There was a propensity, whether conscious or unconscious, towards endogamy, towards choosing wives from amongst cousins, descendants of the same ancestor, heirs to the same inheritance, with whom the matrimonial tie thus tended to bring together its scattered fragments rather than dividing them further. Prudence operated, so that only moderate numbers of offspring were produced, and this limited the number of married couples, thereby keeping a sizeable proportion of offspring unmarried. Finally, there was cunning in the subterfuge employed in the bargaining, care taken to obtain guarantees to protect personal interests and concern on both sides to balance the concessions agreed by the anticipated advantages.

At the end of these interminable discussions there were public words and gestures, a ceremonial which was itself split in two. First there was the marriage, in other words a ritual of faith and pledge, verbal promises, a show of disinvestment and of assumption of possession, the handing over of pledges, the ring, the deposit, the coins, and finally the contract which – in the provinces where the practice of writing had not entirely disappeared – custom dictated must be drawn up. Then there was the wedding, which was the ritual of the couple setting up house. Bread and wine were shared by bride and bridegroom, and the married couple's first meal was inevitably a great banquet; the bridal procession led the newly wed woman to her new home. That same night, in the darkened room, the deflowering took place in the bed; and then in the morning, there was the present expressing the gratitude and hope of the man whose dream it was already to have embarked upon his legitimate paternal role by impregnating his wife.

All these rituals were obviously surrounded by a code of ethics, and I would like to concentrate on three of its principles.

This society was not strictly monogamous. To be sure, it allowed only one wife at a time, but it did not deny the husband, or rather his family group, the power to break the marriage at will, to dismiss his wife so that he could seek another, and to this end start the hunt for a good match again. All the marriage vows (the *sponsalicium*, the *dotalicium*) had among other objectives that of protecting the material interests of the repudiated wife and her lineage.

The area of male sexuality, and by that I mean lawful sexuality, was not at all limited to marriage. Accepted morality, the morality which each individual pretended to respect, did indeed require that the husband content himself with his wife, but did not prevent him from having other women either before marriage, during what, in the twelfth century, was called 'youth', or after marriage, during his widowerhood. There is much evidence that men made extensive and very conspicuous use of mistresses and of prostitution, and enjoyed amorous adventures with the servants, as also of the exaltation of male prowess in the value system.

On the other hand, in girls what was exalted, and what a whole series of related restrictions carefully sought to guarantee, was virginity, and in wives what was praised was constancy. The natural depravity of women, those perverse creatures, would be liable, if there was not vigilance, to introduce into kinship with the heirs to the ancestral fortune intruders, born of another blood, whose seed had been secretly sown – those same illegitimate children whom the unmarried men of the lineage blithely and generously placed outside the house or within the ranks of their servants.

The morality which I have outlined applied to the family. It was private. The penalties which ensured that it was observed were also private: vengeance for an abduction fell within the province of the girl's male relatives, whilst revenge for an adulterous act was the responsibility of the husband and his blood relatives. But since people were at liberty to appeal to Assemblies of the Peace and to the prince, abduction and adultery were therefore provided for in secular law codes.

We know far more about the model proposed by the Church, as there are a large number of documents and studies on this subject. It should suffice to highlight five of its features.

The whole ascetic, monastic side of the Christian Church, everything that led it to disdain and reject the world, as well as everything that, in the cultural baggage which it inherited from Rome, related its thinking to the philosophies of antiquity, led the Church to condemn marriage. It was criticized as a blemish, a source of disturbance for the soul, an obstacle to contemplation, on the basis of scriptural arguments and references, most of which were already collected in St Jerome's *Adversus Jovinianum*.

However, since humans unfortunately do not reproduce like bees but have to copulate in order to reproduce, and since amongst the traps laid by the devil there is none worse than the excessive use of the sexual organs, the Church accepted marriage as a lesser evil. It adopted and instituted marriage – all the more easily because it was accepted, adopted and established by Jesus – but on condition that it should serve to control sexuality, to fight effectively against fornication.

To this end, the Church first offered a moral code for a good married life. The intention was to attempt to purge marriage of its two major corruptions, namely the filth inherent in carnal pleasure and the frenzy of the impassioned soul, of that wild Tristan-like love which the *Penitentials* sought to stifle when they banished love potions and other bewitching drinks. When they were married, the couple's one thought was to be procreation. If they were to abandon themselves and to take pleasure in their union, they would at once be 'defiled', for, in the words of Gregory

the Great, 'they are transgressing the law of marriage.'[1] Even if
they were cold as stone, they still had to purify themselves if they
wished to receive the sacrament afterwards. They had to abstain
from all carnal intercourse during holy periods or God would take
vengeance. Gregory of Tours warned his audience that monsters,
cripples and all sickly children were conceived on Sunday nights.[2]

As regards the social practice of marriage, the Church set out
to correct lay customs in a number of matters. In so doing, the
Church visibly shifted the boundaries between the lawful and the
unlawful, increasing freedom in some areas and limiting it in
others. The clergy therefore sought to tone down the act by which
a marriage became sacramentally complete, since their loathing
of the flesh prompted them to shift the emphasis to commitment,
to agreement (*consensus*), to that spiritual exchange in the name of
which, according to St Paul, marriage could become a symbol of
the union between Christ and his Church. They were thus forced
down a path which enabled the individual to be freed from family
constraints, and made the plighting of troth a matter for personal
choice; it was a path which also led, since it was asserted that
the social position of individuals should in no way impede affective
relationships, to legitimizing the marriage of the unfree and to
liberating them from all seigneurial control. Conversely, the
Church tightened its control when, in its attempt to impose absolute monogamy, it condemned repudiation and remarriage, and
exalted the *ordo* of widows, as when it sought to establish a disproportionately broad definition of incest and introduced further
restrictions on marriages between blood relatives and those related
by marriage.

Finally, the priests gradually played a greater role in the marriage ceremonial, making the rituals sacred, especially the wedding
rituals, and surrounding the bridal bed with set phrases and
gestures which were designed to ward off the devil and keep the
couple in chastity.

In the very long history of the progressive and incomplete integration of the ecclesiastical into the secular model, the ninth
century stands out as a decisive period. This is partly because the
revival of writing lifts the veil which till then almost entirely
conceals social facts from the historian. But it is mainly because

that period, in the area of Europe which was under Carolingian
domination, experienced a sort of co-operation, centred on the
anointed king, between civil power and ecclesiastical authority,
which for a while combined their efforts to construct, for the use
of the Christian people, a social morality less remote from the
injunctions of Scripture. This task involved above all reflection
on concrete exemplary cases which occurred in the matrimonial
affairs of the Empire's highest aristocracy and brought into play
what we would refer to as politics. The specific task of the *oratores*,
that is to say bishops, was to study the mystery of marriage
(*nuptiale mysterium*) so as better to guide their flock. They applied
the wisdom (*sapientia*) with which their consecration had imbued
them to the conceptual development of patristic material. In so
doing they set out to construct a theory of marriage for purely
pastoral and practical purposes. At the same time, the work
involved codification in that wider domain where, under the gaze
of the sovereign who presided over the general sessions of court
and council, the secular and the sacred were more closely inter-
twined than ever before. Indeed, by that time marriage was
regarded as coming under both the authority (*auctoritas*) of the
prelates and the power (*potestas*) of the princes, and a system of
sanctions of which the two associated authorities – as Hincmar
says expressly with reference to the abduction of Judith – were
the driving forces in the hierarchy.[3]

Thus, from this alliance, there originated, almost complete, that
normative construct which, as I have mentioned above, must not
be considered in isolation, but which none the less is worth looking
at quite closely during the period when it suddenly emerged from
the Dark Ages. It consisted of precepts and exhortations to better
conduct, thereby offering a model of Christian life for married
couples (*conjugati*) whom the conception of the *ordines*, or orders,
relegated to the lowest level of a ternary hierarchy of perfection.
This hierarchy exalted first virginity and then continence, but it
at least promised salvation to married couples whilst it was denied
to others, to the fornicators who were cast out into darkness
because they rejected the exclusive constraints of a conjugal sexuality which was indissoluble and chaste. To these admonitions
were added rules instituted to maintain the social order, to prevent
and allay the discord which could arise out of the institution of

marriage. It was the role of kings and princes to promulgate these rules and to ensure that they were obeyed, as well as to protect through their solicitude the widow and the orphan, those two victims of the chance break-up of a marriage. It is worth noting that the capitularies and canons legislated above all for cases of abduction and confined themselves in the main to what touched on the secular in marriage.

The one exception was incest. On this point alone, where the sovereign diligently prohibits what the law of the Lord prohibits,[4] the ecclesiastical model came to take its place in the system of public prohibitions and sanctions. This point is of paramount importance. To ensure that no one 'dare to sully himself or sully others by an incestuous wedding'[5] entailed that all weddings (*nuptiae*) 'whether or not they were between members of the nobility',[6] should be public, and that they should be neither outside their proper rank (*inexordinatae*) nor unexamined (*inexaminatae*), and that consequently the degree to which husband and wife were related by blood should be ascertained prior to marriage.[7] The event was thus made public and inquiries carried out – 'relatives', 'neighbours' and 'elders of the people' (*veteres populi*) were questioned – but the priest and bishop were consulted first, called upon in this way legally to perform the wedding ceremonies. They were there not only to give their blessing and to exorcize, not only to moralize, but also to discipline and to authorize. They were there to judge, and therefore to govern.

Let me, however, insist even more on the following period, on the tenth, eleventh and twelfth centuries. I wish to do so not only because I am more familiar with this period, but also because I believe that the principal turning point in the social history of European marriage took place then. In addition, more varied documentation makes it possible to cover the field from that time almost in its entirety, and thus to put the issues more rigorously. I will illustrate this with some final observations – also unduly cursory and subjective – which can be divided into three sections.

Firstly I wish to stress the importance of taking into account the changes which imperceptibly affected the strategy of marriage in aristocratic society. Kinship structures in that milieu seem to have undergone a transformation during the period in question, through the slow popularization of the royal model, that is to say the lineal model, which favoured succession by male primogeniture. This trend was simply one aspect of the general shift through which the monarch's power to command disintegrated and was gradually demolished; royal virtues, duties and attributes were disseminated and passed into countless hands, down to the lowest degree of nobility.

As regards marriage, it determined a number of changes of attitude within the family which were not without consequence. Since inherited wealth increasingly began to resemble a lordship, and since, in the manner of the old *honores* or fiefs, it became more and more difficult for it to be divided up and placed under the authority of a woman, at first there was a tendency to exclude married daughters from sharing the inheritance by providing them with a dowry. This encouraged noble families to marry off all their daughters if they could. Moreover, this increased the importance of the dowry – which ideally consisted of personal property and, as soon as this was feasible, of money – in relation to what the husband offered. It also meant that the morning gifts given by the husband to his wife after consummation (the *sponsalicium*, the *antefactum* and the *morgengabe*) were succeeded by the dower.

This change was widespread. It can be followed in detail in one of the best available studies on the practice of marriage, in the specific context of twelfth-century Genoese aristocracy.[8] Fear of dividing up the inheritance and a sustained reluctance to affirm birthright conversely reinforced obstacles to the marriage of boys and made the twelfth century in northern France the age of *juvenes* – unmarried knights, turned out of the paternal home, gallivanting about, fantasizing about the various stages in their adventurous quest to find maidens who, as they put it, would rouse them (*tastonnent*)[9] but above all, anxiously and nearly always vainly, in search of a situation which would at last allow them to accede to the status of *senior*, a wealthy heiress, a house which would receive them and where, as is still said today in some rural areas of France, they could *faire gendre* ('become son-in-law'). The attempt to marry off all the daughters and to ensure that all sons except the eldest remained unmarried naturally meant that the supply of women tended greatly to surpass demand in what one might be tempted to call the marriage market; consequently, the likelihood of finding a better match for the young men of noble families increased. A structure of noble societies was thus reinforced in which, generally speaking, the bride came from a wealthier and more illustrious family background than her husband. This affected behaviour and attitudes, and strengthened, for example, that pride in the specific 'nobility' of the maternal ancestry attested in so much genealogical literature.[10] Finally, these circumstances explain why, at marriage ceremonies during the twelfth century, the lord increasingly interceded with the parents and sometimes his decision prevailed over theirs. He felt it was his duty to supply wives for his knights, the sons of his 'friends', whom he had fed in his household – that unruly band which accompanied his eldest son as he went from tournament to tournament. He felt it was his duty – and his right since his own interest was at stake – to provide the daughters of a deceased vassal with a dowry, or else to arrange marriages as he pleased, for the good of the fief, for the widows and orphans of his feudal tenants.

As regards marital practices, changes during that period can be perceived only in the upper reaches of society. But it is probable that there were also changes, although not necessarily similar ones, at the lowest level of the social scale. Indeed, it would be fruitful for research to be carried out into seigneurial customs, tenurial status and the right to marry outside one's rank. At any rate, such alterations – which were determined by changes in wealth, in landed property, in the power to command, in the circulation of money, in short, in the relations of production – cannot be ignored by anyone who wishes to understand and to put into context the far more visible changes which, during the eleventh and twelfth centuries, affected the body of ideological proclamations and rules.

If, after the year 1000, in its sustained attempt to reform itself, to cease in part its collusion with secular authority, to set itself up as the supreme magistrature, the Church intensified its effort to examine and to regulate marriage, it was because this activity was closely linked with a struggle in which, at that time, it was engaged on two fronts. First, it was pitted against the doctrine of Nicolaism, the reluctance of the clergy to free themselves from conjugal ties and their claim also to the right to make use of marriage as a refuge from and remedy for fornication. In this struggle the ecclesiastical authorities found support in a strong current of lay opinion which refused to accept that the priest, the man who consecrates the host, should possess a woman, that his sanctifying hands should be sullied by what seemed – and not only to Church theorists – the supreme impurity which separated men most sharply from the sacred.

The second struggle was against an extreme form of asceticism, the conviction that all carnal relationships were fornication, which led to a radical rejection of marriage. This danger, too, was present within the ecclesiastical establishment, on its monastic side, although the slow retreat of monasticism during the twelfth century tended to lessen it. However, it was largely present in the more extreme sections of reform movements, many of which opposed the Church, and in the mass of sects which considered procreation an expression of evil. The first upsurge occurred during the second quarter of the eleventh century, and extended from Orléans and Arras as far as Monteforte. The second upsurge, which took place after 1130, was more virulent and relentless, and increased the number of people who believed, if we are to credit Raoul Ardent, 'that it is as great a crime to possess one's wife as it is to possess one's mother or one's daughter',[11] people who surged into those mixed communities where abstinence was practised. Such places were described as dens of iniquity in the gossip which was complacently spread amongst the orthodox.

Faced with these two deviations, and in keeping with the moral mission of the Carolingian bishops, at the end of the eleventh century and throughout the twelfth century, the Church attempted to complete the integration of Christian marriage within the universal edicts of the earthly city. It did so by refining the theory of the *ordines* and by endeavouring to put it into practice – on this particular point I need only refer the reader to the admirable pages which documents from Latium inspired Pierre Toubert to write. It also proposed the married couple as the normal pattern for secular life, and subsequently completed the circle of rules and rituals by finally making marriage a religious institution, so that the place devoted to marriage in canonical collections and later in synodal statutes grew constantly. At the same time, after the end of the eleventh century, in both northern and southern France a new matrimonial liturgy slowly emerged. Through this liturgy the essential elements of a ritual which had hitherto been domestic and secular were transferred to the door of the church and inside it – by the completion at last of an ideology of Christian marriage. This, in its opposition to Catharism, rested in part on the justification of and removal of guilt from what is carnal.

It is appropriate here to follow carefully this train of thought, partly clandestine and partly condemned, which starts with Abelard and Bernard Sylvester. It started essentially as a notable attempt to spiritualize marriage. Its various aspects are well known, from the development of the Marian cult which led to the Virgin mother becoming the symbol of the Church, that is to say the Bride; to the development of the nuptial theme in mystical literature; and to the relentless examination of texts and their glosses, in order to establish marriage as one of the seven sacraments. In the process, the work of both the canonists and the commentators on the divine page (*divina pagina*) resulted in their basing marriage on mutual consent – or rather on the two successive commitments, first distinguished by Anselm of Laon, namely future agreement (*consensus de futuro*) and present agreement (*consensus de presenti*).[12] For Hugh of St Victor, followed by Peter Lombard, it was the verbal pledge (*obligatio verborum*) that established marriage. Naturally, this was a means of further separating spiritual love from sexuality, and even, as Gratian did, of returning to the rigours of St Jerome. But it also allowed Hugh of St Victor to speak of love as the *sacramentum* of marriage, and to assert openly in his 'Letter concerning Mary's Virginity' – now fully espousing the spirit of the twelfth century and its exaltation of personal responsibility – that man takes a wife 'so as to be united with her in a unique and extraordinary way in shared love'.[13]

Finally, this whole development, which is widely known and of which the Church leaders were the instigators, should be seen in the light of what it is possible to learn about secular thought at that time. Admittedly one can learn very little from the scattered pieces of information which come late and scarcely shed light on the twelfth century or the attitudes of its ruling classes. Nevertheless, it is worth examining these few pieces of evidence. Four main points emerge.

There was a narrow, but appreciable, divergence between the model prescribed by the Church and actual practice. Ceremonies provide an example of this. The 'History of the Counts of Guînes' (*Historia cǫmitum Ghisnensium*), written right at the beginning of the thirteenth century by the priest Lambert of Ardres, contains one of the few precise descriptions of a wedding. The marriage of Arnulf, the eldest son of the Count of Guînes, took place in 1194.[14] There is a perfect correspondence between the overall picture that emerges from the prescriptive sources and the marriage procedure which was divided into two distinct stages, *desponsatio* and *nuptiae*. After long years of 'youth', of fruitless quests and disappointments, Arnulf at last finds the heiress, the sole and most lawful heiress (*unicam et justissimam heredem*) of a castellany which adjoined the small principality to which he was heir – this was her most salient characteristic. The count, Arnulf's father, began lengthy negotiations with the four brothers (who jointly controlled her inheritance) and broke off an earlier betrothal which promised his son a less profitable alliance. He obtained the approval of the prelates, of the bishop of Thérouanne and of the archbishop of Reims, the official lifting of the excommunication which had been placed on his son for robbing a widow, and finally arranged the *dos*, that is the level of the dower. This was the first decisive stage which was sufficient to finalize the legal marriage (*legitimum matrimonium*).

All that remained was the wedding. This took place in Ardres, in the house of the new couple. 'At the beginning of the night, when the bride and bridegroom were together in the same bed', Lambert relates, 'the count summoned us – that is, another priest, my two sons and myself.' (In 1194 the priest Lambert was a married man and two of his sons were priests, an indication of the gulf between rules and their application.) The count ordered that the newly married couple be duly sprinkled with holy water, the bed censed, the couple blessed and entrusted to God – all this according to the strict observance of ecclesiastical injunctions. The last to speak, the count in his turn invoked the God who blessed Abraham and his seed, and called down his blessing on the couple 'so that they might live in his divine love, continue in harmony and so that their offspring would increase in the fullness of time for ever and ever'. This formula was indeed that propounded by twelfth-century rituals in this area of Christianity. The significant point is that it was the father who pronounced it, that the father, rather than the priest, was the principal officiant.

The second main point relates to the influence on secular literature of an anti-matrimonial attitude which was expressed at the same time in some ecclesiastical writings, such as the *Policraticus*, where it is apparent that for John of Salisbury marriage with the most chaste of brides can only be a last resort, hardly worthy of consideration. One should, of course, remember that the poems, songs and romances written in the language of the courts never provided more than a decorative backdrop for a social game whose rules were at that time being formulated; this game served as derisory compensation for the frustrations of knights forced into living unmarried by the constraints of the inheritance system. The game revolved around the most daring of adventures since, transgressing all prohibitions and braving the most cruel revenge, it consisted of winning the lord's wife, the lady, in spite of the jealousy of other men. This clearly represented an assertion (similar to that made by Héloïse in the *Historia calamitatum*) of the superiority of free love, which was viewed as less continuously lascivious, less 'adulterous' than the ardour of husbands who were too enamoured of their wives.

The perspective which this literature fostered resulted, on a totally different level and context, in the same spiritualization and liberation of marriage towards which the Doctors of the Church were striving at that time. To exalt a love that was less dependent on material considerations, a union with a similar symbol, a ring (but one that was worn, according to Andreas Capellanus, on the little finger of the left hand, the finger which becomes least soiled); to claim the right to choose in the face of all social pressures – this came close to the demand by the ecclesiastical authorities that *consensus* or agreement triumph over all the ploys and cunning tricks of family strategies. The love based on choice which courtly lyrics described also claimed to unite first and foremost two beings rather than two families, two legacies, two networks of interest. Henri de Lausanne, the monk hunted down as a heretic because he wanted to free the institution of marriage from all the restrictions imposed upon it by conciliar decrees, was preaching precisely the same thing at Le Mans in 1116 when he urged that questions of money should no longer affect marriages, and that instead they should be based exclusively on mutual consent.

After 1160 another prevalent feature in secular ideology expressed in courtly literature was the positive value set upon conjugal love. It is at the heart of *Erec et Enide* and indeed of all the surviving romances of Chrétien de Troyes, that is, his most popular works. The anti-feminist mood persisted – and in this area both lay and clerical thought converged once more – and was now transferred to the couple; it was motivated by fear of the wife and by the threefold anxiety that – as people felt and knew – she was at once inconstant, lustful and a witch. There was still considerable emphasis on respect for marriage and on the emotional riches which it fostered. Thus, although eulogistic literature readily acknowledged the licentiousness of its heroes as long as they remained unmarried, once they married, and their wives were living with them, there were references only to the love which they bore their wives. It was this affection which made Count Baldwin of Guînes break down when his companion died, after fifteen years of marriage and at least ten pregnancies. This hard, fiery man, who had spent most of his life on horseback, took to his bed for days on end. He no longer recognized anyone, and his doctors despaired of saving him.[15] He suffered from the same madness which afflicted Yvain when his wife rejected him; he remained thus, languishing for months, until he recovered, and set off restored to health, a sprightly widower once more in pursuit of young female servants.

My final point is, I believe, the most important. At that time (the last three decades of the twelfth century) there were signs that restrictions on the marriage of sons were beginning to be relaxed in aristocratic families. It was now no longer only the eldest son who was allowed to marry. The other sons were married off and homes prepared for them; here branches would take root, separated from the old trunk which the prudence of the nobility had maintained unramified for at least two centuries, planted alone at the centre of the inheritance. In order to confirm this view, more research should be carried out and precise genealogies reconstructed; archaeologists should be consulted, for they too can see evidence of new fortified manors growing up beside the old castles from this date onwards. In addition, one should question the reasons for this relaxation; they should be sought partly in economic growth, in the increased affluence which spread throughout the nobility from the principalities whose resources were multiplied because of changes in the fiscal system, and partly in all the subtle changes which imperceptibly altered mental attitudes. The paths of exploration are wide open, especially in the field of the sociology of medieval marriage, an area still shrouded in mystery. To the extent that this darkness is lessened, light will then be shed on what we already know better, though still imperfectly: law, morality and the opacity of the normative structures surrounding them.

2

What do we Know about Love in Twelfth-Century France?

I shall not be speaking about the love of God, and yet, how not to speak of it when so many reasons, compelling ones, ought to force us to start there? Indeed, within the development of European culture, there was a shift, or rather a decisive turning point, in the way that men regarded the feeling we call love, and we historians can perceive it first in the writings of churchmen.

It was in northern France at the start of the twelfth century that some men were pondering over the affective relationship between the Creator and his creatures – in the cathedral school of Paris, at Saint-Victor, at Clairvaux and in other Cistercian monasteries, and from there this interest soon spread to England. These men were caught up in a renaissance movement which encouraged them to read avidly the great works of classical Latin; they, too, were involved in the progressive internalization of Christianity, and in the repercussions of the Crusades; they, too, were drawn into the recent sustained attention paid to the teachings of the New Testament. For these men soon turned away from a self-centred conception of love, that of patristic tradition, of Augustine and Pseudo-Dionysius, to picturing it – inspired by Cicero and his model of *amicitia* – as a voluntary leap out of 'self', forgetful of 'self' and disinterested, leading, through a gradated process of self-purification, to fusion in the other. On the one hand, the fruits of these reflections did not remain enclosed within the cloisters and cathedral schools. They were disseminated throughout aristocratic society, initially through the osmosis created by the close domestic fellowship that existed between clergy and laity in the households of the nobility, where the two orders, clerics and knights, inter-mingled. Later on, in the course of the twelfth century, they reached the ordinary people, the faithful, through the progress of pastoral work and a determined effort to educate by means of exhortation and preaching. (Many of the texts dwelling on the development of the love which the Christian is called upon to evince for his God were written to serve that very purpose, namely to educate.)

On the other hand – and this is what counts most here – this meditation by theologians and moralists on *caritas* tended very quickly and naturally, merely through the operation of metaphors found in the Scriptures, to develop into a meditation on marriage, on the nature and the quality of the affective relationship of the married couple.

But I shall not be speaking about the love of God, and for a good reason. I am not a historian of theology or morality, and other people, more qualified than I, have already discussed it at length after scrutinizing all the texts. I am a historian of feudal society. I try to understand how this society functioned, and to this end I analyse behaviour and the mental attitudes governing this behaviour. From the outset I must clearly define the scope of my research, the first results of which I am presenting here. I am not concerned with charting the evolution of love as a mere history of feelings, passions and 'mentalities', which would be independent, isolated from the history of the other components of social education, disembodied, so to speak. On the contrary, I am concerned with placing this evolution in the material context of social relationships and daily life. Indeed, the prominence which these twelfth-century religious thinkers whom I have just mentioned gave to the Incarnation should be enough reason for me to do so. This research is the natural development of my recent study of the institution of marriage. It serves as a prelude to the exploration of a relatively unknown area into which I am venturing cautiously when I pose the problem of the condition of women in the society which we call feudal. In consequence, I shall discuss the love which has women as its object, and the love which women themselves feel, in its rightful place, in the most fundamental unit of the social structure, that is in marriage. My specific question is: what do we know about love between spouses in twelfth-century France?

We know nothing, and I doubt if we will ever know anything, about the vast majority of marriages. In northern France, during that period of history, the married life of ordinary people went entirely unobserved. The rare insights which we have all concern the upper echelons of society, people in high places, the rich, the highest reaches of the aristocracy and the princes. These were the ones who were talked about. They paid, and they paid highly, to be talked about, for someone to sing their praises and to denigrate their enemies. They were all married, of necessity since the continuation of their family line depended upon them. As a result, beside them the outlines of a few wives emerge from the shadows. In places, there is an occasional reference to the feelings that bound couples.

These accounts – the best are to found in the genealogical and dynastic literature which flourished in this region during the second half of the twelfth century – all limit themselves to what convention then dictated could be expressed. The accounts remain superficial and show only the façade, the posturing. When the tone is aggressive, directed against rival powers, the husband who is to be discredited is first referred to as deceived, and people mock him. He is also referred to, in the Latin of those texts which are all written in the language of the educated classes, as *uxorius*, that is to say, in thrall to his wife, emasculated, deprived of his necessary pre-eminence. This weakness is denounced as a consequence of *puerilitas*, immaturity. For the man who takes a wife, whatever her age, must act as a *senior* and keep this woman in check, under his close control. Conversely, when the discourse extols the hero, in other words the patron or his ancestors, when it is laudatory, the author takes care not to mention disagreements; he stresses the perfect *dilectio*, that condescending feeling which masters must show towards those they protect and which the husband displays towards his wife, who is always beautiful, always noble, and whom he has deflowered. If he is widowed he is depicted, like Count Baldwin II of Guînes, as sick with grief and inconsolable. A veil is thus drawn over the truth of people's attitudes, for the ideology expressed by this kind of text acts as a screen. It was an ideology which gained ground amongst the nobility during the twelfth century, and coincided, at certain critical points, with the ideology of the clergy.

Firstly, this agreement was based on the principle, obstinately asserted, that women were weak creatures who had necessarily to be subjugated because they were naturally depraved, that they were destined to serve men in marriage, and that men had a legitimate right to make use of them. Secondly, there was the associated idea that marriage was the bedrock of the social order, that this order was based on a relationship of inequality, on that exchange of love and of respect which is not dissimilar to what was referred to, in the Latin of the scholastics, as *caritas*.

When, however, in looking for other, more explicit clues about marriage, one attempts to go beyond appearances, to pierce the outer veneer of ostentation and to reveal genuine attitudes, then one can see that the display of *caritas* within marriage was, at that time, hindered by substantial obstacles. I have divided these into two categories.

The most serious obstacles resulted from the conditions which brought people together as couples. It is clear that in this social milieu all marriages were arranged. It was men that spoke to one another, either fathers or men in paternal positions, such as the lord of the domain in the case of widows or the orphaned daughters of a dead vassal. Often the interested party himself would speak, for instance the *juvenis*, the knight seeking to establish himself, not addressing the woman he wished to attract to his bed, but speaking instead to other men. Marriage was a serious matter and thus a male affair. Of course, since the middle of the twelfth century the Church had introduced into the upper ranks of the nobility the notion that the conjugal knot should be tied by mutual consent, and all the evidence, particularly genealogical literature, asserted this principle clearly – the woman who was being given, whom one man was giving in marriage to another, should have her say. Did she?

References to rebellious girls are certainly not lacking. But these bids for freedom were denounced as reprehensible when the girl refused to accept the man who had been chosen for her, and declared that she loved another, specifically invoking love, and the heavens were quick to punish her. Alternatively, this resistance was praised when it concerned another love, the love of God, when marriage was refused out of a desire for chastity. (The heads of families did not, however, appear to be inclined to respect this desire: the cruelty shown towards Guibert de Nogent's mother by her dead husband's family who wished to force her to remarry against her will was scarcely less harsh, if not less effective, than the cruelty displayed towards Christine, the recluse of St Albans.) Generally speaking women were in men's power. The strict rule was that girls should be given away at a very early age.

The *sponsalia*, the ceremony in which the agreement was concluded between the two families and mutual consent was expressed, took place extremely early, and if the girl was too young to speak, then a smile on her part was taken as a sufficient sign of her agreement. The wedding, too, was at a very young age. The moral code and custom of the day permitted that as early as the age of twelve a child could be taken from the cloistered world of women in her home, where she had been cocooned since her birth, led with great pomp to the marital bed, placed in the arms of a greybeard whom she had never seen before, or of an adolescent scarcely older than herself, who, ever since he himself had left the care of women in about his seventh year, had lived only to prepare himself for combat through physical exercise and the exaltation of male violence.

With so little real evidence to draw on for this study of the early history of love, the historian must take these practices into account and imagine the inevitable repercussions which they had on the emotional life of the married couple. Naturally, little is known about the first sexual encounter (despite the fact that this was a semi-public event). Although the documents are silent on this matter, some clues to its dire consequences can be discerned. For example, Pope Alexander granted dispensation to an inexperienced youth who, through his rough treatment, had irreparably damaged a young girl. He was thus able to take a new wife. More often than not, in the minds of husbands, desire (*amor*) was rapidly transformed into hatred (*odium*) on the marriage night (it is worth noting that the husband's emotional reaction is the only one which is taken into account). Given how little is revealed about such matters, it is surprising how many allusions there are to the impotence of young husbands and to the consequent fiascos. The greatest stir was that caused by the failure of Philip II of France to consummate his marriage with Ingeburg of Denmark.

Such deep scars were perhaps exceptional. Yet we should consider the couple's bedroom, that workshop at the heart of the aristocratic residence where the new link in the dynastic chain was forged, not as the setting for those banal idylls perpetuated by the current sudden and disturbing popularity of historical novels, but as a field of a battle, a duel whose fierceness was hardly conducive to the strengthening of intimate bonds between husband and wife based on concern for the partner and forgetfulness of self, that opening of the heart which is what *caritas*, or affection, means.

Obstacles of a different order were raised in all innocence by the ecclesiastical moralists themselves, a great many of whom were haunted by their fear of the female sex. In a period of increasing pastoral instruction, the priests endeavoured to comfort the female victims of unhappy marriages who must have been so numerous at that time and in that social milieu, women who were scarred, abandoned, repudiated, held up to ridicule, defeated. From the many letters of spiritual guidance which were addressed to married women, I have chosen one which dates from the end of the twelfth century. It came from the abbey of Perseigne, one of those Cistercian monasteries where an attempt was then being made to adapt a moral code for the use of the laity, and where edifying homilies were being refined for teams of preachers from the secular clergy. Abbot Adam, in this studiedly elegant letter, undertook to console and to guide the Comtesse du Perche. The countess, who undoubtedly wished to withdraw and to deny herself, was nevertheless uncertain, and asked herself what the duties of the married woman were, how far she should acquiesce in the demands of her husband, what exactly was the amount of her debt, or *debitum* – moralizing literature used this term of depressing legal dryness to define the foundations of conjugal affection (*affectus*). The abbot endeavoured to enlighten her troubled spirit. The soul and the body, he said, reside in the human being. God is the owner of both. In accordance with the law of marriage which he himself established, he granted to the husband (in the same way as a feudal tenure was granted, that is to say by handing over the use of the property while retaining ultimate ownership) the right which he held over the body of the wife. Thus the husband became the feudal tenant of the body and was authorized to use and exploit it, and make it bear fruit. But, Adam of Perseigne went on to say, God keeps the soul for himself alone: 'God does not allow the soul to pass into the possession of another.' In marriage, the individual therefore finds him or herself divided. The countess should not forget this: in reality, she had two husbands whom she must serve fairly – one who was invested with the right to use her body, and the other who was the absolute master of her soul. Between these two husbands there was no jealousy whatsoever, so long as the wife was careful to give each his due: 'It would be unjust to put the right of either to an inappropriate use.'

Let us be clear: it would be injustice, the denial of justice, if the wife, too deeply wounded, and incapable of overcoming her repugnance, withdrew and refused to give her body to her husband, thereby leaving her debt unsettled. (It is worth noting that at no time does Adam of Perseigne ever contemplate that the wife herself might make demands, that she too might be the feudal tenant of her husband's body, and in a position to insist on her due – and yet that is what canon law states.) But an injustice would also have been committed if, when she gave her body to her husband, she gave her soul too. Adam of Perseigne concluded this little moral treatise by saying that the countess had no right whatsoever to refuse to give herself to her husband. However, 'when your carnal husband becomes one with you, derive your own joy [this word was deliberately chosen and belonged to the vocabulary of marriage; in courtly language it was used to celebrate carnal pleasure] from remaining spiritually attached to your celestial husband.' In other words, she must act as if she were made of stone, without the slightest quiver of her soul.

But this letter, in the form in which it has come down to us, was not intended for private perusal only. It was written to be circulated, so that the message could be widely disseminated, as if it were a sermon, and so that it could teach all the princesses and ladies in their entourage – anxious either about their frigidity or their sexual impulses – how to love in marriage. Indeed, the faithful echo of this exhortation can be found in many texts, notably in those biographies of saintly women which proliferated at the end of the twelfth century out of a concern to correct the behaviour of the laity through the example of the virtues. Thus I have found the same idea, expressed in almost the same terms, in the *Vita* (*Life*) of St Ida of Herfeld, who likewise was 'careful [whilst having intercourse with her husband] to give to God his due, containing in its just measure her carnal love so that her mind [this is clearly a reference to the dichotomy between body and soul] was in no way soiled by a frivolous attachment'.

It would therefore seem that, in the minds of the ecclesiastics – whose influence was strengthened during the twelfth century through the slow diffusion of the practice of individual penance – as far as women, those fragile beings, were concerned, the voluntary leap of the soul out of itself (in other words, love as it was defined by religious thinkers) could lawfully be directed only towards God. Obviously, it was not possible for every girl to be consecrated, given over entirely to the divine lover. Clearly some had to be given up to men, but they had to remain faithful to that primary love, taking nothing away from it, and mindful not to give themselves entirely. Their duty was not to divide their love, but to divide themselves. Dissociation, splitting themselves in two – that was their fate: on the one hand (that side which was earthly, carnal and inferior) there was passive obedience; on the other, there was a leap to the heights, to passion – in short, love. Thus the self was divided in two in marriage, but only for the female partner. It was forbidden to imagine that, in the heavenly sphere, a man might have another companion to whom he remained, in the words of Adam of Perseigne, spiritually attached during the sexual act. For a man only ever has one wife. He had to take her as she was, frigid in the acquittal of her debt, and he was forbidden to arouse her.

Is it far-fetched to imagine that husbands were sometimes exasperated at feeling that between themselves and their wives there was the presence not of the heavenly husband, but of the priest? How many men – such as the one whom Guibert of Nogent wanted to convince his readers was mad – went about shouting, referring to their wives who were stubbornly impassive: 'The priests have planted a cross in this woman's loins'? Fortunately for our evidence some of the literate clergy expressed a different moral viewpoint, that of the courts. One such cleric was Gislebert, canon of Mons. I shall now turn to his account, which is exactly contemporary with that of Adam of Perseigne.

He was, in fact, a *curialis* (courtier), one of the increasing numbers of intellectuals whose talents were employed in the service of princes. Brought up since childhood in the household of the counts of Hainaut, he had been a scribe there and was close to Count Baldwin V, his friend. When the latter died in 1195 Gislebert, ousted by the companions of the new count, was forced to leave the court. After his departure, he began writing a chronicle about the principality in honour of his deceased patron. He endowed the count with every imaginable quality, praising him in particular for having married off his children so well. He had long been on good terms with the chief members of the house of Champagne; his son was to take a wife from that family as soon as he came of age (1185). Gislebert noted the age of the husband and wife: Baldwin (the future emperor of Constantinople) was thirteen years old and Marie was twelve. Then, in a single sentence, Gislebert described the behaviour of the newly-weds. He cast a cold and sharp eye over the couple, with the look of an administrator concerned with the practicalities of life. The way he expressed himself was critical, for Gislebert did not like Baldwin VI, who had forced him to leave his position. Let us look at what he says.

Firstly, he dwells on the subject of the youth of the husband and wife: she is referred to as 'very young' and he is described as 'a very young knight'. It was precisely because they were young that the life which they chose seemed strange, improper, even reprehensible. Indeed, Marie had shut herself away and withdrawn into a world of religious devotion, of prayer, night-time prayer, the prayer of enclosed nuns and recluses, a world of abstinence and fasting. She continued living as she had in the convent which was her home and which she had recently left, and imposed upon herself a self-discipline more suited to virgins or widows than to brides. Everyone found this retreat quite indecent, this refuge in which the newly wed girl decided to cocoon herself, a gesture of penitence, but also a defence against assaults which she found repugnant.

Her husband had not turned away from her – far from it. In the same sentence Gislebert showed that Baldwin had completely given himself over to love. This fine writer, author of the *Chronique de Hainaut*, deliberately chose not to mention *caritas* or spiritual love, but used the term *amor* (physical love) instead, for it was indeed that – a burning, urgent desire which according to courtly propriety befitted a *juvenis miles* (a young knight). It is important to clarify the meaning of this expression: at that time someone referred to as a 'youth' was a bachelor, a knight who was not yet married. Indeed, this desire was even more ardent since it was not satisfied. *Amor*, which is the issue here, was not fitting – and this is the point – for a man in possession of a wife. It seemed risible that, after his marriage, the young Baldwin should continue to behave like a bachelor, still full of desire for his wife, and that he should not satisfy this desire in the bridal bed, or that he should not transfer this desire elsewhere, that he should remain – as Gislebert emphasized – 'attached to one woman', his own wife who refused him. He then commented that such an attitude was almost unknown amongst men. Was this intended as praise? No, quite the opposite in fact. In the courtly milieu of which Gislebert was the accurate and lucid representative, an individual with such an opinion became the object not of admiration but of scandal, and even of derision. At Mons and Valenciennes, people laughed about this stripling who, by getting married, had joined the ranks of the *seniores* and who, right from the start, should have behaved like a *senior*; people laughed at him because he had respected his wife's wish to remain chaste, because he had not taken her by force; above all, people laughed at him because he did not transfer his desire elsewhere, because – the text which I am using stresses this – he was content 'with her alone'. In other words, he was an eccentric, a ridiculous man.

I said earlier that, in marriage, the woman was divided. It is now clear that the man was also split in two, but the way he was split in two was different; whatever desire, passion and love there was in men was not channelled, as female love must be, into sublimation, into spiritual feelings. He too escaped from the matrimonial yoke, but without leaving the earthly and carnal world. He turned away, towards courtly pastimes and the wide open spaces of frivolous leisure. These are the very words used by the author, in all probability male, of the letters ascribed to Héloïse: '*amorem conjugio libertatem vinculo preferebam*' (I preferred love to marriage and freedom to slavery). At any rate, marriage was not the place for what was then defined as love, since the husband and wife were forbidden to rush at each other in fierce ardour. This is precisely the meaning of a particular carved capital in the nave of the church of Civaux in Poitou: husband and wife are shown side by side, not looking at one another but staring out; she looks skyward, but where is his gaze fixed? Towards the *meretrix* (the harlot), or venal love, towards the *amica*, or free love, love as play.

This should not surprise us. Philippe Ariès and Jean-Louis Flandrin long ago pointed out that, in all societies except our own, the feeling which binds men and women cannot be the same within marriage as outside it. This is because the social order rests entirely on marriage and because marriage is an institution, a legal system which unites, alienates and imposes obligations ensuring the continuity of social structures, particularly the stability of power and wealth. It is not fitting that marriage should embrace frivolity, passion, fantasy and pleasure; when it starts to do so, the institution may well already have lost some of its functions and is tending to disintegrate. Seriousness and gravity are fitting in marriage. Montaigne said that in marriage – that 'religious and devout' attachment – pleasure should be 'restrained, serious and mingled with a touch of severity', and sensual delight should be 'cautious and conscientious'. Laclos – under the name of the Marquise de Merteuil – writes in Letter 104 of the *Liaisons dangereuses*: 'It is not that I disapprove of a gentle and honest sentiment embellishing the conjugal bond and softening in some way the duties which it imposes [the Marquise is writing to another woman]; but it is not the role of marriage to inspire such a feeling.' *Affectio* (affection) and *dilectio* (pleasure) were acceptable, but love was not. In the twelfth century all men, churchmen and courtiers alike, were agreed on that point.

Describing this dissociation, this outpouring of love outside the wedded couple, leads me to turn, in conclusion, to those rituals of aristocratic social life pertaining to the sentiment which specialists in medieval literature have termed courtly love. So far I have not mentioned courtly love. I will not say much more about it than I have said about the love of God, because I am not a historian of literature, and because others have already discussed it exhaustively; but particularly because it is debatable whether the sentiment ever existed outside literary texts, and because at any rate it is clear that the pirouettes of gallantry at that time never formed more than a sophisticated charade, a ceremonial dress which veiled the truth of affective relationships. However, the comments I have just made with regard to conjugal love require me to make three brief observations regarding *fine amour* (courtly love) which should help to clarify the words which describe this love, as well as to situate it better within the context of the social behaviour of the period.

Firstly, it seems to me that the position accorded to marriage in the organization of feudal society through marriage alliances and the morality constructed to justify these practices, explains perfectly why all poems and maxims place courtly love outside marriage. For *fine amour* (I am not referring here to dark and fateful love in the style of Tristan, which was something altogether different) was a game whose territory should not be that of obligations and debts, but that of carefree adventure.

It was a game – and this is my second point – which performed a fundamental role (I have emphasized this elsewhere), parallel to that played by marriage, in the distribution of power within the great princely houses. I have also remarked that it was a man's game – specifically masculine, as was indeed the whole literature which revealed the rules of this game and which exalted only male values. In this game the woman was a lure. She fulfilled two roles: on the one hand, she was offered (up to a certain point) by the man who had her in his power and who was conducting the game, and she was thus the prize in a competition, in a permanent contest between the young men of the court, which inspired the competitive spirit in them, channelled their aggression, disciplined and tamed them. Moreover, it was the mission of women to educate these young men. Courtly love civilized. It formed one of the main cogs in the pedagogic system for which the princely court was the setting. It was a necessary exercise for youth, an education. In this school, the woman took the place of the master. She taught even more effectively because she stimulated desire. It was thus fitting that she deny herself and, above all, that she should be forbidden. It was also fitting that she should be a wife, and better still that she should be the wife of the master of the household, his lady. This very fact meant that she was in a dominant position, waiting to be served, sparingly dispensing her favour, in a position parallel to that which the lord, her husband, enjoyed, at the centre of the network of real power. As a result of the ambivalence of the roles attributed to the two members of the seigneurial couple, this love, *amor*, true love, restrained desire, appeared in fact as a school of friendship, of the friendship which one thinks of at the very moment when it should strengthen the vassalic bond, thereby reinforcing the political foundations of the social structure. On the basis of recent research concerned with detecting the homosexual tendencies concealed in courtly love poetry, one may well ask whether the figure of the *domina* or mistress was not identified with the figure of the *dominus*, or the lord, her husband, the head of the household.

My final observation is that a hierarchy was necessary. The pedagogic relationship, the confusion between the image of the lady and that of the master, and finally the logic of the system dictated the submissive posture of the lover. But it is important to point out that this lover was, of necessity, a *juvenis*, a youth. Married men were ruled out, naturally – something which Marcabru and Cercamon continually emphasize. This brings to mind the opinion of William of Malmesbury regarding King Philip I of France, a married man who, pursuing a woman he had taken a fancy to, was behaving like a young man: 'Majesty and love do not go well together and do not reside in the same place.' *Amor*, *fine amour*, that educative game, was reserved for single men. And gradually literature introduced courtly displays besides prenuptial rituals. This was already well established at the beginning of the thirteenth century, when Guillaume de Lorris wrote the first *Roman de la Rose*.

However, Gislebert of Mons informs us, the *seniores* were not in the habit of settling for only one woman. The place reserved for the master's illegitimate children in genealogical literature confirms this. They are obligingly listed by hack writers, for the patron wished that both his ancestors' and his own sexual prowess be celebrated. When Lambert of Ardres described the light-hearted procreative exuberance of Count Baldwin II of Guînes, he asserted that the children of the count who were born out of wedlock – there were thirty-three of them, together with their legitimate brothers and sisters, weeping at the funeral of their deceased father – were all begotten either before the wedding, in the accepted loose living of youth, or after the dissolution of the conjugal tie, in the rediscovered freedom of widowerhood. Gislebert of Mons is more cynical: his hero, the count of Hainaut, had married too early, and had become a widower far too late; he had clearly known many other women besides his wife whilst he was married. These companions, moreover, are all described, like lawful companions, as beautiful (this was a pretext), noble (convention demanded it) and often virgins (thereby highlighting the count's exploits). Yet nowhere is it stated that they were courted or that before possessing them their seducer had celebrated their being with the liturgies of *fine amour*. He simply fornicated. For this man was no longer a 'youth', he was a husband. But marriage, by its very nature, because, by definition, it could not be the place for physical passion, did not fulfil the function of offering the relief which St Paul ascribed to it in I Corinthians. Baldwin of Guînes, Baldwin of Hainaut and many others besides might be married men: they still burned.

3

The Matron and the Mismarried Woman

In northern France the conflict between the two concepts of marriage held by the laity and by the leaders of the Church passed through a critical phase during the half-century around 1100. By then, the episcopacy had reformed itself. Its intellectual framework was strengthened, supported by the diligent work of the canon lawyers. The bishops set out to remodel society's moral code, placing their bets on that major institution, marriage. They forbade clerical marriage, regarding sexual abstinence as the guarantee of a superiority which would place the clergy at the summit of the earthly hierarchy. Conversely the bishops prescribed marriage for the laity in order to control them better, to supervise them and to curb their excesses. They enjoined them to form couples according to rules and principles made increasingly sacred by the development of ritual and of religious thought. They affirmed the indissolubility of the marriage tie; they imposed exogamy in the name of an exaggerated perception of incest; they repeated that procreation was the sole justification for copulation; they dreamed of removing all pleasure from this act.

In reality, the order which the prelates were determined to impose was not facing disorder. It came up against a different order, another morality, other practices that were all just as strictly regulated, but were not designed for the salvation of souls; instead, they tended to facilitate the continuity of social relationships within existing structures. This secular morality, these secular matrimonial practices had themselves become more rigid at the end of the eleventh century, at least amongst the ruling class, the aristo-

cracy, the only section of lay society whose behaviour can be
glimpsed under the impact of changes which affected the distribution of power. Knights and nobles consequently jibbed at the
admonishments of the bishops. It was not simply that they wanted
to enjoy life. If they were the heads of households, responsible for
the fate of a lineage, they would readily repudiate their wives if
they did not provide them with male heirs, and marry their cousins
if this would enable them to keep the inheritance intact. When
they were unmarried, they indulged freely in the erotic rituals
appropriate to 'youth'. In the aftermath of Gregorian reform, the
clash between the two ethical systems sharpened. Amongst those
who held religious power, some of the leaders conducted the
struggle fiercely – the pope, from afar; his legates, closer at hand;
and a few ecclesiastical extremists, such as Yvo of Chartres, on
the spot. They led the struggle on several levels. Thus, they
compelled the nobles, who set an example, starting with the king,
to follow their instructions – and there were some spectacular
incidents, such as the excommunication of the Capetian Philip I,
which was renewed three times. Everywhere they disseminated a
model of conjugality by developing a pastoral concept of good
marriage. Amongst the most effective instruments of this propaganda, at any rate amongst those which are the most accessible
to the historian, figure some edifying narratives, the biographies
of a few heroes whose behaviour the faithful were exhorted to
imitate and who, because of this, were ranked amongst the saints.

At first sight the saints' lives are unappealing. This is because of
the rigidity of this literary genre and the weight of formal tradition.
But if one takes these writings for what they are, that is to say,
some of the most polished weapons of an ideological struggle, then
they prove to be very instructive. They show how the memory of
actual experience is manipulated for the purposes of a particular
cause, how it is dislocated, revived to secure indoctrination. I have
chosen two of these texts, one of which was written at the beginning
(1084) and the other at the end (1130–6) of this decisive period
in the history of marriage in our culture. Both come from the
same region, that is the western borders of the principality of
Flanders, between Boulogne and Bruges. They were both written
in the same type of workshop, the *scriptoria* of Benedictine monas-

teries. Each text presents a woman for the veneration of the
faithful. Both texts, therefore, depict an ideal image of womanhood.
Both advocate marriage in the form in which the Church wished
it to be practised by the laity. They reveal two conflicting positions
through what is said and what is not said, and through the way
they rectify experience, by embellishing it or by painting a black
picture of it.

It is best to begin with the later text. It is the less rich and,
paradoxically, the more traditional. It relates the virtues of the
Countess Ida of Boulogne. The biography was written some twenty
years after the death of its heroine (1113) in the monastery of
Vasconvilliers, which this woman had reformed and filled with
good Cluniac monks, where her body, after bitter disputes, had
been buried, and where a cult had grown up around her tomb,
in the context of the funerary liturgies.[1] In accordance with the
rules, the narrative begins with childhood, with all the portents
of an exceptional life, and notably with those virtues which were
handed down by blood in noble lineages. Then the account moves
on to adult life, describing the wonders which distinguished it; it
then reaches her death and finishes with the miracles which
occurred after it. All this formed a well-ordered file of evidence
(including that odour of sanctity which emanated from the tomb
when, at an uncertain date, it was opened) designed to justify the
official authorization of a cult, for the ecclesiastical authorities
were by that time being more scrupulous in their canonization
procedure.

Ida was born around 1040. A lady of the highest nobility, she
was the eldest daughter of the duke of Lower Lorraine, a sovereign
of the first rank, and of a mother who was 'no less eminent'. By
birth she was favoured with power (*potestas*) and wealth (*divitia*),
the two attributes of nobility. Everything predisposed her to mag-
nanimity. Her biography showed absolute respect for the established order which assumed that, providentially, the nobles and
the rich were good, and recognized natural correlations between
the hierarchies of temporal and spiritual values. This *Vita* (Saint's
life), written in the Cluniac spirit, was careful to avoid suggesting
that Ida had ever dreamt of stooping below her dominant position,
that she ever wanted to suffer physically, or that she ever scourged
her own flesh. This saint was neither a martyr nor an ascetic, nor

one of those fanatics who wanted to be poor at any price. She was a perfectly happy wife. The morality that was preached here was the fulfilment of femininity in marriage.

The moment when, at the appropriate age, Ida ceased to be a virgin and became a wife (1057), is therefore the central part of this biography. The author took care to show that this transition took place correctly in accordance with social and moral proprieties. The man who deflowered Ida belonged, necessarily, to the same social rank, and was a 'hero', 'of very noble birth', 'of the blood of Charlemagne', 'of exceptional renown', and one can see that emphasis was placed both on marriage between equals and on the role of reputation which allowed 'people of valour to marry'. Indeed, it was the girl's reputation, what was reported of her morals and her beauty, but especially 'the dignity of her race' which tempted Eustace II, count of Boulogne.[2] He was the widower of a sister of Edward the Confessor and had no legitimate male offspring. He desperately needed a wife. He obtained one with propriety – there was no abduction, no seduction. He sent messengers to the man responsible for her marriage, her father. The latter took counsel. Ida was 'surrendered' by her parents. Then, escorted by members of the two households, she was taken to Boulogne where her bridegroom awaited her. This is where the wedding took place solemnly and according to the practice of the Catholic church ('Pro more ecclesiae catholicae'), as the text says, perhaps in allusion to the nuptial blessing. By 1130 this ritual had taken root in the region, although there is nothing to indicate that it had been introduced there as early as 1057. Subsequently Ida is seen as a spouse (*conjux*) deploying her virtue in marriage (*virtus in conjugio*) and therefore appearing as the paragon of a good wife.

First and foremost, she was submissive to her husband, who supported her, guided her and directed her towards the best. She was devout, but 'in harmony with her man and in accordance with his will'. How can we imagine a woman achieving sanctity in spite of her husband? She was dutiful, therefore, but also discreet (with Cluniac *discretio*) in the running of the household, in the way she treated guests and was on friendly terms with the nobles, yet she was 'chaste'. Chastity, in fact, was responsible for good marriages. Thus 'in accordance with the apostolic precept' it was by 'using her husband as though she did not have one' that Ida gave birth. For her principal virtue was to be a mother. She brought three sons into the world (the text does not mention daughters): the second was Godfrey de Bouillon, the last, Baldwin, king of Jerusalem. Ida undoubtedly owed the attention she received in her sixties, and the odour of sanctity which surrounded her tomb, to the destinies of her two children, to the fact that the two first sovereigns of the Holy Land were her own offspring. The sanctity of marriage was indeed measured by the glory of the males who were its fruit. Ida had been made aware of this glory during her adolescence. One night, 'as she was surrendering herself to sleep', she had seen the sun descend from the sky and stay for a moment on her breast. Hagiography delights in portents and gladly describes dreams. Admittedly, it is dangerously coloured with prepubescent eroticism. The monastic writer was very conscious of this and was wary. Ida was asleep, he says, but her mind was turned 'towards higher things'. This dream did not, therefore, draw her downwards, towards pleasure. It proclaimed that the virgin would be a mother, that the fruit of her womb would be blessed. It proclaimed a holy motherhood. The entire *Vita* represents a celebration of childbirth.

Noble birth, offspring, nobility (*genus, gignere, generositas*): these words punctuate the first part of the account. It is worth noting their carnal connotation: they emphasise blood, good family, birth. Ida's function – like that of all girls who were introduced into noble households by the rites of marriage – was to form 'by the grace of God' a link in a genealogy.[3] She gave birth to and nurtured males. She was not praised for nourishing her sons spiritually, or instructing them, or preparing them through their education for the exploits which made them illustrious. It was for having breast-fed them, refusing to allow them to be given milk from any other breast, so that they should not be 'contaminated by bad morals'.

This childbearing function apparently took another form after Ida was widowed in around 1070, 'deprived of the comfort of a man'. She was 'gladdened nevertheless by the nobility of her sons', 'enriched by the love from above'. Under the authority of her eldest son, Eustace III, who had succeeded his father as head of the house, her virtues were perpetuated. She was still prolific. But her virtues no longer issued from her body. Henceforth Ida gave birth through her wealth – more precisely, through her money. After the deaths of her husband and father, she had come to an arrangement with her relatives to sell off her own possessions, exchanging them for money. She used this money, whose source was still the paternal clan (*genus*), to give birth to new sons, this time spiritual ones: monks. She did not act alone, naturally, but always in agreement with the male under whose power she had fallen. With her son's 'advice' and 'help', she enriched the Boulogne region, reconstructing, reforming and founding three monasteries in succession. They were monasteries for men: in a fleshly context or not, only the male offspring counted. She did not become a nun herself. 'Her mortal husband having died, she moved on,' naturally, 'to be united with the immortal husband through a life of chastity and celibacy.'

Admittedly, she gradually removed herself from her son's protection and attached herself to another family, a spiritual family. Hugh of Cluny adopted her 'as a daughter', but she remained, as was fitting, in a position of subordination, still submissive to men. When she went to live near the last monastery which she had had built, the Capelle Sainte-Marie, at the gate, surrounded by her followers, it was under the authority of the father abbot. Psalm-chanting, but 'in moderation', she was above all a foster-mother who fed the poor and fed the monastic community. She was 'serving' men, as it was proper that women should never cease to do.

That the major *virtus* of this saint was that of motherhood, emerges again in the details of two of the miracles attributed to her. She performed the first during her lifetime, in the monastery of Capelle Sainte-Marie. Amongst the people whom she supported was a little deaf and dumb girl. One feast day, at matins, the child's mother brought her to church in the retinue of the countess. It was cold, and the little girl was shivering. She snuggled under Ida's cloak. It was as if the odour of the clothing had given her new life: she could suddenly hear and speak. What were her first words? *Mater, mater.* Provided with a prebend by the abbot, the miraculously healed child nevertheless sinned: she conceived and gave birth, thereby losing not only her virginity, but also her stipend and her health. However, Ida saved her twice from the

weakness to which she had twice succumbed, purifying the sinful
motherhood which the girl was guilty of, and finally becoming a
foster-mother twice, for with each rebirth the prebend was restored.
The other miracle took place at her tomb, no doubt shortly before
the biography was written. Once again, a woman was the ben-
eficiary – this time it was the daughter of Eustace III, Ida's own
granddaughter, Matilda. In the throes of a bad fever, 'confident
and assured of the sanctity of the blessed woman', she had made
her way to Ida's tomb. She was the first pilgrim. She was cured,
her grandmother preferring to project her healing powers on to
her own line, a sort of tree of Jesse springing from her bountiful
womb.

The evidence shows nothing exceptional about the life of this
princess: at the end of the eleventh century it was normal for girls
of her social rank to marry brave warriors so as to give birth to
still more, and when widowed to distribute their bounty to monasteries with the agreement of their eldest son, and finally to be
associated with monastic liturgies. There is nothing exceptional
in this apart from bringing Godfrey de Bouillon[4] into the world.
If two of Ida's sons had not been so famous, would her effects
have been argued over in 1113, would her tomb have been opened
later, and would she have been declared a saint in around 1130?
The instigator of this official recognition was undoubtedly that
same Matilda who had been cured by her grandmother from
beyond the grave. Heiress to the county of Boulogne, she had
married Stephen of Blois. Her other grandmother was Margaret
of Scotland, who was already considered a saint, and who is
depicted in the earliest of the biographies (dating from 1093–5)
as accepting marriage with the sole intention of being a mother.
The cult of St Margaret had just been established, at the same
time as that of Edward the Confessor[5] by Edith Matilda, the wife
of King Henry I and sister of the mother of Matilda of Boulogne.
Whilst they were planning to transfer the seat of the bishopric
from Morinie to Boulogne, Matilda commissioned the monks of
Vasconvilliers to write Ida's biography.

It seems to me that the monks were a little embarrassed, somewhat troubled at finding only a talent for procreation as the
principal argument for sanctity in the documents. One senses this
from the prologue which sets out to justify this point of view. The

world, the author says, is moving towards its end. The devil is increasing his attacks. Where could one turn but to the prayers or virtues of the saints? Happily, Providence has distributed sanctity across all the 'degrees' of society. Even women were to be found amongst the saints; even married women, provided of course that they were mothers. In that case they might be 'inscribed in the book of life on account of their virtues and *those of their sons*'. Nevertheless, in order to overcome any lingering reservations, the biographer deemed it necessary to show what was good about the married state. To justify marriage he quoted Paul: 'It is better to marry than to burn' ('melius est nubere quam uri'): marriage was a remedy for lust; he recalled that, 'according to the law', prolific fertility glorified it. Finally he asserted that marriage should be lived in chastity, 'without which there is nothing good': 'virginity is indeed good, but it is proved that chastity after childbirth is great.'

Once these principles had been set out as a guide it was permissible for a Benedictine monk to establish that a married woman could be a saint. He did this discreetly and cautiously, in the best Cluniac tradition, with a keen sense of social expediency. He set out an image of good marriage which was absolutely in keeping with the teachings of the Scriptures and of St Augustine. None the less, since the biography served the interests of a house of the upper nobility, he took care to prevent there being too much discrepancy between the example which he proposed and the moral code to which the high aristocracy subscribed.

The two systems of morality, that of the Church and that of secular dynasties, are reconciled here. I am not merely talking about a celebration of the power and wealth that each of the deeds of the heroine illustrates. The two models of behaviour meet principally on two levels. Firstly, it is asserted that woman's condition is to be dominated: by her father who gives her to whom he pleases; by her husband who controls and watches over her; and later by her eldest son; and finally, when the latter drives the mother with whom he is burdened out of the house, she is dominated by the monks of the family monastery, one of whose roles is precisely to open its doors to the women of the noble family who are marginalized once they have ceased to be useful. Secondly, there is also agreement on the principle that the wife is bound to co-operate in upholding the renown of the family line by providing it with children who are both male and valiant. It was stated that the image of femininity and of marriage common to all the heads of noble houses had at the beginning of the twelfth century corresponded to the divine plan; this was, in fact, the best way to make them concede, at the same time, discreetly, without too much emphasis on the conjugal pact being concluded according to the 'practices of the Catholic Church' that it was desirable that the married couple should show at least the appearances of chastity.

Some fifty years earlier another picture was presented by a text, or rather by two, since two successive versions of the same biography dating from the eleventh century have been preserved. This picture is different, since the system of representations to which it claimed to correspond was not, I believe, an aristocratic but a popular one. The heroine of this tale, Godelive, is well-born, 'of famous parents'. She bears a Teutonic name; the second biographer even felt it was necessary to provide a translation: 'dear to God' ('cara Deo'). This name is eminently suited to a saint, so much so that one might question whether the name, and indeed the character herself, are not mythical. However, there is no doubt that Godelive really existed. The details which are supplied about her ancestry are indisputably precise: her father, Heinfridus, from Londefort in the Boulonnais region, was also mentioned in the charters of the period. He was a knight in the service of Eustace of Boulogne, Ida's husband. He was not of such high birth as Eustace. Nevertheless, his family ranked far higher than the common people. They stood beyond the strict limit which the seigneurial means of production drew between the dominant and dominated. I have used the term 'popular' above because the biography which I am analysing was not written at the request of an illustrious family by the monks attached to the household.

The devotion which Godelive inspired took root in Ghistelle, the village in maritime Flanders, 10 km from Bruges, where she was buried. The earliest biographer refers to this: he wrote, urged on by 'many of the faithful'. He was not lying. What he recounts of the forms of piety which took place at the tomb, and of the miracles of which he was shown the signs, testifies to the fact that the cult did indeed spring from the peasantry. He saw the earth near the tomb magically transformed into white stones. He saw those stones which people had taken home with them 'out of devotion' turn into jewels. He saw people sick with fever, invalids, coming to drink water from the pool where Godelive had been plunged. He was told that some of them were cured. The Church leaders had their hands forced by this fervour; they yielded. On 30 July 1084 the bishop of Noyon-Tournai, Radebod II, instituted the elevation of the relics of a woman who had died there, perhaps fourteen years earlier. He did this at the very time that he entrusted the church of Oudenburg to Arnulf of Soissons in order to establish there the Benedictine monks who had come from Saint-Bertin, and with the same intention – that of strengthening the ecclesiastical structures on the borders of his diocese. Nevertheless the prelate wanted the legend to be adapted so that it might serve the function of improving the moral conduct of a population which was still very primitive.

The legend has obviously been manipulated. Yet traces of the original narrative remain. These are very clear in the version of the *Life* published by the Bollandists[6] from a manuscript originating in the abbey of Oudenburg, which is later (though only slightly, it would appear) than the date of the canonization. They are even clearer in the text which this reworking completed, in the account which Drogo, a monk of Bergues-Saint-Winock, wrote immediately before the intervention by the bishop of Noyon to prepare for it.[7] How far was this official action, this attempt to set things in order taken? It seems that the flow of religiosity which the elevation of relics aimed to stem was from the outset very heterodox. This theory was formulated cautiously by Jacques Le Goff when I was commenting on this document in one of my seminars. He pointed out that witches were hardly mentioned in eleventh-century litera-ture. Might this be because the Church was then appropriating such women for herself, those at least whose memory was still alive amongst humble people, because they had perished tragically, killed by the *ministeriales*, the repressive agents of civil power? Were they systematically exorcized by the 'conversion' of their reputation and transformed into saints? I am not sure that this hypothesis should be pursued too far.

The fact remains that Godelive may well have been canonized

in order to remove controversial elements in the cult surrounding her. The character of two of the four miracles recalled by the first biographer supports this hypothesis. Godelive was a healer and cured paralytics. She came to the aid of a man and a woman whom heaven had punished for working at a time which was forbidden by the ecclesiastical authorities. The man was harvesting on a Saturday evening; his hand remained stuck to the ears of corn. The woman, after mass on a feast day, was stirring a cauldron of dye with a stick. It stuck to her hand. That Godelive should have freed these two labouring hands, cancelling the effects of divine wrath, put her on the side of the people. She had triumphed over the fulminations of the priests. Surely she must have been celebrated as the champion of resistance to clerical oppression? This leads one to detect snatches of a different, popular discourse beneath the edifying, soothing prose of the biography. Nevertheless the original discourse was remodelled with one main purpose. Like the biography of St Ida, but perhaps in another social field, it was to help propagate the ecclesiastical morality of marriage.

In a typology of sanctity, the daughter of Heinfridus, knight of Boulogne, would take her place among the martyrs. But would she also take her place among the virgins? This is what the Bollandists asserted. Her virginity, they wrote, could not be questioned: at Ghistelle, she had always been regarded as a virgin. One may search these two eleventh-century texts in vain to see what might support such an assertion. These accounts do not say anything about virginity. For their authors – remarkably enough – this was not an important feature. They emphasize the martyrdom. It was, however, the martyrdom of a wife. Godelive was the victim of a bad marriage. The writers of her *Life* proclaimed this loud and clear, with the intention (amongst others) of showing with a negative image what constituted a good marriage.

The word *virgo* is applied to Godelive only once, to describe her condition before her parents gave her away in marriage. Her fate, like that of all girls, was to be married off at the end of her childhood (*pueritia*). Unlike the case of Ida, corrupt procedures were employed from the beginning, from the betrothal (*desponsatio*) to the conclusion of the agreement. This virgin was devout, as were all the saints in childhood. Nevertheless she was sought after by a host of suitors who were inflamed with 'love', according to both texts. Faithful to the lay models which they were rewriting, they gave a place to physical desire, to the attraction of the female body. Both versions of the biography stress the young girl's charms. Her only fault was that she was dark, with black hair and eyebrows. But Drogo immediately set the record right: her skin appeared all the whiter for this, 'something which is agreeable, pleasing in women and which is held in honour by many'. One of these young men (*juvenes*), Bertulf, was 'powerful', 'distinguished through his blood relations', an officer of the count of Flanders in the district of Bruges.[8] He was the one who won her. Not that Godelive herself chose him. She had no say in the matter. The gallant, moreover, did not speak to her, but to her parents, the masters, who gave her away. The agreement was mishandled on two counts. Firstly, Bertulf had acted according to his own 'will'. His mother later took him to task for not consulting either herself or his father, and these reproaches were valid: good marriage was not the concern of individuals but of families. Unless his father was dead, as was the case with Eustace II of Boulogne, the boy, too, should leave the decision to his parents. The second defect was that Godelive's mother and father 'preferred Bertulf for his dower' (*dos*) – he was the richest. This reflects popular wisdom, which held that a marriage for money was a bad marriage.

The union started badly and was further corrupted in its second conclusive phase. After the plighting of troths, Bertulf took Godelive home, that is, to his mother. The latter lived apart from her husband, perhaps repudiated by him, and either providing a home for her son or living in his. In any event he could take a wife because, in this house, the matrimonial bed was empty. But his mother was also living there, which did not help matters. Here a classic theme arises, that of the complaints of the unhappily married woman. The journey was fairly long and required an overnight stop between the region of Boulogne and the outskirts of Bruges.

During this journey the Evil One suddenly struck the mind of the newly wed man, who started hating his wife. The example of Philip Augustus and Ingeborg naturally comes to mind: it was not a fiasco (the queen of France bitterly denied this) but instant revulsion. Bertulf was strengthened in this attitude by the talk which his mother gave him on his arrival. 'All mothers-in-law', wrote Drogo, 'hate their daughters-in-law' (he was merely repeat-

ing what the common people said, as was his wont). 'They desperately want to see their sons married, but immediately become
jealous of them and their wives.' This woman not only upbraided
her son for not having consulted her, but also mocked him for his
choice: the girl he had brought home was a foreigner, and was
also swarthy: 'So there were not enough crows here – you had to
go and track one down.' Bertulf then withdrew, refusing to take
part in the wedding ceremony. He stayed away during the three
ritual feast-days on the pretext of financial or legal business.
Appearances were kept up, joy was feigned. The rites were
inverted, however: a woman, his mother, took the husband's role.
It was a transgression of the moral order, of the sexual order, an
improbable turn of events, such as forms the plot of fairy tales.

The corruption of the union was completed in the period which
followed the wedding ceremonies. Scarcely had he returned than
Bertulf was off again, this time to stay with his father. His wife
remained in the marital home, abandoned. She fulfilled her role
as best she could, ran the house and managed the servants. She
was, nevertheless, in despair (*desolata*). At night her solitude was
more oppressive, and so she prayed; during the day she spun and
wove. She filled her time as nuns do, anxious to conquer idleness,
the enemy of the soul, by work and prayer. The author of the
second version (a Benedictine monk) emphasized this point: 'With
the help of this shield, she repulsed the darts of those daydreams
which usually overwhelm adolescence.' In an attempt to make the
first biography more convincing, the concern of the hagiographer
is to reassure the reader that, when left alone, this girl did not
become unchaste, asserting that no gossip was ever peddled about
her. These were necessary precautions: according to popular opinion, women, especially young women, who were naturally
depraved, succumbed to sin, that is to say to lust, as soon as one
took one's eyes off them. It was precisely because of this that the
husband had to stay close to his wife.

Here the text addresses an exhortation to husbands: they must
be there, in adversity as well as in prosperity, to bear for them
their burdens, given that they are bound by law (*de jure*) to support
their companion, to live with her 'patiently' until death, because
they are two in one flesh, because, rather, they form a single body
by 'conjugal coupling' (this reference to the effects of copulation

or *copulatio* makes it clear that Godelive, in the eyes of those who promoted her sanctity, had achieved womanhood).

However perverted, the tie was nevertheless not undone. Bertulf now took counsel of both his parents. He was trying to rid himself of his wife. It is astonishing that the simple idea of repudiating her did not cross the minds of these evil people, according to these didactic tales. Had it already become improper in these circles of the lesser nobility for a man to drive his wife from his house, by his own impulse (*motu proprio*)? In fact, the only plan was to 'hold in contempt' (*deturpare*) the young bride; more precisely, in Bertulf's words, to 'take her colour away'. She was put on a diet of bread and water whilst the servants gorged. Godelive did not waste away, however: some obliging neighbours and female relatives secretly provided her with food. (There was no miracle, no intervention from heaven; instead, as is so often the case in popular narratives, earthly creatures gave their assistance.) Nevertheless, worn out by all these insults, she fled. This is what they were waiting for. Leaving the home was a transgression, and this transgression was to be her downfall. The monk Drogo did not realize this, but his colleague, who improved the first version, felt it was judicious to recognize that Godelive was thus transgressing the precept of the gospels, which forbade the separation of what God had joined together. How could this be allowed in a woman who was being put forward as a saint? Drogo then advanced the excuse that her flesh began to tremble, something which happened to many martyrs.

Additions of this sort suggest that Godelive's reputation amongst scholars was not so secure at the outset as not to need the support of arguments. This led to the first biography being rewritten and amplified. Starving and barefoot, Godelive went back to her native land. She was not alone but with a companion, for women of good repute did not travel the roads alone. She demanded justice, but through her father, since it was unseemly for a woman, who was always subordinate, to defend her rights herself. She had to delegate them to a man; if not her husband or her son, then a male in her family. Heinfridus received her and decided to make a complaint to the wicked husband's lord, the count of Flanders, whose *ministerialis* Bertulf was.

At this point the tone of the two saints' lives changes; they cease preaching morality and talk of law – of the new law which at the end of the eleventh century the Church was working to have accepted by secular society. Both versions proclaimed – the second even more vehemently – the exclusive competence of episcopal jurisdiction in matters of marriage . I have not previously found this claim expressed so clearly in northern France before this double manifesto grafted on to a story of a dishonoured wife. The monk Drogo skilfully placed in the mouth of the count who figured in the story the speech which was in fact addressed to the current count, Robert the Frisian, to urge him to behave properly and, as his predecessor was supposed to have done, to curtail his prerogatives. The good prince was therefore heard to pronounce that he renounced the right to judge, that it was up to the bishop of the diocese to have cognizance of matters of this kind, as they belong, he says, 'to Christianity', that is, to the Church.[9] Those who 'deviate from the holy scheme of things' must be put back on the straight path by the prelate; they should be 'restrained' by the discretion of the Church (*discretio ecclesiastica*), by anathema, the later version specifies – stating more clearly that these causes must be settled 'only' before judges of the Church. 'I am only the auxiliary (*adjutor*)', admits the count (the second version says *vindex* or punisher, the term also used for the king of France when striking with the temporal sword those whom God, through his Church, had condemned). Authority (*auctoritas*) versus power (*potestas*) (the monk of Oudenburg, who was well versed in the subject, balanced the one against the other) – this perfectly Gregorian division asserted the superiority of the spiritual over the temporal. It also located the jurisdictional power of the bishops in the continuing provisions of the Peace of God which had been established in that region during the previous generation.

The bishop of Tournai ruled that Bertulf should take his wife back. No adultery had occurred, no mention was made of the husband's impotence, nor any doubt cast on the consummation of the marriage. In accordance with the norms set out in the collections of canon law, a divorce could not be pronounced. In such cases, the husband and wife should be reconciled, brought together. Bertulf submitted – according to the revised version – out of fear, especially of secular sanctions, for he was perverse –

but he submitted against his will. In his hatred, in his disgust, he saw only one alternative, crime. This is where Godelive's martyrdom began in suffering, patience and slow spiritual development. The bride was no longer physically tormented. Bertulf promised not to ill-treat her any more. But she remained abandoned, even by her father. She was without a man, which seemed outrageous. Her 'friends', the relatives of her husband, were shocked. They criticized him, whilst Godelive, as a perfect partner in the 'marital union', 'forbade that one speak ill of her man'. They pitied her, particularly for being deprived of the 'pleasures of the body'. She replied: 'I scorn the pleasures of the body.' Hers was a joyful abstinence, and gradually the exemplary bride began to profess disdain for the world and adopted the same features and expressions attributed to the Virgin Mary. The words of the Magnificat crept into everything she said, particularly to the monks of Saint-Winock who came to visit her at that time, and she, a feeble woman, showed them the example of continence and submission. Resounding with the echoes of Marian liturgies and the text of the Gospels, the narrative leads up to the martyrdom.

Bertulf prepared his *coup*. He plotted with two of his serfs and listened to the advice of these ignoble creatures, another sign of his perverse character. One evening before sunset, Godelive saw him returning. She was stunned. He smiled, took her in his arms, gave her a kiss, and made her sit by his side, sharing his cushion (in the posture in which fourteenth-century Parisian painters of popular pictures were to depict courtly lovers on ivory mirror-cases and perfume lids). The man drew his wife to him. Afraid, she drew back at first, then she let herself go, obedient and ready to fulfil all the duties of marriage when the master demanded them. Close to her now, Bertulf cajoled her: 'You're not used to my presence, nor to being thrilled by sweet talk and the shared desire of flesh...' (words, then pleasure: these were indeed the two successive phases of love-making, according to the rituals of the game of love). He could not explain how his mind had become distracted and said it must be the devil.

I am going to put an end to the division of my mind, I am going to treat you like a beloved wife and, slowly leaving behind hatred, I am going to reunite our bodies and our minds...I've found a

woman who has undertaken to join us in staunch love, to make
us love one another forever and more than any other couple have
ever cherished each other on this earth.

The two serfs were to lead her to this enchantress. Godelive then
spoke: 'I am the servant of the Lord. I trust in him. If this can
be done without sin, then I accept.' The hagiographer exclaims:
'What virtue! She first put herself in the hands of God, afraid
that she might be separated from him by magic. Nevertheless, for
that very reason, she chose marriage, so as not to be separated
from the Lord who unites couples.'

If we are to believe Fr Coens, the editor of the earlier version,
this scene took place on 30 July 1070. On 17 July Count Baldwin
died and his subjects took sides: the people of maritime Flanders
(Bertulf's home region) took the side of Robert the Frisian, and
those from the Boulonnais region (Godelive's home) took the side
of the count's widow. This caused great turmoil. The moment
was ripe to act. Night fell – the time of mishap, the time of evil
– and the two servants came to fetch the lady. They escorted her
in a parody of the bridal procession, heading towards sin, in the
silence, in the depth of the night, at that hour when the most
heinous of crimes are set in folk tales. They led her backwards
from the bed to the door, not towards a husband but towards a
woman who was far worse than her mother-in-law and truly a
sorceress. Godelive was strangled, plunged into water as if for a
second baptism; she sanctified this water, making it miraculous.
Finally, she was brought back to her bed and dressed again. In
the morning her people found her, apparently unharmed. Soon,
however, first doubts arose, a suspicion that was only murmured
because it arose among the very poorest. And soon, too, the first
miracle occurred, a multiplication of the bread at the funeral
repast, again for the poor. Finally there were immediately manifestations of her cult, water that heals the poor and stones becoming
jewels.

This cult flouted two powers: that of the bishop, in that the
strange power of the martyred woman rendered the prohibitions
he decreed and the sanctions he imposed ineffectual; and that of
the count, for was not the villain of the story, the torturer, with
his sergeants, his henchmen, an officer of the count responsible

for levying his dues? Without going as far as Jacques Le Goff does in his theories, it is possible to see in the primitive forms of such a worship, in the original structures of such a legend, a protest on behalf of the oppressed, of all innocent victims. The heroine did indeed belong to the class which profited from the seigneurial system. The cruelties which were inflicted on her were an attack on her honour, on the regard which her rank demanded. Yet she was a woman, a creature who was dominated, and her husband starved her, as he starved those subject to his lordship in the exercise of his office. In all probability both cult and narrative originated amongst the common people, in the social meaning of the word which suggests conflict. We should interpret this as one of the forms which the class struggle took amongst the free and rebellious peasants of maritime Flanders at a time of upheaval in seigneurial society. Some time later, on the occasion of a reconciliation among the notables of Flanders which was arranged by the Flemish St Arnulf,[10] the count (then leading the investigation into murders committed in the Bruges region) and the bishop, who was then founding the abbey of Oudenburg, agreed to neutralize this cult and to use it to shore up the established order. It was thus that the life of a saint came to replace the moving story of an unhappily married woman.[11]

The established order did not only require deviant cults to be brought back to orthodoxy. It also required that the prescribed rules be followed to educate married couples. The two powers had agreed to impose these norms. The story of Godelive's misfortunes therefore lent support to the exhortation to marry well. This widespread exhortation anticipated by some fifty years the message that was to be conveyed in the *Life* of Countess Ida. It should be remembered that the conjugal knot, tied by God Himself, could not be undone. It was the role of the parents, not the children, to conclude the marriage agreement, and they had to consider morals more than wealth and to avoid *invidia*, that jealousy which destroys alliances.

It was hardly necessary, for it was so evident, to depict the wife as an obedient woman similar to Mary. The advice was added, but in an undertone, to despise the flesh in the name of a devout life based, like that of earlier heretics and soon to be adopted by the

Beguines, on manual labour, abstinence and the fear of pleasure. Nevertheless, it was very strongly asserted – it may be that the collusion between the two powers was still close on this last point – that the right to judge marriage belonged to the clergy. This was the foundation of the doctrine which the monks of the region were required to set forth with moderation, during that half-century.

Against this background, each of these two works, whose meaning and intention I have tried to analyse, contributes something different. Both texts are about women. Taking female characters as the mouthpieces for ecclesiastical ideology had two advantages. It rallied that half of the faithful population to which the Church in the past had paid insufficient attention and whose worth it now regarded more highly. It also focused attention on characters who were naturally passive and upon whom the principles of the submission expected from all lay people could be deeply imprinted.

If, however, the tone of the two works differs markedly, this difference can be attributed to the fact that one text leans towards those who dominate, and the other towards those who are dominated. Since in the biography of the happy wife, Countess Ida, the exhortation is addressed – as in nearly all those which have been preserved from that period – to those in command, to the powerful lineages, to the heads of houses, it emphasizes the genetic, one might almost say genealogical, function of the female body. Whilst the story of Godelive, the unhappy wife, may well have been told to the common people, it also originated amongst them, and placed the emphasis chiefly on love. It is notable that the terms derived from the word *amor* (sensual love) in the *Life* of Godelive are almost as numerous as derivatives of the word *genus* (noble birth) in Ida's *Life*. Naturally this love respected the relationship of necessary subordination which providence established between the two sexes. The love of a husband for his wife is called delight (*dilectio*), whilst that of the wife for her husband is called reverence. Yet it was stressed that man and woman should be united in flesh as well as in mind. They made love – no mention, or virtually none, is made of 'chastity'. It was as much a love of the body as of the heart. This led to an appreciation of the attractions of the female body. It gave permission for recourse to sorcery so as to allow this love to develop fully. When the bishop of Noyon-Tournai, spurred on by what had sprung from popular feeling, elevated the relics of that dark-haired girl with the delectable fair skin, he was inadvertently venturing much further than most of his colleagues were to do for a long while yet.

4

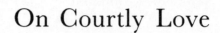

On Courtly Love

It is as a historian, and more precisely as a historian of medieval societies, that I approach a historical subject which is first and foremost a literary subject – that strange phenomenon called courtly love, which when it first appeared was called *fine amour* (refined love). I would like to consider a few propositions regarding what we are able to glimpse of the real attitudes described in poems and fiction during the second half of the twelfth century in France. I shall do so by examining the correspondences between what is revealed in these songs and romances and the real organization of power and social relationships.

I have a feeling that I am treading on dangerous ground. Firstly, because my knowledge of these literary forms is, so to speak, second-hand; and secondly, and more importantly, because I am immediately confronted with a question that is so difficult to answer when applied to earlier times – namely, what kinds of relationship exist between this type of literature, a vicarious literature of dream and escape, and actual behaviour. One fact, at least, is certain. This literature was accepted, otherwise there would be no trace of it (although the state of the manuscript tradition leads one to question whether its reception took place all that quickly). But it was accepted and, consequently, had far-reaching repercussions. For these works to find an audience, they had to relate in some way to the concerns and the real situation of the people for whom they were written. Conversely, they also influenced the behaviour of those who listened to them. This enables the historian to compare the content of these works with what he already knows from other accounts of the structures and development of feudal society.

I shall begin by reducing the initial model of so-called courtly love to its most schematic form, without taking into account the changes which distorted it in the course of the twelfth century. The protagonist is a man, a 'youth' in both senses of the word, in the technical sense that it had at that time (a man without a lawful wife) and in the literal sense, that is, a man young in age, whose education is not yet complete. This man besieges and tries to take a lady, that is to say a woman who is married and thus inaccessible, impregnable, a woman who is surrounded and protected by the strictest of prohibitions imposed by a lineal society – a society based on inheritances handed down through the male line, which therefore viewed a wife's adultery as the most dreadful subversion, and threatened her lover with terrible punishments. At the heart of this model lies danger, and this is where it should be. For on the one hand, the whole spice of the affair came from the danger involved (the men of the period believed, with good reason, that it was more exciting to chase the she-wolf than the woodcock); on the other hand, it was a test in the course of a continuing education, and the more perilous the test, the more educational it was.

I have now, I believe, placed this model of the relationship between men and women in a very precise context. Courtly love was a game, an educational game. It was the exact counterpart of the tournament. As at the tournament, whose great popularity coincided with the flourishing of courtly eroticism, in this game the man of noble birth was risking his life and endangering his body. (I do not refer to the soul, as the subject for which I am trying to find a context was forged to assert the independence of a culture, that of warriors, which was arrogant and, in its enjoyment of life, was resolutely opposed to the culture of the priests.) As at the tournament, the young man was risking his life in the hope of improving himself, of enhancing his worth, his price, and also of taking, taking his pleasure, capturing his adversary after breaking down her defences, unseating her, knocking her down and toppling her.

Courtly love was a joust. But, unlike those duels which warriors fought amid the tumultuous confrontations in which competitors in a tournament engaged, or in the closed field of the judicial ordeal,[1] the joust of love set two unequal partners against one another, one of whom was, by nature, doomed to fall – by physical nature, by the natural laws of sexuality. For that is the point, and no veil of sublimation, none of the make-believe transferences from the body to the heart can succeed in concealing it. There is no mistaking it. Claude Buridant, the French translator of the fine work by Andreas Capellanus, chaplain to Philip Augustus, king of France, gives this work the title of *Traité de l'amour courtois* ('Treatise of Courtly Love'). But Betsy Bowden, a young American medieval scholar, chose a more fitting title, *The Art of Courtly Copulation*, and, more recently, Danielle Jacquart and Claude Thomasset interpreted the text as a manual of sexology. Indeed, the games to which I am referring exalted the value which, at that period, was placed at the pinnacle of male values, and thus of all values – sexual aggression. In order to heighten the man's pleasure, he demanded that the woman suppress her desire.

I have no hesitation in contradicting those commentators who saw in courtly love a female invention. It was a man's game, and amongst all the writings which encouraged individuals to give themselves over to it, there are few which are not deeply misogynist. The woman is a lure, like those mannequins which the new knight threw himself at during the athletic displays which followed his dubbing ceremonies. Was the woman not urged to put on all her finery, to mask and unmask her attractions, to refuse to give herself for a long time, only to give herself sparingly, making gradual concessions so that, in prolonging the temptation and the danger, the young man learned how to master himself, and how to control his body?

Trial, education and all the literary expressions of courtly love should be seen in the context of the vigorous surge of progress which reached its peak during the second half of the twelfth century. They are at once the instrument and the product of this growth, which was rapidly moving away from the primitive savagery of feudal society and was civilizing it. The proposal and reception of a new form of relationship between the two sexes can be understood only with reference to other expressions of this change. I am not thinking – and this may come as a surprise – of any particular promotion of women. Indeed, I do not believe in it at all. The condition of women improved but, at the same time, there was an equally strong advance in that of men, so that the gap remained the same, and women remained at once feared, despised and strictly subjugated, as the literature of courtly love bears out so overwhelmingly. I have in mind, rather, the movement which made the individual withdraw from gregariousness and the twofold influence emanating from ecclesiastical centres of learning, giving fashionable society the small change of the observations of religious writers on the Incarnation and love (*caritas*), and at the same time an echo, perhaps distorted, of the close study of the Latin classics.

The male heroes proposed as models by the court poets and narrators were quite evidently admired and imitated during the second half of the twelfth century. Knights, at least those in the entourage of the greatest princes, were caught up in the game. We cannot doubt it: if William Marshal, still a bachelor, was accused of having seduced the wife of his lord, it was because such occurrences were not exceptional. Knights became involved in the game because the rules of the game helped to pose better, if not resolve, some of the burning social questions of the day. I would like to explain briefly how, to my way of thinking, their characteristics fitted them to the values of courtly love.

I will begin with personal life, that is with the issues raised on the subject of relationships between men and women by the marriage strategies employed in aristocratic society. I have already written in different ways about these strategies and the moral philosophy which supported them. I will sum up my views and add only that they seem to me to have directly prepared the ground for the joust between the young man and his lady. The tight restrictions on the marriage rate of males increased the number of unmarried men in this milieu, who, frustrated, were jealous of those men who had wives to sleep with. I refer not to sexual frustration; there was little difficulty in finding an outlet for that. I mean men's obsessive hope of gaining a lawful companion in order to found their own household and to establish themselves. I mean also the fantasies of aggression and abduction which were fed by this obsession. Furthermore, nuptial agreements were nearly always finalized without the slightest consideration of the feelings of the two betrothed. On the wedding night a very young girl who had barely reached puberty was handed over to a rough boy whom she had never seen before. In addition there was the segregation which, after the age of seven, placed boys and girls in two totally separate worlds. Everything therefore conspired to prevent there being a passionate relationship between the married couple comparable to what we regard as conjugal love; instead there was a cold relationship of inequality which consisted at best in condescending love on the part of the husband, and at best timorous respect on the part of his wife.

Such circumstances made it desirable that there should be a code whose precepts, which were intended to be applied outside the sphere of marriage, would complement matrimonial law, and would be built up in the same way as the latter. Rudiger Schnell in Germany has demonstrated brilliantly that Andreas Capellanus's intention was to transfer into the domain of sexual play all the rules which the Church moralists had adapted for marriage. Such a code was necessary in order to suppress brutality, the violence that existed in the progress towards civility that I have mentioned. It was hoped that by ritualizing desire this code would lead dissatisfied husbands and their ladies (and especially that worrying group of unruly men whom family customs had forced into celibacy) towards regularity and a sort of legitimacy.

The role of regulation and order was thereby fulfilled. This prompts me to consider a different type of question, one relating to public order, a strictly political question which the codification of relationships between men and women was capable of solving. Writers of literary history rightly named this love courtly love. The texts which inform us of its rules were all written in courts during the twelfth century, under the watchful eye of the prince, and had to correspond to his expectations. At a time when the state was starting to emerge from the feudal muddle where, in the euphoria sustained by economic growth, public power once again felt able to mould social relationships, I am convinced that princely patronage deliberately encouraged the institution of these secular liturgies exemplified in Lancelot and Gawain. It was a way of tightening the grip of the sovereign's power over the social class which at that time was perhaps the most useful in the reform of the state, but which was also the least docile. In fact, the code of courtly love served to further the purposes of the prince in two ways.

Firstly, it enhanced knightly values and as far as ostentation, illusions and vanities were concerned, it asserted the pre-eminence of knighthood, which was being insidiously undermined by the intrusion of money and by the rise of the middle classes. Indeed, courtly love, practised with a sense of honour (*honestas*), was portrayed as one of the privileges of courtly behaviour. The villein was excluded from this game. Courtly love thus became the major criterion of refinement. It was by demonstrating his ability to transform himself through an effort of self-conversion similar to the effort which every man had to make if, climbing one step further in the hierarchy of merit, he wanted to be admitted into a monastic community; it was by providing the proof that he could play this game adequately, that the parvenu, the merchant who had grown rich from his business, succeeded in making himself accepted in this particular world, the court which was enclosed in the same way as the garden in the *Roman de la Rose* was enclosed by its wall. However, within this enclosure, courtly society was varied. The prince, counting on this variety, wanted to control this society more closely and to dominate it. The function of this criterion was to emphasize the gap between the different groups which confronted one another around the master. Because of its extreme refinement, this love could be neither that of the cleric nor that of the 'plebeian', as Andreas Capellanus put it, that is to say of the man with money. It distinguished the knight from other people at court.

At the very heart of knighthood, ritual contributed in another, complementary way to the preservation of order, for it helped to control the element of disorder and to tame the 'young'. The game of love, in the first place, was an education in moderation. Moderation was one of the key words in its specific vocabulary. As an invitation to repress impulses it was in itself a factor which contributed to calm and to appeasement. But this game, which was an education, also called for competition. It involved winning the stake – the lady – by outdoing rivals. The *senior*, the head of the household, allowed his wife to be placed at the centre of the competition, in an illusory, and ludic situation of primacy and power. The lady refused her favours to some men and granted them to others. This she did up to a certain point: the code projected the hope of conquest like a mirage on the imprecise limits of an artificial horizon – 'adulterous fantasies', as G. Vinay put it.

The role of the lady was thus to stimulate the ardour of young men and to assess the qualities of each wisely and judiciously. She presided over lasting rivalries. The best man was the man who had served her best. Courtly love taught men how to serve, and serving was the duty of the good vassal. Indeed it was the vassal's obligations which were transferred to the spontaneous pleasure of the spectacle but which, in a sense, also became more intense since the object that was being served was a woman, a being who was, by nature, inferior. In order to gain more self-control, the novice was constrained by a demanding education and, even more effectively, forced to suffer humiliation. The exercise he was being asked to perform was one of submission. It was also one of fidelity and of forgetfulness of self.

The games of courtly love taught *amistat*, as the troubadours called it, that is friendship, Cicero's *amicitia*, fostered, with all the values of stoicism, by the renaissance, by that return to classical humanism which took place during the twelfth century. To desire the well-being of another person more than one's own was what the lord expected of his man. All the evidence – one need only reread the poems and the romances to be persuaded of this – shows that the model of the amorous relationship was friendship, male friendship.

This leads me to question the true nature of the relationship between the sexes. Was the woman anything other than an illusion, a sort of veil or screen, in the sense in which Jean Genet understood this term, or rather simply a medium, an intermediary, the mediator. It is legitimate to wonder whether, in this triangular relationship between the 'young man', the lady and the lord, the major vector which, openly, goes from the young lover towards the lady, does not indeed rebound off the lady herself so as to reach the third person – its true goal – and even whether it does not project towards him without a detour. Christiane Marchello-Nizia's observations in her splendid article compel us to ask the following question: in this military society, was courtly love not, in reality, love between men? I would like to suggest at least part of the answer. I feel certain that, in serving the prince's wife, it was the love of the prince which the young wished to gain, by applying themselves, by bending, by bowing down. At the same time as they served to prop up the morality of marriage, the rules of courtly love reinforced the rules of the ethics of vassalage. In later twelfth-century France these rules therefore supported the rebirth of the state. Thus disciplined by courtly love, male desire would appear to have been used for political ends. This is one of the theories of the tentative research which I am currently pursuing.

5

Le Roman de la Rose

Historians of the Middle Ages have recently begun, as it were, to sift the soil. In some areas – peat bogs, clay beds and sandy soils – it is sometimes possible to collect the remains of the pollen and the spores of the surrounding flora which have been fossilized for thousands of years and accumulated in successive layers. These deposits are like the microscopic archives of the vegetable world. To consult them, date each one of their leaves and measure the part played by each botanical formation, is to gain a clear vision of a field of history where there had previously been only indistinct and intermittent traces, the history of a landscape and its progressive domestication. In the north of France this took place between the ninth and the beginning of the thirteenth century, a period when a slight fluctuation in climate, minute and yet of great significance, given the very rudimentary state of agricultural techniques, made the summers a little less humid and the winters a little milder: forest, scrub and waste land retreated continuously before fields and vineyards.

This process, which was slow to start, gained pace after the year 1000. A hundred years later, it turned everything upside down. Thousands upon thousands of peasant households which had ventured to the edge of heathlands and marshlands, rooted out, burned, drained, started to plough, planted vinestocks, all the time pushing back the unproductive areas.

I have started by describing this lengthy enterprise, these endless labours, because they lead to the orchard of the *Roman de la Rose* ('Romance of the Rose') between 1220 and 1230, and because without them there would have been no prosperity. Indeed, social relationships were at that time based on the seigneurial mode of production, that is, on glaring inequalities, an increasingly sophisticated system of taxes and dues which delivered all the fruit of the peasants' achievements into the hands of a happy few. What we call feudalism left the workers virtually bereft, so that handsome knights with white hands could lie with their girls in the shade of trees in the month of May and make love with a few refined touches.

Nowhere in Europe had rural growth been as intense as in the Ile-de-France; the most vigorous political power, with the greatest resources, most capable of encouraging all creative endeavour, had finally established itself in the heart of these prosperous country areas. It was there that the first part of the *Roman de la Rose* was written, in the triumphant atmosphere of Capetian Paris, after the battle of Bouvines and the military expeditions which brought Languedoc under French domination, at the accession of the very young king soon to be known as Louis, who would be the arbiter of the whole of Christendom. The 'art of France' – Gothic art – could then be seen in all its splendour in the cathedral of Notre-Dame, Pérotin's polyphonies could be heard there and masters were beginning to reveal to dazzled students the whole prodigious and overwhelming range of Greek philosophy. There were already warning signs that agricultural expansion was suddenly slowing down. But no one took any notice; the toil of peasants and the largesse of a victorious king allowed the nobility to live a life of affluence and pleasure.

Imagine Guillaume de Lorris's poem as the pinnacle of a cultural edifice centuries in the making, whose first stones were laid at the very beginning of this period of agricultural progress. In order to grasp the full meaning of the *Roman de la Rose* and to understand what happened to it, we must go back to the foundations of this culture, which contemporaries rightly defined as the culture of the courts. Consider the romance word 'courtly' and the two Latin terms from which it derives. The first word, *curtis*, designates the lord's residence at the centre of a large estate; and the other, *curia*, denotes a quasi-parliament, a group of men assembled around their leader to offer advice on how to settle common interests.

The combination of these two words gives a fairly accurate picture of feudalism, rooted both in rural lordship and in the military system.

Feudalism is the parcelling out of power. The process which helped shape it was already under way at the end of the ninth century when the Carolingian kings ceased to keep a tight rein on the nobility in the regions which made up France. Nobles who had hitherto been the agents of the sovereign, a few adventurers too, founded independent dynasties in the principal strongholds of public defence. These lords proclaimed themselves assigned by God to defend the people and to direct them in the twenty or thirty villages surrounding these fortresses. The owners of the best land, those who lived surrounded by numerous servants and tenants, who had time on their hands, with the means to arm themselves adequately, to train, to take their turn at garrison duty and to join expeditions to distant places, formed a small squad of permanent warriors around the castle and its master. These horsemen, the knights, as people called them, arrogated to themselves a monopoly of military action. The 'poor', those who had to work with their hands and toil on their lands or those of others, the unarmed and the vulnerable had to buy their security from the men-at-arms.

In around the year 1000, the body social was marked by a very clear division which separated the peasants from the warriors. The peasants or *vilains* – people from the *villa* (a word which then referred to both town and village at a period when urban areas had been almost completely absorbed into the countryside) – were judged, punished, commanded and exploited. The military leader took all the savings which they did not succeed in concealing, the rare silver coins which they managed to earn. He would spend them with his men, the knights. His band was not only exempt from taxes, it also shared the profits from them. To be sure, it was also subject to the lord, but by the obligations of honour which constituted the vassalic bond; the rituals of homage, in particular the kiss given on the mouth, to which serfs had no right, were intended to show clearly the essential equality of the leader and his war companions. The latter did not have to serve, except by bearing arms and giving counsel, and these were noble services which deserved a reward: the feudal lord, or seigneur, who wanted to be popular had to be munificent; rich rewards had to be shared continually and freely amongst his vassals. There were no constraints on them other than the constraints of a moral code whose pillars, the virtues of loyalty and valour, supported the entire system of aristocratic values and the *esprit de corps* which they protected. The warriors claimed to face death in order to protect the priests and the labourers. This sacrifice earned them salvation through the prayers of the former who lived off the rents of the latter. It gave them the right to do nothing, other than to exercise their profession as warriors, and to laugh once danger passed. Here we reach the foundations on which the first *Roman de la Rose* is built, the insurmountable barrier which separated the peasants from the courtly world, the wall which completely enclosed the garden of delights, whose narrow gate is guarded by idleness.

The starting point was thus violence and rural life, with the dust of stampedes and infernos blazing before wooden towers to bring the besieged ruthlessly to heel, amid sword strokes, shattered helmets, fierce turbulence. It was a warrior world, violent and masculine, a world which other men, the clergy, attempted to control by fear, and to sanctify, in order to calm the knights a little and prevent them from causing too much harm. On the other hand Guillaume de Lorris's poem is exquisite and finely wrought; Oiseuse, a woman who is not afraid of being treated rudely and who tries to please, succeeds and has men in her power. This refinement, this intrusion of feminine values dates from the twelfth century, at the height of agricultural achievement. As early as 1100 lordship brought in sufficient to give warriors the means and the taste to become more civilized, to distance themselves slightly from the world of plunder and pillage and, at the same time, to adopt a less abject attitude to the clergy. Already there were hardly any castles in France where the children of the master were not educated by tutors. These were priests whose role in the residence was to sing mass, bury the dead and ward off the forces of evil with magic formulas. Their very functions implied that they knew how to read some Latin and that they had been through school. They had not forgotten everything. Most of them could at least teach writing; some used their learning to make courtly games less cruel and, recollecting a few verses from

Ovid, Statius and Lucan, to polish the coarseness of the songs sung for entertainment.

Thus more and more knights could pride themselves on being 'educated'; their wives and daughters were perhaps educated even earlier and more. Words, taken from everyday language, but gradually stylized, fitted to melodies and increasingly removed from popular discourse, formed the chosen language of society and became literature, strictly speaking. For us literature begins with masterpieces, songs that had justifiably commanded admiration, that had been judged worthy of being written down in manuscript, as had only hitherto been the case with the Scriptures, biblical commentaries and the Latin classics. Through this literature the ideology of chivalry was strengthened. A number of intellectuals – that is to say ecclesiastics – co-operated in its construction. But they lived in the house of a prince and sought above all to flatter his taste, and it was a profane celebration which they embellished. The vision of the world which these poems put forward and which all the nobles shared therefore escaped from the grasp of the Church's morality. As soon as courtly culture gathered force, it declared itself resolutely independent of clerical culture, shaped at an earlier date, from whose influence it was strenuously attempting to escape. It was therefore aggressive, and flouted the preaching of penitence, and renunciation, encouraging people to enjoy worldly pleasures. This is the reason why the first *Roman de la Rose* expelled from the garden both Poverty, a chief virtue in the other moral code and Papelardie, or false piety. These were two women, faded and bare, destroyed by the influence of monks, who were to be cast aside.

After 1100 prosperity also encouraged the rebirth of states, and thus the restoration of peace of a kind in Christendom. The Crusades checked the unruliness of knights and directed it to the outside. Internally war tended imperceptibly to take on the appearance of a regulated and codified game, and battles that of sports meetings, amateur contests arranged on set dates in various places during the fine season. In tournaments, simulated battles which were as violent as real ones, howling and furious factions pitted one against the other, eager to take everything, horses, arms and armour, and the enemy for a ransom; but where, on principle, hatred was excluded, knights could at the same time enjoy themselves, pursue their training and strengthen their feeling of social superiority. Princes were well aware of all this and, each spring, they took the warriors from their province on a round of tournaments. The area was thus relieved of these warriors who returned hardened, and furthermore laden with booty and glory. 'France' – by which is meant the Ile-de-France and the adjacent areas – was the chosen territory for these exercises, where the values of prowess were exalted, where as early as the end of the twelfth century 'courtesy' dictated that one lady should choose and crown the victors.

At the forefront of the great spectacles which tournaments had become, 'youth' shone in all its splendour. This word referred then to the group of knights who had finished their apprenticeship and at around the age of twenty had solemnly received the arms and insignia of their profession, but had not yet managed to establish themselves in their own lordships and meanwhile competed in tournaments. Universally considered the 'flower' of chivalry, this age-group – which was large since 'youth' always extended a few years and often did not end – was the best audience of the writers, who did their utmost to please it. Because of the fascination which their way of life held and the nostalgia which those who no longer shared it still felt for these pleasures, and because of the intense ardour aroused by the appetite for seizing what they felt deprived of, 'youth' governed the development of aristocratic values. In 1225 youth still directed them. The first part of the *Roman de la Rose*, furthermore, was also written for young people. Both the author and the hero with whom he identifies loudly proclaim their youth. They see it as conducting a ballet whose dancers are performing in the enclosed garden. Attention is therefore to be concentrated on youth and the peculiarities of its behaviour.

First, it is worth looking at the type of education which 'youth' received. Indeed, this is what is most important: for the *Roman de la Rose* is itself presented as a work of initiation, as the 'art' of good behaviour and the perfection of a style. The natural place for this education was the 'court', the lord's household, the group of boys with whom the descendant of the heads of castles surrounded himself in the year 1000. To receive the sons of his vassals and feed them in his home was in fact one of the first duties of a lord, one which the vassalic contract laid down. It was a duty and a right: this was one of the ways in which the lord could manifest his generosity, and it was also a sure means of ensuring the hold of his successors over the rising generation. The young men were sent to him at an early age, as their childhood was just drawing to a close. They learned to use the sword on horseback in the company of the lord's boys. The lord would dub them to knighthood, provide them with military equipment at the same time as he armed his sons, then 'retain' them, as they put it, for many more years until they succeeded their father in his own fief. This is what the court was first and foremost – a sort of college, a school of knighthood. What was special about it was that this school lasted a very long time, and most of its pupils never left. For this reason the court included young novices and a good number of older companions, former pupils who had, for lack of a better occupation, become monitors. When the time came, the court moved to battlefield or tournament, with the youngest as squires, leading the extra horses, carrying the weapons of the older ones and learning as they watched them fight.

Whether the court was engaged in the turmoil of combat or it devoted itself to the pleasures of peace, it was the lord who supported it with his money. The court depended on his largesse, which explains the position of this virtue at the heart of the chivalric code, at the centre of the imaginary perfections Guillaume de Lorris aimed to present, the continuous eulogy of lordly munificence and the condemnation, the complete rejection of those attributes which are its opposite: avarice and covetousness. Courtesy, and through it all aristocratic society, was based on largesse, and the court clerics complacently pretended to confuse it with Christian charity and with the scorn for wealth extolled by the wise men of pagan antiquity. This particular point enables us to see how economic and ideological structures were articulated: the serfs produced wealth; the lord legitimately seized it, but he was unable to keep it for himself – he had to redistribute it amongst all the knights, and first of all among the young men.

The court was the organ of this process of redistribution – as the court of the king of France remained until 1789 – and the motor force behind it was largesse. Largesse ensured that the 'young' men were kept in a state of dependency – and because of this the court was permeated by envy directed against those who were masters of their money, by an impatience to inherit, to have at last a property and rents which were no longer provided by a lord whose moods had to be endured by the tenants whom he mistreated, and finally by a silent war against the *seniores*. The word *senior* is full of resonances: it refers both to the rich and – this is its first meaning – to the oldest members of society, and clearly marks the confusion that existed between economic position and age-group. Youth was therefore champing at the bit. But it was tamed by largessse. For the lord gave out the prizes. He organized a competition, a contest which lasted the length of the knight's education, extending way beyond the dubbing ceremony in the constant hope of an establishment which he could pass on to his heirs. The winners, those whom the lords helped to leave the ranks of 'youth' first, to establish themselves as lords earlier, were those who were most loyal, the bravest on expeditions, those who engaged in a series of never-ending trials and adventures with the greatest ardour. Largesse therefore made them hold their breath. However, it had no limits: the 'young' always demanded more, the right to devour with gusto all that the lordship produced, and more, and to dissipate the master's resources in extravagant display and knightly pastimes.

Amongst them, games of love constantly extended their domain throughout the twelfth century. Defying the priestly exhortation to continence, knights were forever seeking erotic satisfaction. There were two reasons for this. The first was that since warriors were becoming more civilized and abandoning their armour more often, women gradually came to the forefront of the courtly scene. The second, more decisive, reason stems from a particular aspect of family relationships. To avoid increasing the number of offspring that would have broken up the inheritance and brought ruin on their many descendants, noble families were wisely reluctant to marry off their sons. It was better that only one, the eldest, should found a line. The others remained 'bachelors', unmarried – unless their lord granted them a fief by marrying them to the heiress of a dead vassal and provided them with the means to found their own household without diminishing his own ancestral inheritance. To the young men this gift seemed the best reward of all. All the rivalry centred on the court was directed to this reward. But there was precious little of it. Thus the majority of knights, the liveliest and the most active, lived unmarried. Not, to tell the truth, without women; the generosity of the lords also extended to ensuring that the castles were peopled with obliging girls.

The young men's frustrations were not sexual – apart from the fact that adolescent sexuality, instability and vagrancy were such a long-lasting feature of a knight's existence. Although the court was indeed the place of desire, it was the desire to marry. Marriage meant the attainment of independence; it was a means of setting oneself up. The word *senior*, which is the opposite of *juvenis*, also referred to a married man. Here were the roots of covetousness and of the jealousy which one senses all the 'youth' must have felt towards their fathers at some time, often towards their eldest brothers, and always towards the lord, their benefactor, the head of the household where they were gathered. Every evening, among them, in the large communal hall – which at the end of the twelfth century still contained everything that in courtly life did not take place in the open air, at jousts, in the magic forest that abounded in game, in the orchard – he joined his wife in bed. In Latin the word for lady (*domina*) is the feminine of 'lord'. The temptation to seize her grew stronger, or, at least, the temptation to succeed against all rivals, to shine in her eyes and win her favours.

Thus courtly competition was split in two. A place was made for another entertainment whose arena was the mirror-image of the tournament. It required different weapons, different assaults, different blows to parry, different subterfuges. But the rule was virtually the same: the aim was to win the prize through good, long and loyal service, triumphing over the pitfalls of adventure. The lady here was both judge and prize. Like her husband, she had to be generous. She had to give, to give of herself, by degrees. Her largesse seemed as necessary as that of her lord and master. To prevent the whole edifice of courtly society from crumbling, neither was allowed to behave meanly, the lady by not participating in these games and the lord by keeping her out of reach. Despite appearances, it was he who led these games. He presided over this new competition. He used it, just as he used the other, to tame his young men. With a mirage of adultery, it was perhaps possible to nurture in the knights the illusion of triumphing over the old men, the rich and powerful. Their aggressiveness was offered a kind of outlet, a compensation through play, since courtly love was a commitment freely undertaken, based on fidelity like the mutual friendship owed to each other by lord and vassal, and devoid of all the cunning contrivances which were the prelude to marriage in the interminable discussions between the older men of the families.

Finally, the laws of the new entertainment (which took place within the system of education) introduced moderation, self-control and that semi-monastic virtue, discretion, into the fundamental values of the moral code of knighthood. This helped to quell unruliness more satisfactorily. There is no doubt that courtly love, through the feigned subservience of the knight to the chosen lady, through its lengthy stages, its illusory and gradual satisfactions, was the most efficacious ideological remedy for the internal contradictions of aristocratic society; at the same time it never ceased to be a man's game. The lord, from afar, secretly controlled the sequence of its events, just as he controlled from afar the apparent spontaneity of tournaments. He did this in order to ensure peace and conduct serious affairs as he pleased. Women were never anything other than bit-part players, lures – mere objects. All the poems of courtly love were sung by men, and the desire which they celebrated was always male desire. The first part of the *Roman de la Rose* describes a man's dream. In its disguise, youth is male and the Rose, a fantasy, is a mere reflection of Love, that is to say of the man's desire.

Thus all the pleasure belonged to the knights. Two words suffice to define it, two words which were congruent, combined, indissociable and together expressed the hope of pleasure and the taste of being young: *joi* and *joven*. These two words come from the languages of southern France. Indeed, in the south, the forms of courtly love had taken root in the courts where towards the year 1100, the duke of Aquitaine had assembled a group of young people who were less boisterous; this was not out in the middle of the fields but in cities where, as at Poitiers, the urban layout of the Roman period still survived, and where there were even some echoes of the high culture of Muslim Andalusia. For half a century courtly eroticism remained a distinct feature of southern culture. Then, when agricultural progress had moved north of the Loire, its sphere of influence grew. A number of princesses were undoubtedly instrumental in its dissemination – for example, Eleanor of Aquitaine, after her marriage to Henry Plantagenet, count of Anjou, duke of Normandy and king of England, and later her daughters, who were married to the great feudal lords of northern France. The latter fortified their principalities, dreamed of escaping the control of monarchy and competed with Capetian power.

The games of love initiated in the courts of Poitou seemed to them to be capable of showing their independence *vis-à-vis* the royal culture which, faithful to Carolingian traditions, remained wholly military and liturgical, protected from the temptations of the modern world by a dense barrier of clerks and monks. Over and against the king, the lord of lords, the count of Champagne and the count of Flanders willingly presented themselves as princes of 'youth', promoters of courtesy, and the pursuits it promised, together with all the joys of the visible world. The most vigorous games of love took place in the most sumptuous feudal courts maintained by Henry Plantagenet and his sons. After 1160, all the prestigious chivalric literature radiated from these courts. It was not until another generation had passed and Philip Augustus had defeated the count of Flanders and the king of England, and annexed Normandy, Anjou and Poitou to his own domain, and Paris had triumphed over all the other cities in the west, that *fine amour*, or courtly love, was fully accepted in the Ile-de-France.

When Guillaume de Lorris set about teaching its rules, he was consequently following a powerful and confident historical trend. Thirty years before, Andreas Capellanus had written a treatise on love, probably in Paris, the city of scholars, and at any rate in Latin, the language of the schools, and in a fairly pedantic tone, the tone of scholastic dialectic. In presenting his art of love to a wider public which expected to be entranced, Guillaume de Lorris chose the language of the courts, the French vernacular (*roman*). The same word also already referred to 'romance', a literary genre, the narration of a series of adventures.

The *Roman de la Rose* does indeed fit this description. It was plainly instructive like the stories of the knights of the Round Table, mapping the course of a journey and instructing the reader in the best manners which help people to succeed in the world. Like his model, Chrétien de Troyes, Guillaume de Lorris offers as an example of courtly perfection a hero on a journey who goes from one discovery to another and overcomes obstacles one by one. Although the emphasis has changed, although the thickets of Brocéliande have given way to the order of a domesticated flora which has been cultivated and subdued and is ready for pleasure, and although the characters the hero meets on the way are no longer enchanters, dwarfs or incognito knights, but represent the personification of the values of the system, the *Roman de la Rose* (like the earlier works from which it draws its inspiration) sets out to hold a mirror to secular society and the image it has of itself – the image of a division which isolates good from evil and rejects what each disdains or fears.

A blank wall is thus erected. Beyond it nothing exists. Nothing living is to be seen, only effigies, emblems and mannequins without depth or body, like those burnt on the midsummer bonfires on the feast of St John the Baptist. Nailed against the wall like exorcized objects, this assembly of non-values represents the destruction of what the happy few would gladly no longer see or smell, eyes closed and nostrils blocked to everything that offends them and might tarnish their joy. The orchard is purged of them. It is peopled only with carefree individuals whose gracious company acts out make-believe imaginary relationships, the illusion of a society whose courts provide entertainment, and which conceals from the public gaze the harshness and tensions of life. No one wanted to know the cost of this feast, nor who was paying. Youth and Love – *joi* and *joven* – were kings, and Largesse the director. It excluded peasants and greybeards. It formed couples for the dance. But the Rose – the bud, rather, barely peeping from childhood – is there to be plucked, and its meagre defences are simply there to give the game more spice, to prolong the waiting for a while and to arrange the tests required in the education of pleasure. All the scenery was arranged so that worry was dispelled – the worry of the poor, and the fear of death and what lay beyond. There was no sign of religion. It was as if priests did not exist.

'There is no greater paradise than to enjoy one's beloved': it could not be expressed more clearly. What was the orchard if not paradise profaned. The people who walk there are as beautiful as angels; they sing like seraphim on high, but their song does not rise towards God. The love which they celebrate is physical. Their aim is to take pleasure. Square like the cloisters of a Cistercian abbey, the orchard is their complete opposite – not arranged for the transports of the soul, but the exaltation of worldly delight, the joy of existence, of seizing pleasure in the visible world. Should we go further and ask whether Guillaume de Lorris was continuing the struggle against the sermons of Christianity, and whether the cross-shaped castle where Bel Accueil is imprisoned and on which an assault is being prepared – this model fortress resembles the most recently built castles – is not the symbol of the Church and the constraints which it sought to impose? The Church – and this is worse – is simply forgotten. The field is open, unhampered, to peaceful sensuality, which pervades the entire poem. It bursts out ever more intense at each description of finery, jewels and female flesh. We should acknowledge the perfect fidelity of the premier romance to the models of courtly culture. It perfects them.

None the less, when courtly love finally succeeded in insinuating itself into Parisian culture, it was truly captured, tamed, and made to submit to other laws, and thus to change its appearance in certain respects. For the aristocratic society which gathered in Paris was not the same as that of Aquitaine, Champagne or Normandy. It was not so rigidly insular. This society was subject to other strong influences: from the great intersection of trade routes, where merchants were already making their fortunes and longing to be accepted into the company of noblemen; from the great centre of intellectual work, the most advanced in the world, which was fast spreading on the slopes of the hill of Sainte-Geneviève; and from the institutions of royal government where legal and financial experts were pushing forward to the front ranks. That is why in Guillaume de Lorris's poem chivalric culture, at the end of its very slow development and the path which had brought it from the feudal states situated on the periphery to the heart of the Capetian province, underwent three changes which marked its final refinements. All three move in the same direction, relaxing, polishing the rough elements which remained in aristocratic culture. Under the gaze of the king, the harshness was lessened, and three of the conflicts which had till then divided courtly society, setting the flower of its youth against Schoolmen, married men and 'new' men, lost their bitterness.

The Church is repudiated in the first part of the *Roman de la Rose*. But scholarship, the knowledge dispensed by the university, is not rejected. Guillaume de Lorris, of whom nothing is known, had clearly followed its lessons at length. He had heard commentaries on the Latin poets. He wanted to be a new Ovid, not simply to strive to imitate him like the old scholars who formerly made their career in the courts, but to compete with him, and to employ to this end all the artifices of grammar and rhetoric. Beneath its apparent naivety and pleasing fluency, the work is in fact very learned, written for all kinds of readers, to be understood on several levels, just as the classical *auctores* (the authors), sacred and profane, were understood by the masters of the university, who strove to reveal beneath the surface of the discourse one after another of the multiple meanings with which the terms are imbued. The words of the *Roman de la Rose* are also both open to the gaze and secret. The work lends itself to gloss, to the kind of amorous exchange of thoughts in which the reader patiently draws back the surface draperies and moves towards the deep meaning of the text. In the best schools, those on the banks of the Seine and the Loire, Guillaume had learnt to observe the inclinations of the heart and mastered that inventory of the passions which scholasticism had pursued since the beginning of the twelfth century. Henceforth psychological analysis displayed so much subtlety that romance vocabulary was too crude to communicate the experience.

For this reason, and because the artifices of the theatre were beginning to triumph over all others when it came to transmitting knowledge, Guillaume de Lorris used the allegory which the professors – for lack of anything better – did not hesitate to use themselves. He gave some characters the role of representing abstraction, of miming the subtle progress of love, the awakening of youthful sensuality, on that journey which, from the naive desire to possess, leads, through the gradual discovery of the beauties of body and soul, to the abandonment of self, the elevation by degrees which is not fundamentally different from that pursuit of truth for which the schools were the favoured site. These Parisian schools were also schools of lucidity. They had taught artists to free the romanesque church from darkness. To fill it with light, to purge it of monsters and wild chimeras, to replace the vague swarming of dreamlike vegetation on the capitals of pillars with the intertwinings of real leaves and flowers. Now they invited the poets too to open their eyes to reality. Magic is not entirely excluded from the *Roman de la Rose*. Its fountain, like that which the knights errant of Breton romances trembled to approach, is enchanted and enslaves by its winning enticements. Who knows if Guillaume de Lorris, had he continued his poem, would not have led it for a while into the provinces of a darker love? He too recounted a dream. However, the light in which this dream is bathed leaves no room for uncertainties. It is clear and frank as in a garden on a May morning. Because the meeting of the two dominant cultures, clerical and knightly, had nowhere been pushed further than in the entourage of the king of France, at once priest and warrior, the art of Guillaume de Lorris, independent and more than ever free from any clerical grip, did not hesitate to feed upon all the fruits of the twelfth-century renaissance which had taken place in the cathedral schools of the Ile-de-France.

Through a similar process of opening up, and through the effect of economic growth in the region of Paris, that progressive area, the undue tensions in court society between the 'young' men and those who were older, who had power and wives, could be seen to be relaxed. Inside the orchard everyone was rich. There was no trace of the frustrations which had formerly led troubadours to proclaim loudly that love was irreconcilable with wealth, and that feats and victories in erotic jousts should be reserved for the least privileged, the 'young'. It was no longer a question of marriage – the literature of courtly love neither condemned it, taught how to betray it nor accepted it. Guillaume de Lorris does not breathe a word about it. Is he for marriage, or against it – as courtly love had been most vehemently in its earlier expressions? In fact, marriage belongs to reality, on which the first *Roman de la Rose* turns its back. Like everything that has some connection with the morality of the Church, like everything that one wants to forget when one goes through the door, even if it means finding it again after the dream, marriage is completely absent.

The fact remains that the Rose is far from being in full bloom. The object of the quest, the image glimpsed in the reflection of the fountain, and which inspires desire, is not the body of a lady, of another man's wife; it is the body of a damsel. She is at the age when girls are betrothed. The love by choice, whose development the poem charts step by step, strongly resembles what the period was beginning to dream of, the mutual inclination which it was now good taste to hold as the necessary prerequisite for any marriage, of which no one any longer dared to say, even in court entertainments, that it would not long survive the nuptials. The rise in the profits of lordship, royal favours and the salaries earned in the service of the state really increased the affluence of noble families. They showed less reluctance at the outset of the thirteenth century in allowing their offspring to have children. They no longer so stubbornly refused to marry off younger sons who were not entering the priesthood. At that time a profound change was taking place in the structures of aristocratic society. It imperceptibly freed knighthood from the cultural tyranny of those who were bachelors. A place on the margin of society was valued less highly. The authorities were less concerned with the unruliness of the 'bachelors'. The old conflict between 'youth' and the rest left behind it no more than a pattern of sentimental behaviour. There was no longer any reason to exclude it from marriage. The upper echelons of society (as a result of everything that transformed it) no longer dissociated true love from marriage.

Another boundary was being eradicated, that which tightly surrounded the small group of warriors. In theory, in Paris at any rate, it was no longer constructed so that it followed the line of the enclosing wall which was still just as high, and perhaps steeper, and which forbade access to the non-noble. The *Roman de la Rose* is set in an orchard, not a castle nor the forest of Arthurian combats. There are no more horses or armour. Any show of violence, fits of rage, oaths and sabre rattling would disturb the courtly *fête* (celebration). Distinction is no longer based on exploits and feats, but on the trouble taken to refine language, to care for body and grooming, to move with elegance and restraint. Some ten or fifteen years after the Battle of Bouvines, knights are shown unarmed in the *Roman de la Rose*, as if they had forgotten their military origins, and no longer remembered that the profession of arms was an ennobling one. There was a self-evident reason for this. The knights had recently lost their monopoly of the profession, which was successfully practised by a growing number of people of limited means, hired men and mercenaries, whom the princes were glad to engage since they worked harder at the task. Consequently, it was necessary to use different criteria to distinguish persons of quality: to be precise, the skill used in playing the games of love. Non-nobles were no longer barred from bearing arms, but they had none of the grace, manners or social bearing which won the hearts of beautiful women. Love could not admit them into the ranks of its vassalage. This meant that secular society remained more than ever on its guard, closed, intent on thwarting attempts at intrusion, unmasking the parvenu whose manners gave him away, pointing the finger at his naive lack of refinement, the very gloss of which betrayed it as too recent.

These parvenus were indeed beginning to show their arrogance, and nouveau riche townspeople and soldiers of fortune were already buying lordships and dispensing justice in their turn, receiving the homage of vassals; they too would be holding court if no attempt was made to stop them. They forced their way into the courts of the king and princes, dreaming of passing themselves off as nobles and concealing as best they could their modest origins. The increased movement of wealth, which was nowhere as marked as in the city where the king usually had his residence, made the nobility of birth more conscious of the dangers which threatened the material foundations of its supremacy.

Meanwhile Guillaume de Lorris did not propose anything other than the poetical formulation of the rules of etiquette. Thenceforth a real social barrier was established on the basis of respect for good manners. Was it watertight? Who inhabited the enclosure within it? All the knights, naturally; surely some clerics too, for they did not all come from the nobility; and possibly some members of the *bourgeoisie*. Chrétien de Troyes was still poking fun at the latter loudly. Andreas Capellanus had, however, already portrayed 'plebeians' murmuring sweet nothings to noble ladies – without managing to seduce them, admittedly, but without making fools of themselves either. Guillaume de Lorris was careful not to mention the social status of the man who spoke in his name. He knew well that the writer who wanted to succeed, to please the nobility and gain an audience, must establish a distance between them and the rest of society, but avoid, on the heights where he complacently sets his readers, marking the differences between them too sharply. It would not be fitting, in what inevitably became the court, to jeer too loudly at the sons of the low-born.

Some of the latter were very highly placed, and every one of them pretended to have forgotten his origins.

It is no coincidence that in France the image of chivalry attained its most perfect expression in the account of a dream, or that this dream was Parisian and belonged to a society which was striving to be carefree, which thought itself protected against all danger by the high walls within which it had enclosed itself. It was a society which wished to hear neither of constraints nor of money, and which hoped to stifle, beneath the murmur of tasteful conversation and gentle music, the outbursts of petty quarrels which, in reality, disturbed it. The early thirteenth century had inherited a system of manners and a code of values from the preceding period where, in what was still a peasant world, the seigneurial means of production rigorously defined the position of a self-assured aristocracy, where no one ventured to dispute the power and wealth of lord and knight. People of quality felt vaguely that this ideological framework was the only one capable – now that ecclesiastical prebends, weapons, lordships and fiefs were passing into the hands of all and sundry – of safeguarding the perpetuation of the ruling class and of limiting access to it and smoothing the inevitable intermingling of the nobility of birth, which clung to vanities, with the group of intellectuals who were convinced of their increasing indispensability and the handful of 'new' men, from business or princely service, who were able to get themselves accepted.

The slow development of the relations of production imperceptibly shifted the boundary between the classes. But its mark remained on the original site and neither prince, male heirs nor the most able parvenus thought it advisable to let it disappear. On the contrary, they wished to emphasize it. To this end they set up new boundaries in the same place. These were inevitably the products of illusion, but they had to appear to be true. The value of Guillaume de Lorris's lucid observation stems from this. Turned into a spectacle as Guillaume saw it, the social dream had the convincing strength of reality.

Like all dreams, the first *Roman de la Rose* broke off in midcourse. It is unlikely that Guillaume de Lorris was prevented from finishing his poem. This fine writer was only too aware that his poem would have greater appeal if it were left unfinished. It was captivating. The book was very well received by aristocratic society and by the people who aspired to penetrate it. Its success lasted so long that the ambitious and talented Jean de Meun decided to base his work on Guillaume de Lorris's poem, to take up the story freely, playing with its ambiguities, adding further meanings to it, developing and expanding it. At that time it was not unusual to finish other people's work: cathedrals were never finished, and one master builder succeeded another on the building site. They would take up the draft outline and remodel it as they pleased – witness, for example, Gaucher who chose to place the statues which had already been executed by Jean Le Loup in a completely different manner on the façade of the cathedral at Reims. Writers behaved in the same way. Chrétien de Troyes left the task of completing *Le Chevalier à la charrette* to others.

In the same way, Jean de Meun took over the *Roman de la Rose*. Today there is a tendency to place his work at an earlier date, to situate it in the 1260s, and thus closer to Rutebeuf and the *Péril des temps nouveaux*, the treatise which the teacher Guillaume de Saint-Amour wrote in 1256, before the Second Crusade and the death of St Louis – before the period of extreme instability which, in the last quarter of the thirteenth century, ushered in difficult times. The *Roman de la Rose* in its entirety belongs to this splendid period. The second part very precisely marked its end.

What is certain – and this is what counts – is that forty years separate the second part from the first. Let us imagine Picasso's *Trois musiciens* completed by Soulages. The tone, the writing, are completely different. In the space of forty years the world changed – and just as fast, despite what people believe, in the Middle Ages as it does today. This is what provides the contrast between the two poems. One might think that the author and his hero have themselves aged – and how many commentators have not pictured Guillaume de Lorris as a youth and Jean de Meun as an old man? Jean de Meun was apparently no older than his predecessor. At any rate his age is not an issue. What aged was aristocratic culture. During those forty years, profound changes took place in all parts of the structure which supported it.

These changes started at the foundations, and this was critical.

At the time of Guillaume de Lorris, the rapid expansion of the countryside influenced everything. Subsequently the impetus came from the towns. Revenues from rural lordships remained high. There were not yet any signs of shortages. Savings were hoarded up in cottages: towards the middle of the century peasants from Thiais and from Orly bought their manumission; they found 2,200 and 4,000 *livres parisis* respectively to pay for it, approximately the value of 200 war horses. However, this prosperity belonged to the momentum of an agricultural expansion which for the past forty years had slowed down. Production began to decrease, yields to diminish and fields (sown with cereal crops) were on the decline. Vitality was transferred to the market economy. Henceforth the 'conquerors' were the traders and no longer the peasants who cleared the land. During those forty years great developments affected banking, haulage, canal transport and the means of exchange: France saw the reappearance of the gold coins that had ceased to be minted in Latin Christendom seven centuries before; the first came from Italy, but St Louis started issuing them again in 1263.

European trade was expanding everywhere: in 1241 Europe was still bowed down under the weight of Asia, trembling in Poland and in Hungary at the approach of the Mongol hordes; in 1271 Marco Polo set off for China in the company of silk merchants. This opening mainly benefited Italian cities, and Italy was soon to become the site of great cultural adventures. Less than half a century after the *Roman de la Rose* was completed, Dante wrote the *Divine Comedy* and Giotto painted the Padua frescoes. For the time being France, the great kingdom, and Paris, the great city, prevailed indisputably on account of their wealth and creativity. But the transfer of the means of growth from the fields to the roads, fairs and markets succeeded in changing a great many things. The new wealth was unstable and risky, subject entirely to fortune, and thus abandoned to fate, on that ever-turning wheel which continually raises some and casts others down. This wealth was built up by harsher exploitation of the poor. Destitution was more conspicuous in the towns; it became self-aware and led to revolt. The first strikes in history exploded in 1280. The walls of the enclosed orchard were no longer high enough. The noise of the populace could be heard.

On account of this, power structures were transformed. With money, things were governed differently. The king disappeared behind his officials, his judges and his tax collectors. There was no longer any feudal independence. There was no longer any court. Instead there were courts of justice – institutions. These were so rigid that St Louis considered it fitting to go and sit under the oak trees at Vincennes. What was known as the *Hôtel*, the king's household, consisted of a group of paid experts who rose in rank when they were accomplished at giving judgement, rendering accounts, suppressing riots and patiently enhancing the power and prestige of the sovereign as well as their own. They were, for the most part, experts like Jean de Meun himself, and they came from the lower ranks of the knighthood, the *petite chevalerie*, and some from even lower down the social scale. All of them had frequented the schools of Paris, and those of Bologna where civil law was taught, and which Jean de Meun may have attended. They had qualifications and were referred to by the title of 'master'. They were good students who owed everything to this culture of which they were proud. Some were clerics, others knights.

What actually remained of the contrasts between clergy and knights in a profession and a milieu which had become completely urbanized? The administrative services of the king of France had ceased entirely to be itinerant and rustic. They established themselves in the city which acted like a magnet, attracting the world's best teachers and craftsmen. In the space of forty years Paris had truly become the capital; a century before Gian Galeazzo's Milan, the Prague of the Emperor Charles IV and Pope Clement's Avignon, Paris was the great workshop of the thirteenth century. Here there was a merging between the 'court', that is, what the court had become, and the 'city', or what the city was becoming. This encounter resulted in a new audience, which was already the audience of Rutebeuf and the second *Roman de la Rose*. It still consisted of nobles, of warriors, of the 'young' and the not-so-young in great numbers, but now it was accompanied, at a distance perhaps, by people from the household of the king, from the university, from the clergy of all the churches of Paris, and from that fringe of townspeople who were no longer completely unsophisticated and now enjoyed intellectual games.

This wider audience remained fascinated by the same aristocratic model – the feudal model – which was created in tournaments and princely assemblies. We should cease, once and for all, talking about the 'bourgeois spirit' in this respect. The audience endeavoured to cut any remaining links with the bourgeoisie. In its eyes, the orchard had lost nothing of its appeal, nor indeed had love well enacted, that is to say, love according to the rules. The audience knew the first part of the *Roman de la Rose* by heart. It jealously valued its own pre-eminence, fiercely repulsed interlopers and put up the same insurmountable barrier to exclude the low-born. But it was looking from above. It was curious about everything, about the universe, about itself; and it was more determined not to be fooled. For this reason this audience made greater use of irony, with winks and smiles directed towards its own members. Like Guillaume de Lorris, Jean de Meun was writing for an elite which regarded itself as such and wanted to be one, but at every turn was jostled by all the hustle and bustle of the city, wresting it from its dream and forcing it to look at life.

Spiritual life underwent even greater changes. Forty years earlier the first disciples of Francis of Assisi had only just begun to arrive in Paris. They were suspect. These men, who were clad in rags with their hands outstretched and who spoke of the poverty of Christ, were viewed as heretics. They were in danger of being burned. In Jean de Meun's time Franciscans dominated the university with those other mendicants, the Dominicans. They ruled over the consciences of princes, and first and foremost over King Louis, who no longer laughed; instead, he dressed in black and took to kissing lepers. His friends deplored the fact that he had begun to live like a monk. Franciscans and Dominicans started to dominate the beliefs of the entire populace, at any rate in the cities; they dominated it through sermons, through spectacle, through the increasingly dense network of the Tertiary Orders, that large net in which the laity increasingly found itself caught, and through the Inquisition, which they undertook. They themselves were dominated by the pope and the cardinals, who used them to subjugate the world. What remained of the great outburst of evangelism of earlier times? There was indoctrination, a contribution to repression, pietism and the rebellion of the 'spiritually minded' who already in the south of the kingdom were brandishing the legacy of St Francis against the injunctions of the Holy See.

There was, however, one complete success: convents had been founded in every city and Bonaventure and St Thomas Aquinas were leading intellectual research. That was not all. Christianity was invigorated, and became for the first time a popular religion, through simple teaching, frequent confession and spiritual advice. Proper dialogue was established at last between God's servants and the faithful, which, beyond the rituals, called for people to open up their hearts. The success of the mendicant orders affected the cultural milieu which received the *Roman de la Rose* in three ways.

In the first place it stirred up the jealousy, rancour and hostility of all those whom the Franciscans and the Dominicans dislodged from their comfortable positions. Above all it posed a danger to academics, secular teachers, whose prestige was threatened, and many of their students, whose aspiration to occupy one day the best places in the Church and in the entourage of princes was jeopardized by this formidable competition. On the other hand, the preaching of friars, and the new image of Christ which it presented, overcame the obstinate resistance of secular culture, which had formerly strained to escape from clerical control. Finally, to proclaim, like St Francis, that the world is not such a bad place, that water, air, fire and earth are also blessed, that the Creator placed Adam in the garden of Eden to enjoy it and to work at making it even more beautiful, that nature is the daughter of God and thus deserves to be looked at, observed and understood – this meant following a desire to embrace reality fully which tormented so many people at that time. None the less these people demanded more and more. They did not understand why, at a certain point, they were forbidden to go further. For although Christianity, by becoming more vigorous, had attained to optimism, it in no way denied abnegation or the spirit of penance. Thus, the success of the mendicant orders sharpened the dispute. This is where the new contradiction arose, the contradiction which incited Rutebeuf and his followers against pretence, the hypocrites and the excessively devout. The world is good, life is beautiful, the sky is more luminous than ever. Can one enjoy happiness on earth without losing one's soul? Many in the Paris of 1260 did not hesitate for a moment in answering yes to this question.

During those forty years the boundaries of knowledge had also moved. This was because scholars had discovered what in Aristotle proved to be most alien to Christian thought and which was noted by the philosopher's Arab commentators, starting with Averroës, whom they had discovered as well. It was also because, in the meantime, the paths of knowledge had changed. For Guillaume de Lorris, for all his audiences, even the most learned, and for the masters who took as much pleasure in hearing him as the young nobles, these channels continued to be St Bernard and Abbot Suger. It was a progression by leaps, from word to word, from image to image, through metaphors and analogies, through reflections which rebounded from mirror to mirror, in a shimmering comparable to that of stained-glass windows. At the same time, learning for Jean de Meun's readers assumed the clarity, the rigour and the slightly dry elegance of radiant gothic architecture. Like the latter, learning was built on logic. In the universities and in all the ways of thinking which disseminated from them, *disputatio* or debate prevailed. This was a joust of words, where the adversary had to be unhorsed by sharpened reasoning, the equivalent of the tournament, a game where each strove to win honour. The prize was power, and these polemical attitudes roused the fighting spirit in high culture. In the second part of the *Roman de la Rose* they gave rise to battle postures, to an epic mode completely absent from the first part. Unnecessary embellishments would impede these mental skirmishes, which had to reject all complacency and constantly demanded to know more: to catalogue nature and books; to label and classify in order to show skill in laying hold of new weapons; to learn everything systematically.

Guillaume de Lorris was expected, through the paths of initiation, of pursuit, of adventure and lyrical effusion, to give instruction in the ways of good behaviour. Jean de Meun was expected to communicate a science. He was addressing men for whom life and the taste of happiness would not cease after the age of twenty-five, and who were well aware that the women of the day were learned – men who knew that however handsome they were, however agile in the military game or in the assaults of love, they could no longer shine in secular society if they knew nothing about Cicero, Suetonius or the poets and could not recognize in passing a particular quotation, and at least pretend to know about the books which were discussed in the Faculty of Arts. A marvellous popularizer, Jean de Meun generously distributed this small currency of erudite knowledge. He made libraries more accessible, and made it easier for people to find their way along the shelves. What authors did he not quote? There were Virgil, Livy and Juvenal, Alain de Lille, John of Salisbury, Andreas Capellanus, Abelard, what Chalcidius knew of the *Timaeus*, and many others not yet traced in the *Roman de la Rose*, such as Bernard Silvester, not to mention astronomy, optics and all the areas which scientific research was just beginning to investigate. Having included these references, he made them accessible and amusing, and wove them into proverbs, combining them with folk wisdom. He used everyday words, the language of hunting and gambling and the vocabulary of the streets and the woods to describe what was most abstract, most austere and most arduous. And – like Molière – he always returned to good sense, to robustness and to generosity.

Through his supreme art Jean de Meun even succeeded in minimizing the discordances between the work of his precursor and the very long sequel which he set out to write. Ultimately the two works complement one another. But this underlying harmony stems mainly from the fact that the upper ranks of society, in the general upheaval, remained attached to the same value system which, like a soft garment, yielded to the movements of the body. It did not stray from these values. Jean de Meun's work provides the best evidence of this permanence. He lived by his pen; indeed, he made a very good living from it. He served the greatest princes, Robert of Artois and Charles of Anjou, the brothers of St Louis, whom perhaps he praises in the *Roman de la Rose*, Jean de Brienne, and certainly King Philip the Fair. He therefore worked for those spheres of society which were the outposts of snobbery – and which also demanded other books from him, notably translations of Latin authors in the scholarly tradition.

What did he translate? What was he commissioned to translate? Boethius – and this interest in philosophy perhaps reveals a new flexibility, but it was the only instance. Everything else formed part of the web of chivalric culture. At the end of the thirteenth century people with influence were interested above all in military techniques. Jean de Meun translated Vegetius. His audience liked excursions to the roots of the 'matter of Brittany' – he translated the 'Wonders of Ireland'. Spirituality appealed to them, the usual spirituality which was directed along the paths of mysticism – in other words, Cistercian spirituality. Jean de Meun translated Aelred of Rielvaux. Finally, the dialectic of love fascinated them: he translated the correspondence of Héloïse and Abelard, and some people wondered, not without strong reasons, whether he had not invented it himself.

The ideology of the second part of the *Roman de la Rose* was still based on the *courtoisie–vilenie* polarity, the antithesis between courtliness and the non-courtly. This opposition simply became more marked. It assumed that new bitterness which the growth of an urban economy and the irresistible invasion of money conferred on antagonism within society. Since everyone now knew that everything was for sale, since earning too much created difficulties, Jean de Meun always praised the spirit of selflessness and generosity, but he did so with vehemence. In that ardent and furious tone which the century adopted, inspired by Alain de Lille, he renewed the diatribe against the wicked rich, writing with passionate sincerity, and denouncing poverty equally strenuously and a hundred times more insistently than Guillaume de Lorris.

No doubt, as well as the poor, he intended to attack the mendicant friars who through the pope had triumphed over the secular clergy in the university, and of whom the majority of his readers were jealous. No doubt he was trying to suppress the bad conscience which Franciscan preaching had created among the well-to-do, and once again it was the friars whom he was attacking when he proclaimed that people should support themselves by working and not beg for alms. But they were not his only target. He criticized all the poverty-stricken who had poured into the suburbs in dangerously large numbers on account of the rural recession, and who were beginning to be feared. All society, decent people as well as reprobates, was scandalized by destitution. The poor had to be locked up, forced to work, cared for like the sick, punished like guilty people and destroyed in the same way as heretics were destroyed. When Jean de Meun spoke – and no one had ever before spoken so well – of equality and liberty, when he scornfully crushed all those who claimed that, because of their birth, they belonged to the nobility when their souls were soiled with baseness, it should not be interpreted as a call for a change in society. For him society was naturally divided by a wall, by ramparts which he wanted to strengthen further because the dangers were increasing. He remained on the right side, in safety. He demanded equality and liberty, but within the enclosed garden which had to be open not only to birth but also to merit. The right to taste its delights was promised to anyone who attained a certain degree of perfection, a certain 'prize'. This is precisely what Guillaume de Lorris and the troubadours before him had said. The only difference now was that the criterion for perfection was no longer courtly love but knowledge. For the 'young' knights no longer imposed their tastes on the upper ranks of society. The tone was now set by the intellectuals. The first *Roman de la Rose* sought to eradicate the distinctions between knights and clergy. The second demanded precedence for the clergy.

This partly explains the most profound shift, the most marked crack which can be discerned in the ideological veneer. But at the root of this turning point there were also the victories over ritualism and heresy which had been won in the reign of St Louis by the new Christianity, which was joyful, critical and robust. Like Rabelais, Jean de Meun despised canting hypocrites. Nevertheless he was a staunch supporter of the Gospel, which explains why he proposed replacing the first garden by another garden, which was round rather than square, marking the symbolic transition from the earthly to the heavenly, and the perfections of eternity. At its centre was a fountain which no longer represented death but symbolized life. This new garden was the garden of the mystic Lamb. It was no longer seen as the negation of the cloister, as a desecration of paradise. It was the true paradise, that of Adam reconciled – as the visible and invisible, flesh and joy were reconciled, in both the second *Roman de la Rose* and the sculptures of Notre-Dame.

After a century of doctrinal struggles against the Cathars, against all those sermons which had professed contempt for matter, following the speculation of the doctors of Chartres, the Cistercian attempt to preserve the incarnate in mysticism – after the '*Canticle of Creation*' (of St Francis), and while the impetus of progress exalted the value of work and showed mankind co-operating in this continuing work of the creation – Jean de Meun and those who paid heed to him called for the rehabilitation of Nature. Nature was the 'vicar and constable' of God – in other words it was his lieutenant who was responsible, just as the constable was to the king of France, for leading his expeditions on horseback, directing his battles and doing his will. Nature, the source of all beauty and all goodness, commanded the squadrons which were to force back corruption. Jean de Meun's vision remained Manichaean, but the dualism shifted. The battle was no longer between the carnal and the spiritual, but between the natural and what thwarted it – hypocrisy, violence, cupidity and sin. To sin was to transgress the laws of God and thus to disobey nature, whose function was to apply them. For the kingdom could not be divided against itself nor the constable act against the master's will. Whoever follows the orders of nature therefore embarks on the path of salvation. In joy and crowned with flowers, he progresses towards the garden where heaven and earth meet, where the joy of living is transformed. He goes towards the Rose, which not only represents the young female lover, nor as in the intentionally overt realism of the final act, the flower of her sex. Through the inexhaustible multiplicity of symbolic meanings, the rose in the poem, like the rose-windows which Jean de Chelles had just placed in the transept of Notre-Dame, represents continuous creation, its emerging mystery, the expansion of God as light through the ordered universe, the procession of divine love, the return of human love and the triumph of life over darkness and death.

Imagine Jean de Meun standing before the secret of the world. He is free in spirit, with that true freedom which constitutes true nobility. He intends to confine its exercise to the order of creation, which in human society must separate the base from the rest – by opening people's eyes and fighting, sometimes vehemently but more often through irony. The entire work is pervaded with irony. To ignore it would be to refuse to penetrate the depth of its meaning, as well as to deprive oneself of the best pleasure, and especially to miss seizing this challenge in its full force. Its aim was not solely to entertain. It set out to rectify what was distorted by the advance of corruption which Aristotle called irresistible.

The world had been perfect in the golden age. It had not experienced avarice and poverty, those same vices whose effigies were shown pinned to the walls of the orchard in the first *Roman*. The world now knew these vices. It had been sapped and destroyed by them. It was therefore necessary to raise meagre barriers against corruption, namely coinage, the state, lordship, inequality, the feudal mode of production – a yoke where freedom is stifled, an inevitable yoke until the day when humanity is at last entirely redeemed by the progress of learning and self-knowledge and has returned to the garden, until the Final Judgement. The end of time and the triumph of knowledge coincide in fact.

Until then men should at least attempt to follow the laws of Nature, to react against what distracts them from it and what Jean de Meun, after Rutebeuf, inveighs against. They should fight against lies, starting with Forced Abstinence, unwillingly accepted Chastity and its companion Pretence, i.e. Tartuffe: the mendicant orders and the plot which they had hatched against true Christianity. They had also to fight against false marriage – and here Jean de Meun is taking up again the arsenal of anti-matrimonial writings which had accumulated since the time of St Jerome, but it was to redress the deviations, to put an end to unsound marriages, to the tyranny of husbands and the licentiousness of wives – and especially against false love.

On this point the second *Roman* is in conflict with the first, just as the new courtliness was in conflict with the earlier one, being no longer satisfied with either the game or the fantasy. Love, sentimental love, physical love, has nothing to do with simpering manners, endless ostentation, feigned subjection of the suitor to the lady, repression of desire, or the turmoil of passion. Real love is friendship and charity. It should be the free inclination of a soul freely given, in faith, in justice and in the integrity of the early period of the golden age. It should be a natural physical ardour, free from both sophisticated eroticism and puritanical constraints. Love should be shared. Can Jean de Meun be called an anti-feminist? He subordinated Love to Venus, that is to say men's desire to women's desire which courtly love had disregarded. He did this in order that people should make love naturally, in freedom and equality, so that its pleasure should be shared. This is the 'prize', the reward – quite simply, happiness on earth, some ground gained in the fight against corruption, recaptured once more by nature, that 'art of God' as Dante was to say. Finally the door was bolted against *contemptus mundi* (contempt of the world), against that rejection of the world which the priests had been preaching for ten centuries, as well as against that unreality into which those who were intoxicated by *Lancelot* dreamt of vanishing.

All this was expressed admirably, with a skill in writing most of which unfortunately escapes us, since we have lost the key to rhetoric. Jean de Meun is not popular. He is given a rough ride by all the critics who cannot forgive him for having slightly crumpled the Rose, for having called a spade a spade, and for having considerably pruned the first orchard of its mawkishness. Yet he was by far the greater of the two writers. He excelled through his inspiration, his witty elegance, the strength of his verbal inventiveness, his supple idiom, passing from the tender to the violent; through the complete mastery of immense learning, the ease with which all priggish pedantry was avoided and with which he described a star-studded sky like an aviary of magic birds; through his good humour, and through his boldness, a courage that equalled that of Siger de Brabant, his friend, who like him, defied the condemnations of ecclesiastical authority. That greatness was perceived by the century which saw in *Le Roman de la Rose*, once it was finished, the culmination of all secular literature.

The work immediately became a classic. There was not one noteworthy writer at the end of the Middle Ages who, in some way, did not refer to it. It gave rise to the early forms of literary criticism, notably between 1399 and 1402, in the Paris of Charles VI and the Limbourg brothers, which was more than ever an enlightened city, in the most sophisticated courtly milieu in the world where international gothic art was at its height. A controversy grew around the book. People took sides. Those who were against Jean de Meun were firstly pretentious women, Christine de Pisan lamenting the 'pollution of sin' before Isabeau of Bavaria, and the extremists (such as Jean Gerson) who proposed burning the poem because it corrupted young people by suggesting that people should love better. In the other camp were the first humanists, highly educated men, the king's secretaries in the palace, who sowed the seeds of a Renaissance in France which, but for the hardships of the Hundred Years War, would undoubtedly not have copied the Italian models in such a servile manner or so peremptorily have renounced gothic art. The dispute began at the very moment when, driven out by rioting, betrayal and the English occupation, the upper nobility and the princes were leaving Paris for their castles on the Loire. From then on, and for long after, the court stayed away from the city. But whilst one disastrous crisis succeeded another, there were still many successes. Some three hundred manuscripts of the *Roman de la Rose* bear witness to this, as do all the reprintings until 1522. Only eight years before the foundation of the Collège de France and only ten years before *Pantagruel* appeared at the fairs of Lyon, printers were making a fortune by publishing the joint work of Guillaume de Lorris and Jean de Meun. This book summed up, as did the tradition of cathedrals, what was best in a culture, the culture of feudal France. But this culture was condemned. The French renaissance repudiated it. The art of Fontainebleau triumphed over the *Roman de la Rose*. It never recovered from that defeat. Guillaume de Lorris's elegance might have seduced the romantics; Jean de Meun's forthrightness repelled them. What is more, the French language has changed so much that this work cannot be understood unless it is translated (and in the process betrayed). No one has read Jean de Meun. But who has read Dante? If both are read, one bows before the formal perfection of the *Divine Comedy*, before the Florentine poet's skill in expounding an inaccessible theology. But it is no less astonishing to discover in Jean de Meun so much generous strength, so much simplicity and closeness, and to feel as if he were indeed our brother.

6

Towards a History of Women in France and Spain

In my opening speech I thought it would be fruitful to compare the current state of research in Spain and France on the condition of women during the Middle Ages.[1] I feel that this was a particularly useful comparison despite the difficulties presented by language barriers and despite a number of omissions, two of which I shall now mention. Firstly, no contribution was made to the Spanish art history debate from the French side; secondly, as regards literature, no reference was made to the autobiographies of women. Nevertheless I think the enterprise proved successful. I shall now make several subjective observations which are, in the main, observations on method.

Firstly, I have realized that it would not be very helpful to separate the history of women from that of men. The development of the condition of both sexes should be studied together. It is the only way, for example, to examine the question of the advance of women during the period of progress of the Middle Ages. There is little doubt that the condition of women improved, but at the same time the condition of men was also improving, so it is debatable whether there was ever any appreciable change in the gulf between the two sexes. Similarly, in a study of religious life, the history of female recluses cannot be separated from that of male recluses, nor the development of Mariology from that of Christology.

The comparable nature of the condition of men and women stems from the fact that the foundation of social organization during the period with which we are concerned was the family, and more precisely, the house, or *domus*. In the introduction to his speech, Paulino Iradiel urged us to accept this evidence. Underpinning feudal and post-feudal society is the marital couple, one man, one woman, both in a dominant position, surrounded by other men and other women. One should clearly look first at this domestic society. This should shed light, in particular, on the age that little boys were removed from the world of women (this is one of the questions raised by Reyna Pastor) in order to be introduced, often abruptly, into the world of men which they were virtually never to leave. Moreover there was a division of roles within the domestic group. Men were involved in outdoor, public activities, whilst women usually found themselves forced to remain indoors in that room which, in the heart of the house, was like a womb. In this enclosed existence we can recognize what were then the essential female functions – procreation and the control of the most mysterious secrets of life, those associated with birth and death (washing the bodies of the newborn and the dead). There was thus a natural metaphorical correspondence between the inside of the house and the female body.

Not only was there a division of roles within the domestic group, there was also a division of power, and this is worth emphasizing. We historians must not rely too heavily on written sources, for all the documents we have, in both France and Spain, were written by men. It is only in the late Middle Ages that women's voices began to be heard. In France the first reliable expressions of female utterance (unlike, for example, the letters of Héloïse, whose authenticity can legitimately be questioned) are the depositions made by the female villagers of Montaillou to the Inquisitor. Later there was the trial of Joan of Arc. Between the two came the work of Christine de Pisan, but that was also of a very late date. If we were to believe everything written by men we would be in danger of mistakenly thinking that women had no power whatsoever, and were thus in a position of 'poverty' (as Carmen Lopez reminded us, poverty is the absence of power).

Indeed, once the truth is uncovered, either because of some disturbing event such as those events discussed by Martinez Gros, or else because the sources suddenly reveal what is naturally concealed, we perceive that the female world was highly structured, like a little monarchy – that monarchy wielded by the master's wife, the 'lady' who dominated the other women in the house. This monarchy was often tyrannical. The chronicles of French families at the end of the twelfth and the beginning of the thirteenth century, paint a picture of shrews reigning brutally over servants whom they terrorized, and over their sons' wives whom they tormented (for example, Blanche of Castile, mother of Louis IX). Indeed, a female power existed which rivalled that of men; the domestic sphere can be regarded as a field of a permanent conflict, of a battle between the sexes.

This internal conflict was responsible for the fearful attitude which at that time was one of the major components of male psychology. Men were afraid of women, especially their own wives, afraid of being incapable of satisfying a being who was seen both as a devourer and as a bearer of death, that, like all weak creatures, employed depraved weapons like poison and magic. This anxiety was mingled with contempt for women and was inseparable from another feeling, nostalgia for the maternal breast. I have already described how many young boys at the age of seven were suddenly separated from their mothers, plucked from a female world in which they had been cosseted. A study of biographies such as that of the monk Guibert de Nogent, reveals that men had difficulty in overcoming this traumatic experience, an experience whose after-effects influenced some of their most basic attitudes towards women throughout their lives.

This situation explains the force of an ideology which clearly had several aspects. It regarded the natural submission of women to men as necessary and providential. Women had to be ruled. This conviction was supported by the texts of Scripture and provided the model image of the male–female relationship. This relationship should be hierarchical, taking its place in the universal hierarchy; men had to keep a tight rein on the women entrusted to them, but they had also to cherish them, and women owed respect to the men who had power over them. This exchange of *dilectio* (love) and *reverencia* (reverence) established order within the domestic group, starting with its nucleus, the married couple. But in the relationship between man and wife, the Church moralists judged that that other feeling, which was different from *dilectio* and was called in Latin *amor*, should be excluded, because sensual love, desire and physical impulses signified turmoil and disorder. Normally *amor* should be expelled from marriage and confined to the sphere of gratuitous pleasure, the place which is accorded to it by that diversion of society called courtly love. Marriage was a serious matter and demanded austerity; passion should play no part in marital affairs.

The whole structure of civil society was based on marriage and the image of the house, a house where there was a single procreative couple, and within which power and roles were shared hierarchically between the master and wife. A woman had neither legal status nor even, it could be said, existence, unless she was married; she climbed up another step when, as a married woman, she fulfilled the function for which the man had taken her, and gave birth. She then gained an indisputable power, that of the mother over her son, indeed over all her sons, a power which increased when she became a widow. As a result outside the domestic unit the woman was in a position thought dangerous. Society did not acknowledge single women, those 'poor' women who were bereft of that power which was really a reflection of the power which men exercised over women. There was thus a move to put all these single women into institutions where they would be confined and protected, institutions organized as 'houses', that is, substitute homes – monasteries and *béguinages* (devotional communities of lay women), but also brothels. As for women who remained completely alone, it was the responsibility of public power to guarantee their protection. It was originally one of the functions of royalty – a function which gradually spread as the process of feudalization took hold – to protect widows and orphans and, as far as possible, to reintroduce them into the framework of marriage by providing them with the means to be taken by a husband, the dowry which made them attractive. Alternatively they were simply given away (as the king of England did at the beginning of the twelfth century), as presents which were greatly appreciated by good vassals, when the woman thus awarded to them was a rich heiress.

We are accordingly confronted with a powerful domestic model in actual social relationships, a model which was transferred to the sphere of the imagination, in particular to the sphere of religion. I think that the area of women's participation in religious life, of which relatively little is yet known, could have been examined in greater depth. In medieval Christianity women were excluded from the ministry, and specifically from the ministry of the Word. All sermons were delivered by men. And this was in spite of the fact that the lady, in her domestic role as mistress of the house, was urged to be the teacher of her servants, her daughters and her nieces. The home was the setting for female pastoral care, an area not readily accessible to research, but I think we should be able to discover some traces of it through a careful examination of the texts. Furthermore, medieval Christianity gradually accepted, however reluctantly, that women could take part in religious life. This medieval trend constitutes, in my opinion, the major difference between Christianity and Islam or Judaism, which left women in a far more marginal position.

During the rapid economic growth of the twelfth century and amid all the upheavals which this growth produced, there emerged the 'woman question' (*Frauenfrage*), the problem of women and acceptance of their own specific spirituality, and it is entirely credible that women demanded this acceptance. It seems that heretic sects were the first to respond to women's expectations. Nevertheless, heresy also forced the official Church gradually to respond by freely opening the churches to women and by setting up monastic refuges for women (hitherto there had been very few). However, access remained limited, and it is important that we should try to define more clearly what prevented its growth. Female monasticism was at first viewed with caution. How should these convents full of women be organized? Robert d'Arbrissel provoked outrage by daring to place under the power of the abbess the community of men attached to the monastery of Fontevraud, a move which looked like a transgression of the natural order. Another persistent question was where in the Christian value system to situate women who were not ruled over by men, who were not *uxores* (married women). They had to choose between two comforting but opposing role-models – the *virgo* (virgin) or the *virago* (warrior maiden), the strong woman of the Scriptures.

At the same time, I think that it would be fruitful to study further the question of the progressive feminization of Christianity. Was it not under pressure from the domestic, conjugal model, that it became necessary to place a lady beside the lord, Our

Lady next to Our Lord? Hence the theory, discussed by Marie-
Christine Pouchelle, that Jesus should also be seen as a mother-
figure, a solution which was quickly abandoned because it entailed
the androgyny of God. On the other hand, the Marian cult bur-
geoned in the twelfth century, with the figure of Mary embodying
the two complementary values of virginity and maternity. With
the Virgin, other women little by little invaded the territory of
devotion and of the saints – there were few saints who were
mothers but many more self-denying virgin saints, saints who were
converted sinners as well as saints who staunchly defended their
virginity against that familial power which wanted to hand them
over to men. The themes of the Spanish gothic paintings which
we saw are also evidence of the frequent appearance of saints in
pairs. On one particular reredos there are four male and four
female saints: once again the silhouette of the married couple, the
model, is outlined.

In conclusion, our discussions have convinced me that it is necessary to examine carefully the connections between ideology and
reality. Indeed nearly all the sources that we can usefully draw
upon tell us less about reality than about the dominant ideology,
for they place something like a screen between our eyes and what
our eyes want to see, that is to say real attitudes. All our sources
transcend social reality, to borrow the phrase used by Matilde
Azcarate. I am not referring simply to artistic or literary works,
but to all the normative rules, all the legal documents which reveal
a formal exterior rather than that which it covers. I am also
referring to stories, chronicles, even autobiographies, since the
person who says 'I' remains a prisoner of the ideological system
which dominates him or her. Our sources of information reflect
reality to a certain extent, but all or nearly all of them were
inevitably written at some distance from this reality. Our problem,
as historians, is to measure this distance, to perceive the distortion
for which the pressure of ideology may have been responsible.
Obviously, the extent of this gulf depends on the type of source
and, according to the period, the images we find are more or less
stylized or realistic. However, it is my personal conviction that
this screen can never be completely penetrated. We must give up

the positivist dream of attaining past reality. We shall always be separated from it.

However, every ideology has its history; ideologies combat and transform one another, carried away by a movement which cannot be dissociated from that which promotes material culture. The worst error of method would therefore be to isolate the study of these ideological screens by separating them from what accompanies their modification on a material level, about which we are better informed by less misleading sources. Consequently we must take into account the history of women, or rather the history of the image we perceive of women within the context of society – a development which perhaps took place more rapidly than we used to think. I have therefore noted some significant changes on the subject of prostitution which took place over a short period of time. Within a particular social context I shall attempt, as far as is possible, to connect the ideological education of courtly love on the one hand with political development, the changes in power which took place in twelfth-century France and, on the other, with the history of the institution of marriage, which is absolutely inseparable from courtly love, as well as the history of the feudal and vassalic institutions where courtly love offers a ludic outlet, and with the history of wealth and aristocratic inheritances. I must ask, for example, to what degree the game of courtly love was gradually modified in the course of the twelfth century, when there was a relaxation in the control exercised by domestic power over the marriage of boys in order to preserve inheritances.

II

FAMILY STRUCTURES

7

Family Structures in the West during the Middle Ages

There is no need to emphasize the importance of kinship bonds in the society we call 'feudal'.[1] They are its inner framework – so much so that many relationships outside the family adopted a similar structure. That is so with all the 'fraternal' associations, short-lived or permanent, uniting men unconnected by blood, as in membership of fighting units, in the bonds of vassalage, in the oaths of mutual assistance sworn by fellow townsmen, and, strongest of all, in the families – as we may rightly call them – formed by monastic communities.

It is clear that demographic change is largely governed by the form of family structures, and that economic processes rest on a base of production and consumption by family units. Kinship plays a great part also in the unfolding life of politics, in the game of alliance and opposition, and in the advancement of careers.

Lastly, family structures have a powerful effect on the way people view the world, with a particular influence on the evolution of religious forms. Eleventh- and twelfth-century Christianity owes them several of its main features, for instance the way in which family consciousness shaped the extensive developments in the commemoration of the dead, the multiple parallels between meditation on the ancestry of Christ, devotion to the Virgin and the emotional bonds developing within the family. There is scarcely a single aspect of medieval civilization that is not in some way illuminated by knowledge of the structure of kinship.

Legal historians have long contributed significantly to this knowledge. Their contribution is, however, far from being entirely satisfactory, since the bulk of their work is based on late case-law texts, and also because it is difficult to measure the inevitable and sometimes pointed discrepancies between the rigour of the statutes and their application in everyday life. Indeed, social relations, the dictates of custom and, more importantly, the dictates of the moral code proposed by the Church presented a model which was undoubtedly closely linked with the reality that they set out to order, but which corresponded but imperfectly to group behaviour. Take, for instance, the very strong tension which clearly existed between the lay world and the religious authorities on the subject of conjugal morality. The question should be approached by alternative routes. Among the documents which allow us to do so are firstly the genealogies, both those that historians reconstruct from a thousand scattered clues, and those no less valuable ones that were drawn up during the tenth, eleventh and twelfth centuries, which reflect the image people at that time had of their lineage and kinship group. This material permits assumptions about the evolution of kin relations in the upper echelons of Western European society between the end of the Carolingian era and the twelfth century.

Several studies devoted to the Rhine region and later extended to the northern part of the kingdom of France[2] suggest that in these regions the family structures of the aristocracy changed considerably during that period. Indeed those historians who have attempted to go back through noble lineages from son to father to the most distant ancestors have not succeeded in extending their research beyond a certain point in time – the end of the ninth century as far as the most important princes were concerned, and the whole of the tenth century in relation to less powerful lords. The genealogists at work during the feudal period could not pass this barrier without inventing legendary ancestors.

However, the existence of this threshold cannot be explained by the paucity of the sources, but stems instead from the fact that they no longer provide clues which make it possible to establish descent from father to son with any certainty. One might therefore think that this was the boundary between two successive stages in family relationships. Previously the individual found himself at the heart of his kin as if in a flexible and, so to speak, horizontal grouping where marriages counted at least as much as ancestry.

In a milieu where success depended mainly on the good will of a patron, on the grant of personal and revocable benefices, the important thing for all was to attach themselves to the 'house' of a benefactor, and where possible to that of the king. This was achieved through close relatives, whether they were blood relatives or not. Later, however, because men were no longer recipients of a benefice but heirs to a property and authority passed down from father to son, they felt that they formed part of a vertically aligned kin group, a lineage of males. Thenceforth ancestral memory occupied a far more significant place in their mental pictures, since it endeavoured to go back as far as the founder of the 'house'. Genealogical awareness can be dated to this foundation, the achievement of independence based on the possession of a hereditary 'honour'. It occurred at precisely the moment when family ties started to be limited to the strict framework of lineage.

It is legitimate to regard the gradual strengthening of these lineal structures as a specific feature of feudal society. Indeed this movement coincided with the disintegration of regal powers. The oldest genealogies are those of the territorial princes who freed themselves from royal patronage from the end of the ninth century. There followed the genealogies of the counts when they freed themselves from the protection of the princes, and subsequently the genealogies of the lords of ordinary castles who in turn became independent of the counts. Finally, in the north-west of France the lineages of knights gradually came out of the shadows as the knights emerged from their primitive domestic position and induced their lords to establish them on lands of their own and founded their own lineage there. The change in kinship relations seems therefore to stem from two linked transformations which developed over more than two centuries. Firstly there was a change in the political structures which fragmented the pattern of authority. Secondly, a change in economic conditions was evidenced in the dispersal of groupings of 'friends', who had formerly been incorporated in princely houses, in the dispersal of wealth from the upper reaches of society down to the bottom of the seigneurial class, and in the way in which members of the aristocracy gradually became more firmly rooted in their inheritance.

New research would be required to test the value of these theories and to confirm whether it is possible to apply them to the European West. An accurate survey[3] of the aristocratic families living in the immediate vicinity of the abbey of Cluny in 1100 shows that at least 80 per cent were firmly established on heredi- tary lands before the year 1000, and that more than a quarter were already securely in this position before 950. It also emerges that the lineages of the lords of the three castles in this region cannot be traced back as far as those of some of their neighbours who, at the beginning of the twelfth century, were merely simple knights. Finally, twenty-eight of these thirty-four lineages were apparently branches of six aristocratic houses whose landed wealth extended over the whole territory at the end of the Carolingian period. Thus, in the south of Burgundy, the seigneurial class as a whole appears to have been a hereditary society, firmly estab- lished at a very early date; for that reason, they were very conscious of their genealogy.

Yet through the study of filiations, it has become clear that, although the tenth century was a period when inheritances were divided and original family units were broken up into numerous, increasingly independent lines, conditions changed around the year 1000. Thereafter a period of rapid concentration began: in 1100 aristocratic lineages were no more numerous than 100 years earlier. That these families stopped branching out can be attri- buted to the contraction of kinship ties within far more strictly defined lineal structures. Analysis of archival documents confirms this. Thus indivisibility of property amongst brothers, almost unknown before 950, is attested in a quarter of deeds during the second half of the tenth century, a third of deeds between 1000 and 1050, and half of the deeds between 1050 and 1100, as possession in common was gradually extended to the most distant relatives. Furthermore, the names of the mother and father sud- denly became less common in witness lists after 950, which proves that during the lifetime of their parents sons had already virtually ceased to own personal property.

Finally, the *laudatio parentum*, the consent of lineal relatives to the transfer of part of the ancestral inheritance, suddenly became a necessity from the middle of the eleventh century onwards. All these details together demonstrate a gradual strengthening of the solidarity of blood relatives around the family inheritance. Another indication of this was the change in the *sponsalicium*, the settlement agreed to by the husband for his wife; after the year 1000 its significance completely altered through extension of the rights of the husband. This transformation accompanied the prevailing influence of customs which tended to exclude women from inheritance. In the eleventh century married women no longer received anything other than their dowry, and their sisters who remained in the paternal home received only negligible amounts for their funeral costs, generally drawn from their mother's dowry.

These lineages thus became male lineages after the year 1000. However, it was only at the end of the eleventh century, and in the very limited milieu inhabited by the lords of the castles, that there emerged the first measures designed to favour the eldest son: in customary practice, those rules which prescribed the equality of heirs of the same rank were, without doubt, the most tenacious. Using different means, through the practice of joint possession, and especially through a sustained policy of limiting the number of marriages, knightly lineages in this region in the eleventh century were instrumental in averting the dangerous effects of the successive division of inheritances. These families stoutly gathered together to defend their economic position. They succeeded, and for close on two centuries seigneurial society was remarkably stable.

These observations raise new questions. What effect did the establishment of these lineal structures have on the expression of chivalric culture? The development of genealogical writings in France during the eleventh and twelfth centuries provides a few answers.[4] Others can be found by studying poetical works of entertainment written for knights. In the themes of the epic and love literature of the twelfth century, it is possible to discern signs of a conflict resulting from the marriage practices of knightly society, between the *seniores* who were married and managed the family fortune, and the *juvenes* (young men) who had been compelled to remain unmarried and who, on account of the rigidity of the lineal structure, had no economic independence and no hope of establishing themselves except through the hazards of adventurous quests.

What were the effects of the improved economic conditions from the end of the twelfth century on structures of kinship which had been formed to protect rights based exclusively on the possession of land? The few existing studies on the nobility of thirteenth-century Europe allow us to catch a glimpse of the break-up of old family groups and the proliferation of new households. Recent research in north-western France[5] shows that after 1175 the number of written agreements sealed by large family groups decreased and was compensated for by an increase in documents sealed by couples. It would seem that in the aristocracy lineage began to give way to the household of the married couple 'of which the Church and the peasant and bourgeois groupings appeared to be the champions'.

This observation should prompt us not to limit our study to the upper echelons of lay society on which the surviving documentation initially led scholars to concentrate. Research must be extended to rural and urban populations. The sources shed very little light on the peasant family; however, in the Carolingian period they generally start to show evidence of small groups centred on married couples. The legal framework of tenure, varying greatly from one domain to another,[6] undoubtedly continued to exert decisive pressure on the structure of rural kinship, notably through limitations on the means by which inheritance was handed down.

Nevertheless, it would seem that throughout the period of agricultural expansion which marked the entire economic history of the West between the tenth and thirteenth centuries, peasant societies usually succeeded in circumventing the rigidity of seigneurial custom. At the outset, it is worth noting the conclusion of a recent study of archives from Picardy. Between the tenth and twelfth centuries the development of family structures was diametrically opposite in the aristocracy and the peasantry; while kinship ties were becoming strained amongst the nobility, they were becoming more relaxed among the peasants.

What one is able to discover about urban societies suggests that, in the new areas of expanding towns, immigration and forms of wealth in which chattels were markedly more important than in all other sections of society made family relationships much more flexible than elsewhere. This rendered artificial and complementary fraternities much more necessary and stable. However, this impression deserves closer examination. And it is worth remembering that the appeal of the aristocratic cultural model was responsible for the institution – in those sections of the bourgeoisie which had access to wealth and which, as early as possible, acquired land – of structures of kinship, 'lineages', '*parages*' and '*consorterie*'. These structures were formed in a similar way to those amongst the knights and just as strictly, following a rigidly patrilineal filiation.

After the end of the thirteenth century, in the wealthiest regions, the state archives and those of notaries provide statistics which shed light on some aspects of family demography in the overall population established in a specific area, rather than on legal frameworks or mental attitudes. A statistical survey of the information contained in the Florentine *catasto* (land register) of 1427–9[7] reveals what one can expect from this kind of source. During that period in Tuscany, in the countryside as well as in the towns, married couples formed the basis of virtually all families (92.25 per cent in Florence). Larger households, which usually included married brothers within the paternal inheritance, were found in the villages, but in towns the largest households were in fact the wealthiest (in Florence the proportion of family units based on married couples fell to 77 per cent in the most affluent social strata).

It was on the basis of wealth that the most distinct differences were established. Since their children were more likely to survive, rich families were considerably larger (six children per family in Florence, where the average was 3.8); there were also more older and collateral relatives; and there was a higher proportion of unmarried men and of married women. The age difference between husband and wife was also more marked. The incidence of male offspring became higher amongst the richer members of the hierarchy (up to 158 in Florence for every 100 female ones, with an average of 116). These statistics, drawn mainly from a study of notarial registers, provide the starting point for a more sophisticated analysis of social relationships as regards matrimonial and succession practices.

These are a few of the areas where research is already being carried out. In this work it is vital that methods and problems be presented according to the established fact that there was a close link between the history of the family and that of the economy. This link was striking in Tuscany during the fifteenth century, in the area around the abbey of Cluny during the eleventh century and in the suburbs of the towns in the thirteenth century. Relationships of kinship, at any rate, those that emerge from the sources, were formed on the basis of inheritance, whether of land, rights or money, but the family structures, the customs and practices which ensured the survival of these relationships and the assumptions based on them, also played their part, often indirectly but always decisively, and slowed down or speeded up the development of the means of production and the hierarchy of wealth.

8

The Relationship between
Aristocratic Family and State
Structures in Eleventh-Century
France

I shall limit myself to posing a methodological problem that arises
where two lines of research intersect, one concerning the structures
of the state, the other the structures of aristocratic families, a
subject in which I have been personally involved for a number of
years. My aim is simply to look at the relationships in tenth- and
eleventh-century France which could have linked the development
of state structures and the development of family structures in the
upper aristocracy. For this purpose I shall begin by putting forward three observations.

Some years ago my German colleague Gerd Tellenbach and
some of the medievalists influenced by him, notably Karl Schmid,
drew attention to the fact that when historians attempt to trace
the lineage of important families in Frankish countries in order
to discover their most distant ancestors, there always comes a
point at which research can go no further.[1] For the leading families,
that stage, the chronological threshold which genealogical research
cannot cross, occurs at the end of the Carolingian period or, more
commonly, in the first half of the tenth century. Until then the
historian can delve into the past and go back from son to father
in one continuous chain of descent. But once that threshold is
reached, he is able to trace only individuals whose marriage
alliances are documented; often he can discover the identity of

the wife but not of the father. This is not because there were fewer documents then, but because family structures had changed significantly. Previously, at the watershed of the ninth and tenth centuries, men who came from the highest aristocracy had belonged to a fluid, ill-defined kinship group which appears to be a body of close kinsmen where alliances between families carried at least as much weight and psychological resonance as descent. However, after that period, men were strictly integrated into a clear agnatic line.

I shall compare these observations with what we know about the gradual political dissolution of the kingdom of western France through the excellent work of my friends Jan Dhondt, and Jean-François Lemarignier. Large principalities were established at the end of the ninth and beginning of the tenth century. Then the process continued on the periphery of these great regions with the formation of political groups which, towards the middle of the tenth century, were virtually independent within the *pagus* (country district) and in relation to the count. Finally – and this was the end-result of the process of fragmentation – between about 980 and 1030 the *pagus* itself was split up into a multitude of autonomous castellanies.

My final observation concerns documentation, and in particular a category of sources which I have been using for some time in my research on the kingdom of France, the genealogical literature of the eleventh and twelfth centuries. There are relatively few of these written sources in France, and they all come from the western part of the kingdom. For the most part they were written for very powerful families. The latter, anxious to bring fame to their noble line, commissioned a household clerk in their employ or one of the monks attached to the church under their special protection, and where they buried their dead, to write the history of their lineage by going back to the most distant known ancestor. These works have the advantage of showing the image which the families had of themselves and their origins, an image which often was actually very different from the one that was reconstructed much later through the studies of modern genealogists. Furthermore these sources are useful in that they provide some answers to my preliminary question concerning the relationship between state and family structures. I have concentrated on the study of these texts and I shall confine myself to offering some very brief examples here.

Some genealogies, written for the most illustrious families, trace a line which goes back as far as the ninth century, sometimes even further. This is the case, for example, with all the genealogies which were written for the rulers of the principality of Flanders. However, I shall not be examining the most important lineages here, those of dukes and heads of large regional principalities. I shall be limiting my observations to the lower ranks of the nobility, to counts, *vicomtes* and castellans, that is to say, the masters of those smaller political entities which were set up in the last stages of the disintegration of the feudal state. I shall begin by drawing on one of the works, the *Historia comitum ghisnensium* ('History of the Counts of Guînes'), which contains what is perhaps the most fascinating information. Written in the last decade of the twelfth century, this text describes one of the satellite *comtés* situated in an independent position on the southern borders of the principality of Flanders, and reconstructs the lineage of its masters. However, since neighbouring castellanies had become linked to the inheritance through alliances, this source also charts the genealogy of several less powerful families, notably the family of the castellans of Ardres. I shall be examining two levels of nobility, two types of political grouping, a *comté* and a castellany.

The author of the *Historia*, an educated clerk who drew on extensive documentation, was able to trace the line of the counts of Guînes from father to son as far back as 928. This is where he placed the 'auctor ghisnensis nobilitatis' (founder of the noble Guînes family), a character who appears to be mythical and whom he treats like the hero of a courtly romance. Sifridus is presented as a Viking adventurer. On the one hand – and this is what counts – he is depicted as the builder of the castle of Guînes, the fortress which was to become the centre of the *comté* and the material and topographical foundation of the lineage, the comital house. On the other hand he is depicted as the seducer of one of the daughters of the neighbouring prince, the count of Flanders. Through this illicit union Sifridus became the root of that tree of Jesse which the Guînes genealogy ('genealogia ghisnensium') formed after him.

The family power gained its legitimacy with the bastard son, when his uncle, the new count of Flanders, who adopted him as a godson, armed him as knight – another mythical transference into the past of the values with which dubbing was endowed at the end of the twelfth century – raised his land to the status of a *comté* and granted it to him as a fief. Such is the image which the counts of Guînes formed of the origins of their family at the end of the twelfth century. For them, lineal descent began in the 920s through the union between their ancestor and the daughter of a prince who was himself descended on the distaff side from the Carolingians. For them, the origin of the lineage coincided exactly with the establishment of autonomous power based on the fortress, the title and the powers which were attached to it, and which thenceforward was to form the heart of the family inheritance. It is worth noting that once again it is in connection with the count, who died in 1020, that the first reference in the *Historia* is made to succession by primogeniture. If one now turns to the other important lineage which he describes in the same text, that of the lords of Ardres, who were not counts but simple castellans, one can see that this family presents the same lineal and agnatic structure but – and this is the main difference in my opinion – this lineage goes back much less far into the past; the most distant ancestor mentioned lived in about 1030. Thus, the memory of lineal descent reached back to the first thirty or so years of the tenth century in a count's family, and only to the first thirty years of the eleventh century in that of a castellan. These two chronological points seem noteworthy.

In order to draw a comparison I shall now turn from the extreme north-west of the kingdom of France and concentrate on the south-west; I shall be examining another genealogical work, the *Historia pontificum et comitum engolismensium* ('History of the Bishops and Counts of Angoulême') which was written a little earlier than the other *Historia* discussed, in about 1160. According to this work, the record of the lineal and agnatic descent in the family of the counts of Angoulême does not go back quite as far as that of the counts of Guînes. But the work also starts with another legendary hero, Guillaume Taillefer, who fought the Normans armed with a magic sword, and died in 962. Here the title of count, linked to that of the count of Périgord, was for a while shared by cousins – this was fairly common in political groupings in southern Gaul. But this joint possession ceased around the year 1000. Thenceforth there was a strict line of descent from father to son. In about 1020 the genealogical narrative attests to both the establishment of primogeniture for the comital succession and to the formation of satellite castellanies, granted to the count's younger sons, who were deprived by this practice of the core of their inheritance.

There are also examples from Provence which are worthy of mention, notably the case of the *vicomtes* of Marseille, but I shall limit myself to a second comparison and look briefly at the Mâconnais region. Here, in eastern France, we are in a region with no tradition of genealogical literature. There is only a list of counts which was introduced into the cartulary of Mâcon Cathedral at the beginning of the twelfth century. But the research which I have carried out into the charters of this region has shown me that the adoption of the title of count by a lineage was also taking place during the first three decades of the tenth century, and that the appropriation of independent castellanies by families with an agnatic structure also dated from the years 980–1030. Some detailed studies would still be very useful; however, I think that I can safely say that in the kingdom of France as a whole the majority of lineages of counts go back as far as about 920–50, and the majority of the lineages of castellans go back to about the year 1000.

I shall now put forward my research theories. In the kingdom of France the corroborating evidence of the charters and of those very valuable documents constituted by twelfth-century genealogical works suggests that kinship structures in the middle ranks of the aristocracy changed during the tenth and at the beginning of the eleventh century. Previously, without a lineage, there had been no strictly genealogical consciousness, no coherent memory of one's forebears. An aristocrat regarded his family as a horizontal grouping, so to speak, spread out over the present, as a grouping with indistinct and changing boundaries, formed both of *propinqui* (relatives by marriage) and *consanguinei* (blood relatives), of men and women who were linked just as much by blood as by marriage. What counted most for the aristocrat and for his fortune was not so much his ancestors but his close kinsmen through whom he came closer to higher authority, that is to say, to the king or to the duke, who were the dispensers of offices, gifts and honours. Politically he expected everything from a prince; what mattered most to him was his relationships and not his ancestry.

Later, however, the individual felt himself trapped in a group which was far more rigidly organized, based on agnatic descent, with a vertical structure. He felt like a member of a lineage, of a stock where an inheritance was handed down from father to son, a member of a 'house', the running of which was handed over to the eldest son, and whose history could be recorded in the form of a tree firmly rooted in the person of the founding ancestor, the source of all the power and all the renown of the family. The individual himself became a prince; he adopted the mentality of an heir. This new structure – a point remarked upon by Karl Schmid – reproduced in fact the structure that before only the family of the king or the duke had, and it was established around a power that had become autonomous, subject only to the uncertain duties of vassalage.

This new structure of kinship was thus formed at the very moment when the state was fragmenting, when king and duke were relaxing their hold on the aristocracy, which had hitherto been entirely incorporated into their own 'house'. This is where the chronological coincidences between the appearance of lineages and the gradual dismantling of state structures become significant. The new structure of kinship first became apparent in the kingdom of France between 920 and 950 amongst comital families. When the latter gained their independence, they began to hand down to their sons the 'honour' which was by then hereditary and soon to be indivisible (and for that reason handed down by primogeniture), and which was constituted by their title, the fortress with which the title was associated, and the powers which were attached to both the title and the castle.

Two generations later, the power of the counts was itself eroded. In about the year 1000 some castles in their turn became the centre of a tiny principality; a family established itself there, detached from the house of the count; thus freed, it established itself as an independent 'house', and in turn immediately adopted an agnatic structure. A new group of lineages was therefore formed, the line of castellans. I have drawn on my knowledge of Mâcon society as well as on a genealogical note which I have already used elsewhere, and which is perhaps the only one written during the twelfth century on the subject of the lineage of ordinary knights. The text in question is a passage from the *Annales cameracences* ('Annals of Cambrai') of which Fernand Vercauteren has made an excellent study. This leads me to believe that, two generations later, in the third quarter of the eleventh century, other more modest families were in turn freeing themselves from the domination of the castles. Centred around a small fief, a 'house' whose name they adopted, they organized themselves into lineages, followed rules of succession and family customs which had hitherto been reserved for kings and dukes, and later for castellans; they formed the lowest level of lineages, those of the minor nobility of knights.

I shall end here, for my intention was simply to draw attention – by adding to the observations made by German medieval scholars – to a correlation (which seems to me to be obvious and worthy of far more detailed study) between the development of family law in feudal society and that of state structures. My purpose was to highlight a link which seems to me to be fundamental: on the one hand, the dissolution of the power of command, the appropriation of *regalia* (regalian rights) and the development of feudal institutions and, on the other hand, the appearance of new family structures within the aristocracy of the kingdom of France.

9

Philip Augustus's France: Social Changes in Aristocratic Circles

In order to examine social changes in aristocratic circles I shall remain within what I consider truly to be Philip Augustus's France, that is to say that part of the kingdom where the sovereign was active, and where there was interest in everything he did. In other words, I thought it best to establish the area by locating the echoes of the battle of Bouvines, north of Poitou, Berry and the Nivernais.

I shall not venture further south for two reasons. Firstly, because I have the feeling that social relationships were organized differently within the nobility there, and, secondly – and more importantly – because research into medieval history over the past ten years has barely progressed in my chosen field, although it has been prolific in southern provinces on other subjects and other periods.

However, in the last decade, since the publication of Robert Fossier's monumental thesis, some important works have been published which shed light on the events in northern France which I am discussing here. I refer to a study of the lords of Nesle by W. M. Newman; research by E. Bournazel on the knightly class of the Ile-de-France at the beginning of the reign of Philip Augustus; research by T. Evergates on feudal society in the *bailliage* of Troyes; research by M. Parisse on the nobility of Lorraine; and research by Y. Sassier on the nobility of the Auxerrois.[1] Another, no less important contribution which has yet to be published is the study of the lords of Coucy by D. Barthélemy.

These works – three of which were supervised by Jean-François

Lemarignier whose memory I fondly salute – have made it possible, amongst other things, to date more accurately the development of the style by which the rank of members of the aristocracy
was referred to in charters. They have also enabled us to follow
more closely what happened to hereditary wealth as well as the
ramification of kinship ties, and to gain a better understanding of
the relationships between the dominant lineages and the dominant
section of the Church.

It is important to evaluate recent research and to begin fresh
inquiries. The books I have referred to have made an impression
on all scholars of medieval history. To summarize their contribution once more, after so many reviews, does not seem particularly useful. I prefer to concentrate on a problem which it is now
necessary to reconsider because of these works. I would therefore
like to propose two working theories which should provide a new
impetus to the interpretation of these documents. I shall suggest
relating what is known about the situation and the structure of
the ruling class to two changes which took place in the region in
question during the reign of Philip Augustus. The first change is
technical and relates to the modification of military practices. The
second change is social and concerns the modification of marriage
strategies.

As regards the first series of changes I am reluctant to venture
into Philippe Contamine's field of expertise. I shall state a simple
impression that I have – these are merely, I repeat, theories which
I am offering for criticism – the impression that, at the time of
Philip Augustus, two changes had been fully effected, changes
whose beginnings could be discerned from about the fourth decade
of the twelfth century onwards. These are two linked changes
whose relationship to the development of the economy should be
closely studied.

Between 1130 and 1160 the development within the aristocracy
of a new means of combat in which horses performed a significant
role also determined the sudden rise in the cost of knights' equipment. (This is based on the conclusions presented in Barcelona
by V. Cirlot.[2] They minutely compared the evidence of Catalan
iconography with that of the texts.)

In the second half of the twelfth century there was a sudden
increase in the number of bands of professional soldiers of low

birth who worked for money and were armed with weapons which were said to be unworthy of knights; they knew their job and were so efficient that princes did not hesitate to employ them as widely as possible, even though the cost was appalling and the practice reflected badly on their honour (note the care which Rigord took to conceal the use that King Philip himself made of mercenaries).

It is worth examining the effects which these two changes had on the structures, social boundaries, attitudes and self-awareness of the aristocracy of northern France. A third change can be added, namely the improvement of fortification techniques. The assertion that at the heart of the value system there existed a contrast between the noble and ignoble way of fighting the enemy is critical in defining the limits of the aristocratic group and in reinforcing its cohesion around the chivalric code. Was not the challenge issued to knights by warriors who did not belong to their order – but were none the less capable of defeating and killing them – another decisive factor? This not only posed a physical but also a social threat which, although hidden, was more serious – the perceived danger of the rise of adventurers who were favoured by the princes.

Another danger also emerged at that time, that of a rebellion against the seigneurial exactions which seemed so intolerable that military monopoly – the peace-keeping role which justified them – was called into question. Here, it could be most illuminating to examine the analysis of the motives which chroniclers attributed to that wave of rebels who invaded the region of Auxerre as part of the continuing 'Capuchon' movement. Threatened, the aristocracy closed ranks; it was more tolerant of the financial demands placed upon it by the increased cost of military equipment and the burden of princely authority which guaranteed preservation of noble privileges. Under this protection, the commonly acknowledged value of the rituals of dubbing to knighthood, of the title which this ceremony conferred and of the duties which it imposed, rapidly narrowed the gap between princes (*proceres*) and knights (*milites*) within an order (*ordo*) which princely ideology was able to raise to the higher level. A dialectic existed between sword, lance and helmet, and all the systems of classification, all the symbols of social superiority which were displayed in heraldry, in the language of the charters, and revealed in the organization of funeral processions, within churches and cemeteries. I think it is important to trace and carefully date the signs of this dialectic. This will be my first research project.

In my second research project the problem is, so to speak, reversed. I started off by looking at a change in technology in order to note its repercussions on the development of aristocratic society. I now consider a change in the attitude of the dominant lineages in northern France during the reign of Philip Augustus. I would like to place this transformation specifically within the context of what changed in the surrounding milieu – the relaxing of a long-held reluctance to allow too many young men to marry.

Until then, that is until the last quarter of the twelfth century, it seems that the concern to maintain the rank of families of good birth by preventing the diminution of their inheritance, forced the heads of families to allow only the eldest son to take a wife. Naturally, this rule was not inflexible. There were many cases of younger sons who married. But – and C. Bouchard's fine study on the genealogy of the lords of Seignelay[3] provides a convincing example of this – the wedding of the youngest son usually resulted from happy circumstances such as the generosity of a patron displaying largesse towards the young people of his vassalic household who asked him to find them wives. Sometimes the accidental death of the eldest son forced the second son to produce legitimate children who could take over if necessary from his orphaned nephews who were threatened by infant mortality and by the risks of military training.

More often the opportunity arose for a younger son to establish himself as son-in-law in another house by marrying a girl who had no brother and was therefore an heiress. In these cases there was still an attempt to halt the dilution of the lineage and the division of the inheritance by securing ecclesiastical posts for the sons born from these lateral marriages, or by sending them off on distant adventures – in short, by encouraging these chance branches to atrophy rapidly. The result of this was that in the course of the twelfth century the number of noble houses in these regions seems to have remained fairly constant. If there was any change at all it was not an increase but a contraction which resulted in the concentration of wealth.

I have noted the reversal of this trend in the last two decades of the twelfth century. The research which I am suggesting would consist, firstly, of substantiating my theories by reconstructing genealogies. However, I feel that these theories are already sufficiently well established. I have observed the absorption into the aristocracy of northern France of the 'youth', that group of adults who were forced to live unmarried and whose role in the development of chivalric culture I have described. 'Bachelors' were in short supply. To be without a wife was formerly a permanent state which the majority of men from that social background shared; subsequently it was merely a stage, a period in the lives of most men.

The common lot, for sons who did not enter the Church, was to establish themselves, to found their own family line and no longer to produce only bastards but also legitimate sons. This enormous change is reflected in the treatment of the themes of chivalric literature during the period.

If my views on the change in the pattern of marriage behaviour are confirmed, then its importance should be recognized. Firstly, we need to look for an explanation. On this subject I can only ask questions, such as whether this break with the old constraints was not facilitated mainly by a two-fold shift.

The first change which influenced feudal custom resulted from the practice of *parage*[4] which became more widespread: satellite houses were created around the mother house but remained dependent upon it, since the elder son, who succeeded his father in the ancestral home, retained that portion of the inheritance where the lineal memory was deeply rooted. He received the homage of his married brothers since they held in fief from him the possessions inherited from their mother or recently granted to them in order to set up their households. The other change was economic, a loosening of restrictions. During that period the wealth of the aristocracy initially seems to have grown regularly through refinements of taxation, the improvement of land, the increase in the number of households that could be exploited and a general development which increased the profits that powerful landowners derived from their prerogatives. In particular this wealth seems to have circulated more freely, since a greater proportion of it consisted of money. Greater flexibility resulted from the wider use of money, whilst the mass of goods which the rulers of the states (whose capacity for munificence was increasing) redistributed amongst their peers or their knights continually increased.

I believe these new practices had far-reaching effects. Firstly, there was less unrest once so many *juvenes* became *seniores*, settled down and were therefore forced from then on to control their passions. Perhaps a part of the peace that was gradually won during the thirteenth century was the result of the change which I am describing. Furthermore, there was a collapse of authority and a tendency towards systematic exploitation, usually within the parish. At the same time the lord's residence became smaller, and *maisons fortes* or fortified manors – the symbolic replicas of the old *castra* (castles) – became widespread. Finally, let us turn to the proliferation of the nobility. I regard this growth in the aristocratic population, traces of which one begins to discern in the last years of the twelfth century, as being of the utmost importance. It would be useful to attempt to measure this growth, to compare it to the growth which can be perceived in other social spheres, in the Church, amongst the peasantry and the townspeople. The main thing is to compare this new profusion of births with the developments which I have just mentioned, namely the rise in the cost of armour and equipment, the increase in the number of knights' sons who delayed their own accession to knighthood, the appearance of titles and heraldic symbols which guaranteed their superiority by birth, the gradual homogenization of the nobility through the adoption of a standard system of values and images.

The two working hypotheses which I am discussing here do, in fact, coincide. They can be brought together in my final question: how does one resolve the apparent contradiction between the two attitudes? On the one hand, there was the defensive reaction, the aristocracy's reliance on the quality of its blood and on the code which it set up to contend with the threats of destabilization created by new ways of waging war. On the other hand, there was at the same time the relinquishing of the former strict matrimonial policy, with less concern to control births by this means – a relaxation that surprisingly did not have as a corollary a feeling of ease, but whose immediate consequences were to enlarge the nobility, thus making it more permeable, less strictly closed to the rise of the parvenu, and finally weakening it, to the advantage of royal authority.

III

CULTURES, VALUES AND SOCIETY

10

Problems and Methods in Cultural History

In France, cultural history remains an underdeveloped country, not a subject of scientific research. Nevertheless, this topic is being actively studied and is a field for challenging investigations. Two main obstacles continue to hamper progress in this area.

The first is the fact that academic disciplines are rigidly compartmentalized. In the universities, at the CNRS (National Centre for Scientific Research) and elsewhere there is a divide between historians on one side, and, on the other, art historians, historians of literature, philosophy, the sciences, and subjects even more specialized, such as the history of medicine or music. Because for the past century France has been a secular and academically learned country, historians have succeeded in taking over two areas, religious history and the history of education, but no others. The lack of communication between disciplines and our reluctance to cross boundaries are depressing. I think it is not only in France that this occurs. When I received the programme for this conference[1] I noticed that on both the Hungarian and French side 'culture' always meant written culture. Other forms of expression have been ignored in the programme which we have organized. There is no mention of visual images, either paintings, photographs or films, or of music.

The second obstacle is the inadequacy of our analytic tools. Cultural history, which is a latecomer, is still trailing behind economic history, which has been supreme for the last fifty years. Therefore cultural history is at present moving away from the methods of economic history and creating new ones better suited to it, as well as concepts and theories capable of guiding research in these areas. The concepts and theories of economic history have proved to be inadequate in so far as cultural matters are concerned. At the very least it is necessary to adjust them and correct them.

Having stated my position I shall look first at the production of culture and then at the consumption and distribution of cultural objects.

Cultural history sets out to examine the mechanisms whereby cultural objects were produced in the past within the general movements of a civilization, whether this was achieved through mass production or high-quality production, up to that peak when a 'masterpiece' was produced, with all the questions which it raises. Naturally the historian of culture must study production in its entirety and consider the relationships which may exist between what happens at the top of the edifice, at the level of the 'masterpiece', and the relatively inactive foundations of ordinary production which they dominate and influence. This means that separate disciplines, the histories of art, literature, philosophy, even the sciences, are deceptive in so far as they concentrate on the exceptional.

One of the problems of cultural history, and one of the stumbling blocks in the construction of appropriate conceptual systems, lies in the clarification of the relationships between this creative process which brings about the development of a culture and the deep structures underpinning it.

These relationships are evident in economic structures. In examining the pace of cultural production in certain periods, for example during the twelfth-century Renaissance, the historian must question the momentum which at that time spurred economic activity: a fundamental relationship undoubtedly existed between the increased productivity of the work of the peasants of the Ile-de-France and the increased productivity of the work of the masters in the 'school' of Laon towards 1110. Recently, when I chose to study an event in European history, the diffusion of Cistercian art, I emphasized the part played by the organization of farms on the estates which belonged to the Cistercian order, and by the role of money both in the administration of these domains and in the payment of the teams of builders. But I also added that the event could not be simplified in this way, that other factors were involved, that the Cistercian achievement not only meant the success of a particular system of economic production, but that it also meant – and no doubt primarily – two things: the revival of a formal tradition and the illustration of a moral code and of a concept of the world.

Amongst the factors involved in the production of culture (apart from its basic raw material) there is a legacy, a fund of forms on which each generation draws. The principal concern of literary history, of the history of the arts and of philosophy, is to make an inventory of these forms, to show how this fund is impoverished or increased, and how it changes, to specify the genealogy of external forms, to shed light on the effect of taste and fashion and the process of branching out, cross-fertilization and finally eclipse. This can be viewed as a storehouse where there are forgotten shelves, where some are full and others are empty. All this has a relatively independent history, and naturally there is a history of forms.

In the development of this history, it is important to avoid concentrating too much on innovations; the enormous number of features which remain should not be overlooked. Take, for example, Cîteaux. The intention of the Cistercian order was literally to go back to the Rule of St Benedict; the function of Cistercian buildings was the same as that of previous monastic buildings, and Cistercians professed the virtue of humility and tended to be conservative. For these reasons Cistercians revived traditional forms. But since they tended towards asceticism, first they purified these forms, and since, unconsciously, they adhered to the optimism created by the enormous progress of the twelfth century, they adopted the latest technical developments – for example, intersecting ribs – and introduced them unchanged into the traditional forms.

The presence of a legacy of possible forms, starting with language forms, must be taken into account. It was a legacy which was not fixed, but which changed over time. Whilst its changes had only a very tenuous link with the history of the economy, they were very closely connected with the life of the workshops, with all the processes of apprenticeship, and thus with the educational system as a whole: this is where the legacy is handed down from one generation to another, and where it is constantly being sifted. If the twelfth century experienced a 'renaissance' it was the result of education being invigorated at that time, particularly through the gifts of the lay patrons who decided to endow collegiate foundations rather than monasteries, as well as through the greater mobility of the masters and the audience, which strengthened all communications. It was also through a systematic examination of the heritage and the recovery of sources that had been lost in history, notably the forms of pagan antiquity which no longer seemed to represent such a threat.

The second type of factor can be described as ideological. I shall not emphasize the decisive role which is played in every society by the world of the imagination, by the value system and by all the images which serve to explain the world. I shall simply point out that these objects, these immense 'envelopes' which we call ideologies, also have their history, and that this history is linked with changes in material structures. And not only because it echoes their movement, but because a process of superimposition makes it have profound effects on the infrastructure. I shall take the example of the influence of ideological representations which govern, however imperfectly, the sexual practices which influence demographic change. This influence accounts for a considerable number of changes in the population curve for the recent past; for the distant past, such as the one with which I am concerned, the Christian ideology of marriage clearly influenced population growth in the High Middle Ages.

The history of ideologies is also very evidently connected with the history of power. Ideology is a weapon which power was determined to make use of. It controls the principal workshops of the production of culture. An indissoluble union is thus formed between the history of that production and the history of ideology. It is therefore necessary to undertake the study of those institutions which are difficult to apprehend and the study of coexisting and concurrent ideologies. Indeed, the relationship between ideological factors and underlying deep structures is manifest especially in the fact that the confrontations which take place in society are expressed by a permanent struggle between several opposing ideologies.

In any fairly advanced society there is, therefore, not one culture but a number of cultures. This observation leads me to the second part of my comments concerning the distribution of cultural objects. I shall quote from Gramsci (*Marxismo e letteratura*): 'The people is not a single homogeneous cultural collective, but presents numerous cultural stratifications in different combinations.' This remark about the 'people' also holds true for that part of society which dominates it. The people consists of stratifications and different combinations, and I will add that they shift, move and overlap continuously. In France this complexity of the cultural 'domain' has been the subject of a number of valuable studies by historians. They started with the concept of 'level of culture', a notion which corresponds to Gramsci's idea of stratification. This geological metaphor has the advantage of being in keeping with the image of a society which is also stratified, and there is thus the temptation to establish a correlation between the strata of ideology and society. This temptation can be explained not only by the influence which Marxist models of analysis have had on French historians, but also by the fact that, as I have already said, an ideological struggle took place which was not unrelated to the 'class struggle'.

However, this concept has the disadvantage of not corresponding exactly to what one glimpses of reality. Cultural topography naturally presents layers, but it also presents as it were nodules, nappes, fractures, faults and numerous unstable zones – in other words, structures which are at least as vertical as they are horizontal. Therefore I wonder whether it would not be effective to attempt to put into practice instead the concept of 'cultural formation', or education, provided that it is related to the concept of social 'formation' which has already been discussed at length. The concept of 'formation', which also is borrowed from geology, seems to me to give a better account of the complex cultural structures, of the permanence of residual forms, of all the resurgent factors and the unceasing mobility of the elements of acculturation. Furthermore, it does not conceal the fact – which I consider fundamental – that divisions between conflicting or combined cultures are not, in reality, filtered through the body social but through the attitudes and behaviour of each individual.

I shall now turn to what I consider to be the principal contribution made by the French school of history to cultural history. I shall attempt, with the ethnologists in mind, to delve into the lower strata of society, to acknowledge something other than the top of the social edifice, to reach a culture which, generally speaking, is eclipsed by the dominant culture – in other words, popular culture. In espousing this recent and very strong movement which has at last directed the attention of the French towards their peasant origins and towards civilizations steeped in tradition, historians have undertaken a vast survey based on the notion of a clash between scholarly culture(s) and popular culture. They are thus posing the question in terms of a conflict, of a real struggle between those who held excessive power – the knowledge which is contained in books, libraries and museums – and the poor.

Posing the question in this manner makes it easier to examine other factors: for example, the battle which the medieval Church fought to destroy an entire system of beliefs and rituals; or that other battle which was fought from the eighteenth century onwards to wipe out illiteracy, a battle which was unwittingly linked with the struggle sustained by egalitarian ideology, and which represents the final stage in the popularization, the socialization of scholarly culture (that is to say, of written culture, of the alphabet, the culture of books). In France this led to the functions of education being reduced, and finally to the ossification of artistic training, that is, the training of eye and ear. For this reason, at the very time when – during the nineteenth century – there was an attempt to make heroes out of all citizens through conscription, there was also a desire to make scholars out of them all through compulsory schooling.

I have drawn attention to the power of two very old cultural models, of the old typology established as early as the twelfth century within the dominant culture which separated the culture of the clerks from that of the knights. The continued existence of high culture throughout history makes us realize immediately that in this game there were, in fact, not two players but three, and that popular culture was not engaged in a duel but in a far more complex struggle.

Is there truly such a thing as 'popular' culture? Indeed the term disturbs me, because of what I have said in connection with the notion of cultural education and all the cross-fertilization that is implied. I believe that if one limits oneself to the notion of a clash between two classes, one improperly narrows the field of observation and risks impoverishing the results of one's research. In our culture, in the culture of each one of us, however learned we are, is there not far more than a residue of, a nostalgia for, 'popular' culture? Can one talk about the cultural creativity of the 'people'? What is the 'people'? If there are truly creative sources within the 'people', where are they? A multitude of questions remains to be answered.

11

The History of Value Systems

The comprehensive history of a civilization is the result of changes that occur on different levels – on the level of ecology, demography, production techniques and exchange mechanisms, on the level of the distribution of powers and the position of the decision-making bodies and, finally, on the level of mental attitudes, collective behaviour and the vision of the world which governs these attitudes and controls this behaviour. There are close correlations between these different processes, but each process carries on relatively independently, at its own pace. On some levels, particularly in connection with political relationships, changes which are often very rapid can be perceived. My own experience leads me to believe that the history of value systems does not undergo sudden changes.

Of course it can happen that this history is disturbed by processes of acculturation. At a given moment in its development, a culture can find itself dominated, invaded and penetrated by a foreign culture, either through political shocks such as invasion or colonization, or else through insidious infiltrations, for example the effect of fascination or conversion, themselves the result of the unequal vigour, development and appeal of opposing civilizations. Even in this case the change always seems slow and incomplete. The cultures, however unsophisticated they are, prove resistant to attacks and withstand the sudden entry of foreign elements for a long time and with some effect.

It is striking, for example, how slowly Christianity (simply one element amongst others borrowed from Roman culture) reached the populations that the great migration of the early Middle Ages had brought into closer contact with a less rudimentary civilization. Archaeology reveals that Christian symbols found their way only very gradually into the burial places of Germanic cemeteries, and pagan beliefs, under the superficial garment of rituals, gestures and formulae imposed by force on the whole of the tribe by the converted chieftains, survived for a very long time. In the eleventh century bishops were still endeavouring to eradicate these beliefs. They had not yet been completely rooted out at the very end of the Middle Ages, even in those provinces of Christendom which were the most firmly controlled by the Church. Even then the latter had had to agree to make room for many of these pagan beliefs – the most tenacious and no doubt the most fundamental of them – such as the belief in the mysterious survival of dead souls between the time of the funeral and that of the resurrection of the dead.

Similarly, in the last years of the eleventh century the military expansion of Western Christendom led to the discovery in Toledo, Campania and Palermo of the overwhelming wealth of Jewish and Graeco-Arab learning by the scholars who accompanied the warriors. These intellectuals were quick to take advantage of these treasures, but the value system which they espoused prevented them for many decades from drawing anything from it other than techniques, applied either to the art of reasoning, or to making measurements, or to bodily care. No doubt repressive measures issued from the ecclesiastical powers came into play very rapidly to prevent them from also appropriating the philosophical and moral content of the translated works. But such prohibitions were always circumvented; the totalitarian Church of the thirteenth century did not succeed in preventing the 'New' Aristotle from being read and commented upon in any of the great centres of research. Even so, the corrosive power of this body of doctrine had not succeeded, two centuries later, in making any significant breach in the coherence of Christian thought.

The processes which made the value systems change were even slower when they were protected from external pressures. Trends in economic growth or recession (the medievalist is fortunate enough to be able to observe, in this field, signs of prolonged stagnation and regression), which were closely linked with the line of the demographic curve and with changes in techniques, naturally determine changes in the organization of production relationships and in the distribution of wealth at the different levels of the social edifice. But these changes seem to be more spread out over time than the economic transformations which caused them, and in fact these delays and the slowing down are in part determined by the weight of ideological trends. Indeed these trends occur within a cultural framework flexible enough to receive them, but one which proves to be less willing to change, which yields only up to a certain point. This framework was in fact built on a structure of traditions handed down from generation to generation under a variety of guises by the different educational systems, traditions based on the solid support of language, rituals and social conventions.

In actual fact obstacles to innovation varied enormously in strength amongst the different cultural milieux which are juxtaposed and cross-fertilize one another in any society. However, in most of these milieux, conservative tendencies were by far the strongest. The conservative spirit appears to have been particularly strong in peasant societies, whose survival had long depended on the extremely delicate balance of a coherent set of agrarian practices, which had been patiently tried out and which it seemed unwise to disturb. This implied strict respect for all customs and for a wisdom of which the ancients seemed to be the most reliable source. This spirit was doubtless no less intense amongst all social elites, apparently open to the appeal of ideas, aesthetics and new fashions, but in fact unconsciously tortured by the fear of less superficial changes which might challenge their authority. It was perhaps more vigorous than anywhere else amongst the clergy of all kinds, concerned with maintaining visions of the world and moral precepts which were the basis for the influence they exercised and the privileges they enjoyed. Moreover, such resistance to change was naturally reinforced by the trend which very often led the cultural patterns, created according to the interests and tastes of the dominant social strata, to be gradually popularized. It was further strengthened by the fascination that they evoked, causing them to be disseminated stage by stage to the very foundations of the social edifice. The effect of these shifts was to prolong for a considerable time the vitality of certain mental images and the attitudes which they governed, and to maintain, below a superficial modernity which suited the elite, a solid base of traditions on which conservative aspirations could rely.

However, it should be recognized that these aspirations were thwarted at times when the faster development of material structures made the internal and external barriers more permeable and encouraged communications, through the relaxation of family solidarity, through openness to other cultures, or through the upheavals which disturbed hierarchies. The changes which affected political structures stemmed from more direct consequences in so far as the establishment of a new distribution of powers could be expressed by the deliberate intention to modify educational systems. Thus sudden events – war, revolution, the transformation of institutions – can prove to be disruptive. At any rate one has to discover within society which groups of individuals, through professional or political position or membership of a particular age-group, are more remote from the dominance of traditions and more readily induced to combat them. It is also necessary to measure effectively the power of these agents of innovation. But whatever their importance, whatever their potential for subversion, the cultural system provides a firm structure of resistance to their activities. Cracks developed in its articulation, gradually widened and ended by splitting the structure; however, this was achieved through processes of dissolution which nearly always proved to be insidious. Despite the illusion of advance that the turbulence of superficial agitation can maintain, it is only in the very long term that its resonances bring about a collapse, and even that is never more than partial, leaving behind indelible traces of the old system.

In order to support these general remarks with an example I shall examine a milieu that might be thought one of those most receptive to new ideas, the circle of scholars who settled in Paris at the zenith of the Middle Ages. Their meeting place was a city placed on one of the main thoroughfares of the world. It was an urban area in constant growth, whose population was affected more than any other by economic trends and, lying at the heart of the largest state in the West, by political cross-currents. It was the focus of all those who, throughout Latin Christendom, were fired by the

greatest enthusiasm for learning. Their profession, teaching, was
by its very nature bound up in routine, particularly because at
that time it was a professional vocation whose object was to train
the leading members of the clergy. Yet it naturally placed the
teacher in front of people younger than himself, whose demands
spurred him forward. The feeling is expressed very clearly by one
of these masters, Abelard: 'My students demanded human and
philosophical reasons; they needed intelligible explanations rather
than assertions.' As regards the practice of this profession, teaching
methods were based on dialogue, argument, free discussion, on a
spirit of competition comparable to that which, in the tournaments
of the period, spurred on knights; it urged them to the same
challenging boldness in questioning received ideas. Historical
observation has the advantage of surveying extended periods of
time; its limitation lies in having only partial information, which
leaves many questions unanswered about the remoter ages. In so
far as this is possible, I shall try to reconstruct the value system
as it was accepted in about 1125 by Abelard's contemporaries,
and as it was in about 1275 by Jean de Meun's.

This represents a period of 150 years, an era filled with prodigious activity. It was a time of deconstruction, comparable in
its intensity and repercussions to our own and, to my way of
thinking, just as overwhelming. Infrastructures were radically
transformed: at the time of Abelard the towns were only just
emerging from the countryside; circulation of the coinage had
recently been revived, but the sole source of wealth was still the
soil; the only labour was in the fields, despite the importance
craftmanship had already acquired, stimulated by the propensity
for ostentatious luxury of a newly enriched aristocracy which had
benefited from a century of agricultural growth; for all men life
was entirely dominated by the rhythms and pressures of nature.

At the time when Jean de Meun set about writing the second
part of the *Roman de la Rose* the population was no doubt three
times greater; the countryside was permanently developed, but
was by then economically and politically subjugated by the cities.
Within them, there were ways of life which were free from the
tyrannies of nature, which escaped the oppression of hunger, of
cold and darkness; money became the principal instrument of
power, the incentive for social advancement; manipulating it made

Italian businessmen in the rue des Lombards, close to the schools, rich beyond measure.

The changes were no less profound in political relations. At the beginning of the twelfth century they were entirely organized within the framework of lordship. For the great majority of workers, this meant complete subjugation to the masters of the castles and to village leaders; for the rich it meant military specialization, the profits of plundering, the rejection of all constraints, except those stemming from the obligations of homage, from feudal grants and submission to the older members of the family. A century and a half later, a genuine state had been established, based on an administrative framework sufficiently sophisticated for an abstract notion of authority to be revived, and for the personality of the sovereign to be hidden behind that of his servants. This had been made possible by the assuaging of strife; the art of war became a ritual and made battles seem like sporting events; legal rules were set down in writing, and there were experts in procedure to handle them; negotiation became the norm; a sense of freedom grew up, reinforced within associations of equals, of interest groups formed at different levels of society and strong enough in the outskirts of the towns to bring about the first strike movements.

It was a century and a half which saw the development and failure of the Crusades, the pillaging in Spain, Sicily and Constantinople of higher cultures whose brilliance had once made the uncouth simplicity of Carolingian civilization seem derisory, the remarkable pushing back of the world's frontiers, the advancing tide of Mongolian Asia, Marco Polo's journey to Peking, the penetration of the African and Asian borders, no longer by soldiers but by traders and missionaries, who learned to speak other languages and to use other systems of measurement.

It was a century and a half which saw the development of heresy, and which finally saw them contained, dismantled by the repressive control that the Church managed to impose on the whole of Christendom, stifled, weakened, partially assimilated by orthodoxy at the cost of great misrepresentations, as demonstrated by the fate of the Franciscan message.

It was, finally, a century and a half during which aesthetics could be used as a criterion, from the tympanum of Autun to Cimabue and the pulpit of Pisa, from the vaults of Vézelay to those of the Sainte-Chapelle, from Gregorian plainsong to the polyphonies of Notre-Dame.

In a cultural milieu such as this, which was so deeply imbued with the need for truth, the thirst for understanding and the taste for the modern, these upheavals do not appear to have appreciably changed the value system. No doubt, towards the year 1275 the primacy of reason was exalted more resolutely, and we have seen how emphatically it was praised in the second *Roman de la Rose*. But even two generations before Abelard, Beranger of Tours was proclaiming that reason was the 'honour of man'. The clear vision of things which, by the application of reason, the contemporaries of Jean de Meun were endeavouring to attain, was in fact attained through the patient use of the mechanism of logic. In the early years of the twelfth century, the masters of the Parisian schools were learning to apply it in order to remove all ambiguity from revelations of truth in the sacred texts and in the manifestations of the visible world; at the same time, these processes became more subtle and more effective, but they changed neither their nature nor their objective.

In 1275 no doubt the critical mind boldly confronted everything which the intellectuals of the day called sham, religious hypocrisy, the submission of the *papelards* to pontifical command. It rejected the privileges of high birth (which Abelard, who was wholly integrated into this social category, did not repudiate and had never dreamed of challenging), the licentiousness of the courtly game, in which Abelard himself had endeavoured to join to the best of his ability, and the sophistications of the ethics of high society. But here, too, it is evident that in the first quarter of the eleventh century the masters of Paris had always assumed such an attitude and aspired to honesty and to moderation; if their targets were not the same, it was only because the problems presented by the social, political and moral climate were not posed in the same terms. During the last three decades of the thirteenth century, nature, the 'art of God', was the subject of more sustained attention; there was the will to discover its laws, to reach a clear comprehension of the natural order 'from which the paths of honesty lead'; and to reach the solid foundations of an ethic and a faith.

One feels that these elements were already truly alive, less confident no doubt, less assured, still lacking an instrument of conquest, but bent on creating one, in the minds of those who, a century and a half earlier, in the time of Louis VI and Suger, were writing commentaries on the Scriptures, observing the course of the stars and studying the way in which light was dispersed. Finally, there is no evidence that this set of beliefs was seriously affected at the same time. Dante, in fact, referred to the great number of disciples of Epicurus who professed that the soul died with the body. Such views had perforce to remain clandestine, and those who shared them, if they were not unmasked, are therefore hidden from the historian's view.

But in how many intellectuals in Paris did anxiety and the critical spirit in fact produce a tone of ribald irony? Those I refer to seemed to adhere to the basic points of Christian dogma effortlessly and without dissimulation. No doubt their Christianity presented a new face; it was far less objective than it had been fifty years previously in the terrified prostrations and outward appearance of ritualism of the time; now it was directed to a suffering and fraternal God with whom man could try to talk. Many, along with Bonaventure, chose a mystical path, but Bernard of Clairvaux had to a large extent paved the way. Abelard had already read the Gospels closely enough to affirm that sin lay in the intention and not in the act; Anselm of Canterbury had, before him, focused his studies on the problem of incarnation. In fact, what emerges most clearly from all these factors are in fact constants – a technique of analysis, a desire to understand which was sharpened by the methods and aims of education, moral needs dictated by a particular situation within society, a vision of the natural and supernatural world based on texts which were being interpreted with increasing competence.

The only significant shifts I have glimpsed come on two levels. In the first place they consist in an awareness of relativity, starting with time. For the thinkers of the thirteenth century, time was no longer viewed as one homogeneous entity where past and future were consistent with the present and had a spiritual relationship with it. When the Dominican Humbert of Romans reflected on the recent history of Christianity, he sought the explanation in a series of natural causes, and his personal experience of the failures of the Church, of the decline of imperial dignity and the retreat of the Latin institutions of the East prevented him from continuing to believe in the unity and the necessity of the history of the people of God. At the same time the gradual discovery of the immensity, diversity and complexity of creation, the new awareness that the world is full of men who refuse to listen to the message of Christ compelled the most clear-minded to think that Christianity was perhaps not situated at the centre of the world, or at least that it occupied only a limited area. In addition they were forced to recognize that Christian thought was incapable of absorbing or of dissolving the coherent unity of the Aristotelian system.

Secondly, many of these men welcomed unreservedly the taste of earthly happiness, that happiness which, according to Jean de Meun, had been offered to man on the morning of creation, a *joie de vivre* which the retreat of nature and reason before the offensive of Faux-Semblant (in *Le Roman de la Rose*) jeopardized, but whose recovery it was the responsibility of philosophers to promote. These intellectuals resolutely rejected the exhortations to *contemptus mundi* and all the models of renunciation and refusal of which the monks had for long, and even until recent times been the triumphant advocates.

In so far as ideology is concerned, therefore, the changes seem far less pronounced than those which at the same moment in history affected economic activity, demography and power struggles. Value systems are not unchanging; the transformation of material, political and social structures disturbs their foundations and modifies them; but this modification continues steadily and without upheaval, even in those avant-garde cultural milieux whose special role was to work towards adapting these systems; beneath the turbulence fostered by controversies, diatribes and condemnations, the historian sees these systems shifting flexibly and imperceptibly.

On the important question of the predictability of these changes, I shall venture only a few comments.

The task of the historian is to put forward explanations after the event, that is to say, to order the facts which are at his disposal, to relate them and thereby to introduce logic into the unfolding of linear time. This very approach first of all makes him more attentive to new facts, to detecting them in this artificial manner within the broad movement of customs and routines. In addition, when he wants to give an account of these new facts, and especially when these facts are concerned not with events but with structures, he puts necessity before chance. The historian thus manages to establish satisfactory correlations between the assertion at the end of the thirteenth century of the concepts which the words 'nature' and 'reason' intended to express at that time, between the increased enjoyment of life, between the discovery of relative rather than absolute values, and also the rise of urban prosperity, the break-down of divisions in the West, the expansion of certain social groups, the slow decline of the mirages of the heavenly Jerusalem and the more skilful use of syllogism. Similarly, the historian succeeds in explaining the transition from the religion of the Eternal as shown in the church of Moissac (Tarn-et-Garonne) to the religion of the mockery of Christ. But in this way, whether consciously or not, he provides an argument for all the systems which offer hope, for all the concepts which base the succession of the ages of humanity on a sequence of determining causes which thus aspire to prediction. On the basis of an experience of the past, these concepts set out to construct a line which they suppose must be extended into the future.

The convictions of eleventh-century monks, for example, rested on an interpretation of history; their periodic processions set out to imitate the progress of men towards the uncreated light, just like the Eternal Gospel of Joachim of Fiore[1] who ascribed the precise date of 1260 to the coming of the reign of the Spirit. Marxist thought is based on an interpretation of history, and it is worth reflecting carefully on the stance it adopts in relation to the foreseeable nature of events: as Antonio Labriola, for example, wrote,

Historical prediction, which is at the root of the doctrine of *The Communist Manifesto*...implies neither a chronological point, nor its description anticipated by a social configuration. It is the whole of society which, at one crucial point in its evolutionary trajectory, discovers the cause of its destiny, and enlightens us and explains the law of its movements. [This prediction] stems neither from chronology, nor from foreshadowing nor from promises; to sum it up in a word which in my opinion expresses everything, it is 'morphological'.[2]

Evidently, what is considered foreseeable is society's progress towards new forms. This phenomenon can be foreseen in so far as one can firmly establish the repeatability of certain relationships and the fact that they are regularly subordinated to given laws. But when Marxist analysis professes to be rigorously scientific one must recognize that it claims only to establish firmly such relationships and such subordination on the material foundations of the social edifice. On the subject of what he referred to as 'ideological social relationships' ('Who are the friends of the people?') Lenin was in fact very guarded. The major objective which I believe current research in social history should set itself is precisely that of shedding light on how the discordant movements which are responsible for infrastructures and superstructures are articulated, and on the manner in which these movements affect one another. If the break-up of relationships of personal dependency in the midst of medieval lordship appears to result directly from long-term trends, from the improvement of agricultural production techniques, from population growth and from the wider distribution of money; and if, consequently, supposing that there had at the time been means of analysis available similar to those which we use, one might think that it would have been possible to predict this break-up in so far as the extrapolations are not on the whole deceptive.

Who, on the other hand, would have been able to predict the sudden introduction, in the buildings commissioned by Abbot Suger at Saint-Denis, of an aesthetic of light, the establishment of the rituals of courtly love to counterbalance a development of the structures of the aristocratic family and the conjugal morality proposed by the Church, or else the fate of the Waldensian heresy and the forms which Franciscan devotion would take when it was made to conform to papal authority? In the current state of the human sciences it is clear that the 'morphological' prediction of the future of a civilization cannot without excessive rashness take into account anything other than the likely continuation of the underlying trends influencing the history of the economy, population and technology, and perhaps the history of scientific know-

ledge. It must also not conceal that the consequences of a shift
in opinion, propaganda or the decisions of the authorities may at
any moment make the progress of events deviate appreciably from
its predicted course.

This does not mean, however, that the historian cannot offer
the futurologist certain propositions regarding method, which can
be applied to the observation of value systems. One may admit
that the ideological 'envelope', which we have seen is flexible and
does not suddenly break, is quite evidently affected by the movement of infrastructures, but that it tends to respond to such
movement in slow shifts. In this case the important thing would
appear to be first to observe certain strong tendencies, everything
which in the development of demography and the transformation
of economic relations is liable to cause such adjustments by disturbing the limits of thought, by stimulating or by curbing communications between groups, by encouraging transfers, uprootings,
exchange and fusion. Secondly, it is important to detect the points
where there is less resistance to tradition. In addition, it is necessary to test the rigidity of educational systems within the family,
the school and all the mechanisms of initiation and apprenticeship.
The aim is to measure their ability to receive contributions from
outside, and the powers of assimilation of a certain representation
of the world in the face of a possible irruption of elements projected
by outside cultures.

It is also important to take into account events in themselves.
They exist essentially on the political level. It is, no doubt, possible
to regard them as surface agitations, widely determined by the
arrangement of deep-seated structures. Nevertheless, to the historian who has already observed how narrow the limits of fore-
seeability are with regard to the long-term trends which influence
demographic or economic development, events appear fortuitous
in essence; their emergence, or at any rate development, proves
to be particularly resistant to prediction. Short-term effects are
never negligible; in the attempts to create revolution or reform,
in the transfer of activity that they prompt, they affect the institutions which are responsible for the transmission of knowledge,
belief and rituals. Finally, it is the historian's duty to emphasize
the actual importance of history as a particularly active element
amongst those which make up a practical ideology. To a very

great extent the vision which a society forms of its destiny and the meaning which it attributes, rightly or wrongly, to its own history are among the most powerful weapons in the hands of conservative and progressive forces, as critical supports to the desire to safeguard or destroy a value system.

12

The Renaissance of the Twelfth Century: Audience and Patronage

One of the major problems facing the social sciences today is the relationship between cultural factors and the general development of economic and social structures, or to put it in different terms, the interaction between material infrastructures and superstructures, that is to say in the present case, the production and reception of cultural objects which are considered, by contemporaries or by ourselves, the expression of a 'renaissance'.

There are two main difficulties. There is no theoretical proposition on which to construct the problem before carrying out the inquiry. Work is greatly hindered by the current compartmentalization of disciplines in universities and research institutes, by the boundaries which still unfortunately separate economic and social historians from historians of thought, literature and art. Between these territories, which are so jealously delimited and defended, communication is rare: at present there are very few places where interdisciplinary research can be carried out. In fact conditions have not altered appreciably since the time of Charles Homer Haskins. The sole profound and promising change is our growing dissatisfaction, upon rereading *The Renaissance of the Twelfth Century*, at finding in this admirable book scarcely any references to the considerable changes in social relationships within Latin Christendom. We would like to see these relationships correlated with the combined changes in the mental attitudes and cultural forms which both express and govern these attitudes.

In the current state of our knowledge, my contribution on the subject of 'Patronage and Audience' will therefore inevitably be superficial and introductory. I shall be able only to formulate suggestions for research, by drawing virtually all my examples from what I know personally of French history of the period. My comments will centre on three set of questions.

GROWTH AND ITS EFFECTS

The process of development which, ever since Haskins, has been called the twelfth-century renaissance is clearly inseparable from the long movement of material progress which took place in Western Europe at that time. This movement had neither beginning nor end; the 'renaissance' which we are discussing did not have a beginning or an end either, any more than the Italian Renaissance of the fifteenth century. Expressions of cultural development are less difficult to situate chronologically by the very nature of the sources available. However, since these sources lack statistical information, the process of social and economic development cannot be closely followed. Of this we can perceive little more than trends.

The twelfth century seems indeed to have represented – at least in France – the height of this progress. It is worth bearing in mind three criteria: (1) The spread of currency: the first signs of this diffusion appear around 1080 in documents relating to the countryside of the Mâcon region; a hundred years later money was everywhere and dominated everything. No one, from the greatest prince to the humblest peasant, could avoid using it daily. (2) The extent of the land under cultivation: Robert Fossier's statistical analyses for Picardy situate the greatest increase between 1150 and 1170. (3) The increase in population: Fossier's analyses show that it reached its peak in the last quarter of the twelfth century.

Growth was essentially agricultural and took place in what at that time constituted the basic framework of production relationships – rural lordship. Established in France around the year 1000, the institutions of the seigneurial fiscal system were perfected during the last two decades of the eleventh century; they were fully operational throughout the twelfth century. In order to meet the demands of their lords – masters of their bodies, of the land which they cultivated and of the power they had to command them – peasant families had constantly to produce more. Their standard of living does not seem to have improved appreciably before the 1180s. Indeed, the system of rents and taxes transferred to the lords the bulk of the increased resources created by the expansion of agricultural land, greater productivity and the enlarged workforce. The seigneurial class was virtually the only one to profit from the increased wealth of the countryside.

It would indeed appear that the secular aristocracy benefited more from this general progress than the great ecclesiastical establishments. In fact throughout the twelfth century it managed to protect effectively the source of its revenues, that is to say the lordships, from being divided, a process which had severely affected them up until about 1050. This was achieved in two ways: by appreciably reducing donations of land and rights to churches, and especially by limiting the birth rate, by preventing family stock from branching out and in so doing dividing the inheritance. For the entire period, the exclusion of married and dowered daughters from sharing the inheritance, and the celibacy of all sons except the eldest, guaranteed that the number of noble lineages remained constant and therefore ensured the stability of their patrimony, whose profits were constantly being increased by economic growth and improvements in seigneurial taxation. Both the households of princes and the families of knights therefore lived comfortably, for the most part. They continued to spend more, making increasing use of money.

This increase in aristocratic consumption stimulated specialized crafts and trade. It encouraged urban growth, which was very marked in twelfth-century France, to such an extent that during the last two decades of the century development was centred in the cities in this region of Christendom. Thenceforth the city prevailed over the countryside, dominating and exploiting it. This sustained the rise of two social groups, the elite of the merchant bourgeoisie and those who served the great lordships. These people grew rich, some even richer than many nobles, but their ideal remained integration in the rural nobility, acceptance within its ranks and participation in its culture and its way of life.

I have outlined the development of material structures as they directly concern the subject under discussion because of their effects on attitudes and outlooks. Two events, both determined by economic growth and by social transformations, seem to be particularly noteworthy.

Firstly, there was the emergence of an ideological system peculiar to the secular aristocracy. This was organized around the concept of knighthood. The set of values which the term denoted was strengthened and enhanced throughout the twelfth century through the entertainments, tournaments and *joutes amoureuses*, offered to the *juvenes*, 'bachelor' or unmarried knights, the most dynamic section of an aristocratic society reinforced by the matrimonial policy of the nobility. This is borne out in northern France after 1160 by the elaboration of the dubbing ritual and, more clearly, the resurgence in secular literature of the old schema of a trifunctional society. However, this pattern was transformed and desacralized, and the 'order' of knights was given pre-eminence, not only over the peasants but also over the clergy. What is important is that the cultural monopolies hitherto held by the Church were certainly challenged. Chivalric society wished to participate in high culture as well. Its dream was to monopolize 'clergie', that is, the knowledge of the schools. Thus the cultural distinction which separated the ecclesiastical from the secular aristocracy became blurred and the two classes intermingled. It is precisely at this point that the phenomena of patronage and audience are to be found.

The second event which in my opinion is fundamental, arose directly from the spectacle of a world transformed by the efforts of men and of the natural environment being increasingly developed: it was an awareness of progress. The strengthening of this perception can be discerned first amongst the intellectuals who were most closely associated with the secular aristocracy, amongst members of the cathedral chapters – Bernard Silvester seems to me to be typically representative. These men of learning, of written culture and reflection, set about celebrating nature – a nature that was now in favour again. With increasing clarity they imagined man – whose underlying structure corresponded to that of the created world – as capable of influencing the world, as called upon by God to co-operate with all his strength in this work of creation – henceforth conceived as continuing through historical time. Here, with improved techniques and with the labour of settlers constantly reclaiming more land, there developed the idea that civilization grows like a plant, that each generation takes on the task from its predecessors and takes it nearer towards its goal. This was indeed a complete reversal in men's vision of human history. It ceased to be regarded pessimistically as a process of inevitable corruption but came to seem a conquest. It changed direction. Its advance, by then parallel to the history of salvation, no longer seemed to lead inexorably to decline, but to rise from age to age, little by little, towards greater perfection.

Naturally this reversal of the value system came about imperceptibly. Take, for example, the Cistercians. The monks of Cîteaux were entrenched in the past. Convinced that everything was debased by the passage of time, they saw themselves as reformers, but in a retrogressive sense, one that was strictly speaking reactionary, deciding to return to the original principles of Benedictine life. Faithful to the spirit of the *contemptus mundi*, the main expression of an ideology which had developed in times of regression and stagnation, they elected to distance themselves from the tide of life and to escape to the desert. The manual labour which they chose to undertake remained for them something with a negative value, an act of humiliation and of penitence. And yet these men hastened to apply the most modern technological innovations; they worked away furiously at making the waste land where they had settled yield more and more, and thus without realizing it they were taking part in what was most vigorous in the general movement of progress, ending up by placing their agricultural domains at the forefront of economic success. Above all, by placing the mystery of the Incarnation at the heart of their meditation, they were asserting ever more forcefully that, in man, the spirit's strivings towards perfection are inseparable from the strivings of the body. In this way they too joined in the movement to rehabilitate the flesh.

A watershed was therefore reached at the beginning of the twelfth century in the way in which intellectuals in the region around Chartres, the Ile-de-France and Champagne conceived the world and its history. It altered fundamentally the meaning of the word *renovatio*. Each previous renaissance had set out to restore and to rescue from inevitable deterioration works which were admired because they were the heritage of an earlier age, and therefore better: restoration was exhumation. From now onwards each renaissance was regarded as generative. It retrieved the legacy, but did so in order to exploit it as settlers exploited virgin land, in order to obtain more from it. Just as in all seigneurial lineages, the heir in each generation felt that he had been chosen to make the ancestral heritage produce a profit and was confident of his power to increase its yield, so medieval men felt capable not only of equalling the achievements of antiquity but of outdoing them.

PATRONAGE

The continuously growing surplus from seigneurial exploitation was in part used for cultural purposes; this proportion was clearly greater in ecclesiastical lordships. Here the reform of the Church succeeded on two levels. Firstly, it was responsible for the reorganization of ecclesiastical revenues. There was less plundering by the laity and less of the administrative negligence which squandered a large part of the profits. People learned to keep accounts and to plan. The administrative arrangements made by Abbot Suger of Saint-Denis and by Peter the Venerable, abbot of Cluny, bear witness to that organized effort which revitalized ecclesiastical domains. The gains which resulted from this reorganization largely offset the losses suffered by ecclesiastical wealth because of the dwindling of alms in the form of lands donated by the lay aristocracy. Once it was protected and better managed, this wealth produced more abundant resources. Churches established in urban areas became particularly prosperous. They shared in the profits from the lucrative taxes which were levied on the circulation and exchange of money in the growing towns. They collected the pious donations of the bourgeoisie, all the more generously given because businessmen were uncertain of their salvation. Through its offerings, the urban population soon became the main benefactor. Secondly, the reform placed able prelates in decision-making positions. Having triumphed over the secular power, they believed that the resources of their houses should serve to advance learning, to promote the activity of the scriptorium and chantry, and to provide a more sumptuous setting for church services.

So long as it was a matter of embellishing the musical adornment of the office, of enriching the bookshelves, maintaining the school and sending emissaries in search of new knowledge, the cost remained low. It became very heavy when the decision was taken to build. Nevertheless most bishops, abbots and priors did not hesitate. Rivalry drove them to achieve more than others. For a while St Bernard resisted his companions who were urging him to rebuild the monastery of Clairvaux; he finally gave in and authorized the emptying of the coffers in order to take on workmen. Often plans were too ambitious. To carry on with the enterprise exceeded the community's ordinary means. Subsidies had to be found from outside. We know the difficulties with which Peter the Venerable struggled as, deeply in debt, he had to complete the building of the immense abbey of Cluny. However, most of the time lay benefactors came to the rescue. Generous subsidies from the count of Champagne, for example, allowed Cistercian monastic buildings to be renovated in that province. Subsequently, the king of Castile and the king of England were regarded as the true 'builders' of the 'great church' of Cluny, until the prudent generosity of the bishop of Winchester, Henry of Blois, temporarily helped the community out of its financial difficulties. When the chroniclers of the year 1000 spoke of the rebuilding of churches, they often described miracles and the chance discovery of hidden treasure. It was their way of giving an account of the true fact which effectively enabled these projects to be carried out: the release of hoarded money, the circulation of precious metal reserves stored in the sanctuaries. At the same time our twelfth-century sources of information, for example, the author of the *Life* of St Bernard,[1] emphasized very clearly that the architectural works which the Church was promoting were in large part financed by lay patrons.

Their intervention occurred partly because economic growth and the mechanisms of seigneurial taxation meant that money was accumulating in their hands, but mainly because they felt obliged to dedicate their wealth to this sort of enterprise. In the early Middle Ages people looked to kings to participate in the embellishment of religious monuments. This activity was part of the mission of royalty. I have just referred to Alfonso of Castile and Henry II of England who supported Cluny: both were kings, like Robert the Pious who was especially praised by his biographer Helgaud and by Oderic of Sens for contributing generously to the adornment of so many churches. Formerly, the greatest monetary revenues had in fact been in the hands of monarchs, sovereigns obliged to participate in ecclesiastical culture, particularly because of the coronation which placed them amongst the *oratores*, amongst the celebrants of the liturgy. Kings contributed directly to the flowering of that culture by maintaining in their *palatium* the main centre of creativity, the chapel, and all its associated workshops of art, writing and thought; by conferring benefactions on cathedrals and royal abbeys; and lastly by ensuring peace, which was conducive to intellectual work. Originally patronage was the specific function of the king, God's lieutenant on earth, but in the twelfth century the entire aristocracy aspired to fulfil this role. Three factors account for this diffusion of the functions of patronage.

First, there was the feudal system, that is to say the appropriation by a growing number of princes of the privileges of sovereignty. These princes took possession of the powers of the king; we should not ignore the fact that they also wanted to invest themselves with his virtues, and in particular to occupy the place at the heart of religious culture which the king had previously been the only layman to hold. This happened very early on. In the year 1000 the duke of Aquitaine wished it to be known that he too was learned, read books and meditated on the mysteries of faith.

A century and a half later this claim had gained considerable ground; there were even more princes who wanted not only to imitate the king in this area but also to set him an example. In about 1155 an anecdote was added to the second version of the *Geste des seigneurs d'Ambroise*. It testifies to this desire naively but forcefully. It describes the count of Anjou, Fulk the Good who died in about 960: the intimates of the king of France laughed at him because they saw the count singing the Office in the midst of the canons, but they soon heard the riposte he himself had written, that 'an illiterate king is a crowned ass'. The sovereign had to recognize that '*sapientia*, eloquence and letters are as fitting for counts as they are for kings'. At the time of this interpolation, the king had lost his monopoly on participation in learned culture and on the patronage implied by that involvement. All the lords who were responsible for the safety of the people considered themselves responsible also for their salvation. Their duty was therefore to combine, as formerly only sovereigns had done, the learning of the schools and the practice of arms. We are told that Count Fulk of Anjou was admired because 'although he was thoroughly and discerningly initiated in letters, in the rules of grammar and in the arguments of Aristotle and Cicero, he nonetheless surpassed the strongest, the best and the most valiant of knights.'[2]

During the twelfth century people were convinced that the goods appropriated by secular lords from the fruits of peasant toil should not serve solely to conduct war for public defence. These fiscal levies seemed justified only if they were partly applied to the advancement of knowledge and the flowering of religious art.

During this period austerity was encouraged in order to increase the portion of lay seigneurial revenues devoted to intellectual works. The preaching of penance, the exhortation to poverty and renunciation of worldly riches, and the banishment of all excessive luxury from the courts were gaining ground all through the twelfth century. Such preaching undoubtedly encouraged works of charity and care for the destitute. But in the end it called into question the form of patronage which supported the great artistic enterprises. When Peter the Chanter denounced as robbery the taxes levied in Paris on the 'poor', which, thanks to the generosity of Louis VII, went to supplying the money for the building of Notre-Dame founded by Bishop Maurice of Sully, he was condemning royal patronage. However, it is certain that in so far as these exhortations were heeded, some of the money that the rich might have spent on their pleasure and on making their houses sumptuous was channelled into religious establishments, and so into culture. These pleas thus contributed to furthering the renaissance. For example, Guillaume de Saint-Thierry congratulated St Bernard on managing to persuade the count of Champagne to part with the jewels in his treasury. He donated them to the Cistercians who, finding liturgical display repugnant, sold them to Suger. The latter used them in goldsmiths' work, whilst the Cistercians used the money thus earned for building.

Finally one must take into account the irresistible process of imitation which, having popularized the model of royal behaviour, gradually encouraged the mimicry of the attitudes of princes, that is to say of kings right down to the lowest levels of aristocratic society. As knighthood became sanctified, took on the appearance of an 'order' to which a 'sacrament' (dubbing) permitted entry, all the adults of the military caste felt themselves called no longer to show physical courage but to cultivate the virtue of *prudentia*, no longer to conduct themselves *en preux* (with valour), but also as *prud'hommes* (wise men), to take part in some way in high culture, as did the princes and the kings, and to patronize it with their largesse. Three main points emerge from this development which is of particular interest in examining the phenomena of patronage and audience.

Like the Count of Anjou in the legend, all the knights wanted to be regarded as *litterati* (educated men). From the end of the eleventh century there is mounting evidence of young men who did not belong to the high nobility and were not destined for the Church, but were taught at home by private tutors or sent to schools, and learned at least to read and understand a little Latin. The custom of entrusting the education of sons to clerics continued to be widely practised, and at the end of the twelfth century it began to spread beyond chivalric society. It won over some of the *nouveaux riches* such as Durand de Blanot, a humble provost from a village near Mâcon, the brother of a peasant freeholder who, around 1220, sent his son to Bologna to study law.

This appetite for learning led to investment. People spent money maintaining clerics whom they expected to help with the education of their family as well as with the administration of the lordship. Lords of moderate rank were not content simply to contribute, like the count of Champagne, to financing Cistercian buildings, as had for example the lord of Simiane at Sénanque and the lord of Baux at Silvacane in the second half of the century. Instead they founded colleges of canons, if they did not already exist, near their residences. In this way centres of learning developed everywhere. In Champagne members and officials of the count's household alone created more than 320 prebends for canons during the 1150s.

The most significant fact was, undoubtedly, that the generosity of the lay aristocracy increased the number of positions which assured men I shall describe as 'intellectuals' the means to work and to surround themselves with culture. It would be very illuminating – and far less difficult than many other inquiries in this field – to attempt to evaluate the increase during the twelfth century in the number of canons, of those individuals whom people were gradually becoming accustomed to call 'masters', all the clergy who found permanent or temporary employment in noble households. One could better measure the importance of this group of men who played a decisive role in the success of the renaissance if one were able to follow more closely the rapid development which took place in parallel with that of 'courtly' troupes of young bachelor knights, of another *jeunesse* drawn from the clergy, nearly all of whom, for the same reasons, were also drawn from the aristocracy and imbued with the same dynamism. Indeed, these clerics, whom Stephen Langton criticized because they made their careers in the service of lay power instead of meditating on holy texts, were the main agents of this cultural integration which, embracing the concept of chivalry, transferred to aristocratic ideology some of the values and the techniques of scholarly culture.

It is worth studying closely the schools where these intellectuals received their education and the movements which rid these educational institutions of their torpor, increased their number, concentrated them and filled some of them disproportionately. The social and economic study of scholarly institutions during this period has barely been touched upon, but the task is possible. It would permit a closer examination of the material growth, the role of money – begged by scholars from their families, earned by the masters, and sometimes copiously (Abelard boasted about how much his knowledge earned him) – and the role of patronage, the subsidies granted by prelates and princes whose conscientious largesse was deployed in this area of cultural activity well before the first colleges for poor students were founded at the very end of the century. The scholarly milieu would be more clearly perceived, together with the ministry and the wholesale trade, as the scene of the greatest social mobility at that time. Like the *jeunesse* of the chivalric order, the young of the intelligentsia engaged in competitions which were analogous to tournaments (as we learn from Abelard), where some won glory and the 'prize', and all endeavoured to wield more effectively the formidable weapons of reason. They rank amongst the adventurers of this age, more assured than many others of rising in the social hierarchies, provided they had courage and ambition.

If the number of students continued to grow during the twelfth century, it was because more and more careers were opening up for those who had gone to the universities, the most accessible and attractive of which were not ecclesiastical. Secular society required the services of men with this education. It was ready to pay well for them, and all the money that both the upper and lower reaches of the aristocracy paid to have in their service such large numbers of young men who knew how to handle words and figures, could reason and had a smattering of the *quadrivium* (four liberal arts), entitles it to be regarded collectively as the true patron of the expansion and diffusion of knowledge. Demand was so pressing and the response received was so enthusiastic that, during the last decades of the century, the leaders of the Church started to question the purpose of cathedral schools and thought of taking measures to stem the flight of graduates into semi-secular professions. It is important to note that these intellectuals were hired in growing numbers in the courts where their function was increasingly considered indispensable, and received ever greater rewards; they were the craftsmen who brought together lay culture and learned culture – they were the most effective propagators of a 'renaissance', for which the school was the great workshop.

AUDIENCE

In the twelfth century a new form of culture developed which was available to all members of the aristocracy, but also to the newly rich who felt that to adopt it was the best way for them to conceal their origins and to blend with those of noble birth. In the *Ars honeste amandi* by Andreas Capellanus, one of the *litterati* in the court of Philip Augustus, the *plebeius* (commoner), is sharply distinguished, by his birth and by the source of his wealth, from the noble (*nobilis*), the more noble (*nobilior*) and the most noble (*nobilissimus*), the clerk. But he prides himself on sharing their tastes, on speaking their language and on scrupulously conforming to the rules of behaviour which they observe. This culture was largely a reflection of the knowledge and forms of expression which were 'reborn' in the creative centres of the higher reaches of the Church. To examine its formation and expansion poses the question of audience which is inseparable from that of patronage, since they are in fact two complementary aspects of the same phenomenon, itself inseparable from economic and social development. I shall limit myself to a few remarks on the location and chronology of this process of reception.

This culture can certainly be described as courtly: the courts, both large and small, were the locus of both its enrichment and its diffusion. The court was the extension of the seigneurial household. It developed as the profits of the nobility grew. Largesse, the principal virtue of the aristocratic value system, created the authority and prestige of every lord. It compelled him to attract as many members of his household as he could support and to treat them well. Since it was necessary for his reputation for his guests to feel at ease in his household, he endeavoured to occupy them with intellectual as well as physical entertainments. Thus the ethic of generosity made the court a centre of cultural creativity. It was also a school, a permanent gathering where good manners were learnt. With the most munificent princes this initiation was the most extensive and produced the best '*prud'hommes*'. Courtly life was animated by the *juvenes*, knights and clerics, who competed against one another, each one longing to outshine the others, to win the favours of the patron by demonstrating his excellence in arms or in letters. Women, we must not forget, also contributed to court life. Everything suggests that their participation in scholarly culture was more precocious and extensive than that of the males of the secular aristocracy. Adjoining the noble residence was a sort of convent where the daughters of the master were educated. Those who did not remain there all their lives in a semi-monastic condition, probably left less superficially educated or *litteratae* than the knights, their brothers. They played a central role in the cultural competition for which the court was the theatre. This competition took place before them; it was in their eyes that the boys wanted to shine; it was for them to bestow the 'prize'. They were one of the essential links between the 'renaissance' and the upper ranks of secular society.

In this society the encounter between knights and clergy took place. The *senior* and the lady, his wife, each embodying courtly values in complementary fashion, also wanted to appear, like the kings of old, as models of lay piety, by setting a good example to members of their household. They made room in their lives for religious observance. Through their agency close communication was established between their entourage and the monastery where the dynasty's ancestors rested, the community of nuns to which widows retired, the collegiate church where the master went regularly 'in clerical garb', to follow the liturgical offices in the midst of his *confrères*, the canons, reading from a book and ritually distributing alms, as did the legendary Count Fulk of Anjou, or the historical Count Charles the Good of Flanders. Even the least important squire had his chaplain; most of the ruling class at that time were trying out practices which encouraged closer lay involvement in the liturgies of the Church.

This osmosis between the sacred and the secular clearly facilitated the acceptance at the apex of society of those forms whose 'renaissance' underpinned expansion in the ecclesiastical sphere. The renewal of religious art and music, which ornamented the liturgical celebrations to which the knights were invited, had an impact on the setting of secular festivities and led to artistic renewal there as well. Similarly, through *exempla*, through the structure and content of the homilies delivered before 'courtly' audiences, something of the logical processes of scholarly thought and its perceptions of nature, history and the supernatural was communicated to lay thought. Significant relationships can be discerned between the vernacular literary works which have come down to us and what we know of the preaching intended for the people of the courts. I shall confine myself to one example, that of the chaplain of the earl of Chester described by Orderic Vitalis: he preached before this lord's household, his knights, both the young and the not so young. In order to keep their attention he interspersed his comments on the word of God with stories capable of holding the imagination of these men of war, stories of military saints and of William of Orange. A careful reading of the *Chanson de Roland* shows that it could be understood on several levels and was written for audiences of which several at least, although lay, remembered more fragments of the Scriptures than one would have anticipated. Audience? The secular aristocracy's first experience of the 'renaissance of the twelfth century' was through sermons.

The renaissance also reached it through entertainment, since courtly society, exclusive and strictly protected against the intrusion of the non-noble, scornfully looking down at everyone from on high, well established in the wealth and the idleness it sanctioned, lived at first wantonly, for gambling and for pleasure. The principal entertainment was storytelling. The people of the court listened. Works written by clerics but in a form accessible to them, that is to say in verse and in the vernacular, were recited before them. Those works, which we call romances of antiquity (*romans antiques*), clearly represented the most striking attempt to adapt the *auctores* on whom the school grammarians commented, for a lay audience, but none of the works of chivalric literature escaped from the profound influence of the *trivium*.

Nevertheless, in the twelfth century so many Latin literary works were addressed to courtly audiences that one should examine how they reached these audiences. Amongst the lords and the princesses to whom Hildebert of Lavardin and Baudri of Bourgueil dedicated their poems, were there so few people who could enjoy these works without interpretation? The canon who, around 1155, wrote the 'Account of the Lords of Amboise' (*Geste des seigneurs d'Amboise*), specifically citing Boethius, Horace, Lucan, Sidonius Apollinaris and Seneca, and straining to assimilate Ciceronian *amicitia* to the affective bond forged by vassalage, must surely have expected the graces and the vigour of his Latin writing to be appreciated by people other than his *confrères*, the clerics? Should we not assume that there was a considerable growth in the lay audience sufficiently educated to communicate without intermediary in the language and learning of the schools? What could have been the practical function of the 'History of Duke Geoffrey' (*Historia Gaufredi ducis*) which was also written in Latin? Was it read? Where and in what circumstances? How was it read? In translation? With a commentary? This work shows Geoffrey Plantagenet besieging the castle of Montreuil-Bellay; this 'educated commander' (*litteratus consul*) requested that a copy of Vegetius be brought from the abbey of Marmoutier. To be sure, it is not stated that he read the book himself, but he listened as a monk read it to him. In Latin? Translating and commenting on the text? At any rate, the following day, the count set about putting into practice what he had heard.[3] Whether the story is true or – as is more likely – invented, it shows what was expected of a lord of this rank in the 1180s in Touraine and that he referred to classical authors just as an ecclesiastic did. This is good evidence of a state of mind, of how people imagined the achievements of the 'renaissance' made their way into the daily life of the nobility.

It is clear that the social milieu capable of appropriating these achievements grew throughout the twelfth century. No doubt it is impossible to date precisely the stages of this gradual growth. But it would be worthwhile carrying out a chronological survey, something which has not been done so far. Drawing on some scattered information I can provide a few preliminary impressions of this development in France.

The movement appears already well advanced in the last decades of the eleventh century. The upper nobility, naturally, but also the lesser nobility, such as Guibert of Nogent's parents, still made a choice between two types of education for their sons, depending on whether they were destined for knighthood or an ecclesiastical career; the latter were placed in collegiate churches or entrusted to private tutors; it was only the former who were expected to become proficient in bodily exercise and to be faithful to the teachings of the warrior ethic, and it was thought that educating their minds through study carried the risk of spoiling their bodies. Nevertheless it sometimes happened that the death of an elder brother forced an ecclesiastic to abandon his clerical status in order to take charge of a lordship. This is precisely what happened to the canon who, in around 1100, became the head of his lineage and assumed military command of the castle of Berzé in the Mâcon region. Moreover, what is known about the father of Abelard or the childhood of St Bernard proves that the barriers between the two types of education were not impenetrable, that future knights benefited from the lessons which were given to their brothers, and that some could read and write.

In the middle of the twelfth century the connection between secular culture and scholasticism seemed to be strictly established in certain privileged, influential places where the nobility of an entire province periodically assembled for a short while. It was the large courts which set the tone, dictating fashions, showing how well-born people should behave if they wished to be worthy of their rank. At first these courts were those which assembled the feudal princes who were rivals of the Capetians, Henry Plantagenet, the count of Flanders and the count of Champagne, who saw very clearly in the influence of the culture produced and codified around their person a sure way of enhancing their prestige in comparison with that of the king. Paris appeared to be in retreat. In fact, if the adaptation of scholarly culture to the secular seems to be less far-reaching there, the activity of the king of France, which was directly responsible for the scholarly concentration from which the town profited, caused the dissemination, more vigorous there than elsewhere, of the forms of the 'renaissance' which were directly linked with the sacred. In the south this role was played by the cities of Avignon, Arles, Narbonne and Toulouse. But the expressions of the 'Renaissance' which spread from these urban centres were much more secularized. This feature stems from the cultural structures which were peculiar to the southern provinces: since Gregorian reform there had been a wider separation in this region between the Church and lay powers; in consequence ecclesiastics did not have a monopoly of writing there, and an important section of the upper social strata of these towns, judges and notaries, had direct access to scholarly culture.

The documents available to us make it possible to perceive more clearly, at the end of the century, the system of relationships between the centres of the intellectual renaissance and the places where it was received. I am using the exceptionally precise information provided by a text which I have already used and which I am studying exhaustively, the 'History of the Counts of Guînes'. This was written in a small satellite principality of the county of Flanders at the very beginning of the thirteenth century. Its author, Lambert of Ardres, was precisely one of those household clerics who were the most effective agents of acculturation. He boasted of being a 'master' (*magister*), a university graduate. He used the books housed in the collegiate church founded in 1069 near the residence of his masters. His work itself carries the most convincing evidence of cultural assimilation. Written in Latin, it was supported by a reading of the classics, it was skilled in the most learned rhetoric and it also echoed the most modern expressions of secular literature.

Above all the priest Lambert, composing a double panegyric to the glory of his two patrons, the lord of Ardres, master of the household which he served, and his father, the count of Guînes, to whom the work was dedicated, highlights the two levels of the cultural edifice within which the mechanisms of reception operated: the level of the *juvenes*, amongst whom the lord of Ardres still ranked, where the military values of chivalry prevailed, where culture remained entirely oral, preserved in the memory of the *commilitones* of the young hero who recounted, in order to entertain the company in the intervals between their war games, tales of the Holy Land, fables of the 'Matter of France' and the 'Matter of Brittany', and tales of the exploits of the lineage's ancestors. The other level was that of the *seniores*, whose foremost representative was Count Baldwin. This minor *princeps*, who was proud of having been knighted by Thomas Becket and who fought to preserve the autonomy of his lordship, was himself uneducated (*illiteratus*); nevertheless, he endeavoured to achieve wisdom (*sapientia*). He was well aware of the way in which the intellectual activity which he inspired in his household added to his prestige. In order to stimulate that activity he spared no expense. He supported a team of masters; he had discussions with these doctors of arts (*doctores artium*), they initiated him into theology. In exchange he taught them what secular tales he knew; he flattered himself that he reached the 'mystical virtue' of the sacred texts, was capable of playing a creditable part in the exercise of *disputatio* (debate), and when they heard him, people wondered how 'he could be familiar with letters without ever having learnt them'.

He also liked his chapel, with the help of the nuns of the family convent, to be honoured by splendid music. He filled it with books, the writings of the Fathers and the fables of the poets. He paid translators generously, for he wanted to hear read, in the language he understood, not only the Song of Songs, St Augustine, and the *Life* of St Anthony, but treatises summarizing what was known of the physical world.[4] Finally he commissioned the work which celebrated the brilliance and age of his lineage. He wanted this monument to his dynasty from which his descendants would learn, by following his example, to patronize literature, to be written in Latin, in the most classical, the most 'renascent' Latin. Where can the links between the 'Renaissance', its patronage and audience be more clearly discerned than among those middle-ranking lords whose castles dotted the French landscape at the close of the twelfth century?

13

Observations on Physical Pain
in the Middle Ages

I shall not be discussing the psychological pain caused by separation, oppression, humiliation and imprisonment. And yet what better place to do so than where we are today?[1] I shall confine myself to speaking about physical pain and shall make a few brief and very general observations.

Recently historians have been continually extending the field of their research. A few years ago death, and everything that surrounded it in the past, was the subject of detailed and fruitful studies. Now historians are showing increasing interest in the body and its experience, as well as in people's awareness of their bodies in former times. They are studying the history of eating habits, of dressing, of caring for oneself, the history of plagues and famines; and the history of medicine, which has lain dormant for so long, has suddenly become a focus of interest in France. However, historians have not yet directed their attention specifically to physical pain. Now, pain, too, clearly has its own history. The way in which it is perceived and the place which it is accorded within a value system are not unchanging facts. They are patently not the same in the different cultures which coexist under our eyes. They vary according to place as well as period. In a general history of sensibility these variations would undoubtedly warrant a close examination. I therefore urge that research be carried out in this area. For the time being, as regards the era with which I am most familiar, that is to say, the feudal period – which was in fact a very long stretch of time extending from just before the year 1000 to the beginning of the thirteenth century – I can only mark out the ground to be covered by presenting a few, as yet superficial, impressions which I have gained from a lengthy study of the available documents.

These documents are very sparse. Virtually everything that one wishes to know about this period is shrouded in darkness. However, from the outset it is worth pointing out – and this is rather extraordinary – that references to pain are very rare in these few texts. The culture I am referring to was dominated by priests and military leaders – at least, what we know of this culture, the way in which 'intellectuals' of the period (nearly all of them members of the ecclesiastical elite) felt and thought, since they were the only individuals to leave written and visual traces of their ideas and of their reactions to the world. In other words, 'feudal' culture does not appear to have been greatly concerned with physical suffering, far less than our own culture at any rate. There are no references to it in its discourse. This indifference, or rather suppression, poses a problem. In order to account for such an attitude it would be overly simplistic to seek an explanation in the roughness of manners, the savagery and the far greater burden which nature imposed on people. Instead we should look beyond the constant hardships experienced by a rural population whose material living conditions until the mid-twelfth century had apparently barely changed since the neolithic period, and who were still poorly protected from cold and hunger; otherwise one is liable to assume that people were hardened by all this. It is far more useful to consider the fundamentally male and military character of the ideology which prevailed at that time. This ideology relegated women to a position of total subordination; it exalted the male values of aggression and tenacious resistance to all attacks; in addition it tended to conceal weaknesses, or at any rate not allow pity for physical failings. However, it does seem possible to progress a little further in the interpretation of the texts.

For this purpose it is useful to examine the Latin vocabulary which was used by intellectuals. It established a quasi-synonymy, or at least an equivalence, between the word *dolor* (pain) and the word *labor* (work). This semantic arrangement sheds light on the place of physical pain within a value system which in this bookish culture rested on two major foundations – principally on the Bible and secondly on what had been preserved of the moral treatises of classical antiquity.

In the Judaeo-Christian tradition pain is depicted as a test and as a punishment inflicted by God in his wrath. The Almighty afflicted Job in order to put him to the test. But he chastised Israel. He began by punishing Adam and Eve for their disobedience. Everything stems from this, from our first parents and their sin. Because they succumbed to temptation, men and women were doomed not only to die but to suffer. Women were condemned especially to pain – 'In sorrow thou shalt bring forth children' – and men were destined especially for work – 'In the sweat of thy face shalt thou eat bread.' The punishment was deserved. Men are born sinners, and it is natural that they should suffer – it is not only natural; it is also necessary. Does avoiding suffering not run counter to divine will? Is it not questioning the order established by the Creator? As we know, some of these mental representations have endured to this day.

It follows from this that pain is firstly a matter for women, and that in consequence men should despise it. A man worthy of being called a man does not suffer; in any case he must not show that he is suffering, for fear of being made to look less manly, of regressing, of being brought down to the level of the female condition. But it also follows that physical suffering, because it is associated with the idea of toil, seems particularly unworthy of free men. The Graeco-Roman tradition reinforced this, since it identified freedom with leisure and considered all manual work servile. Therefore, like manual work during the feudal period, pain was considered debasing. It was viewed as enslavement. This was the main reason which prevented priests and warriors from expressing their suffering – they were the only men who were truly free because they belonged to the two classes which dominated the third, that of the workers, that is to say the serfs. This concept is clearly reflected in the system of criminal punishment: only inferiors, women, children and subjugated peasants were subject to corporal punishment; members of the ruling class had fines imposed on them rather than physical suffering, which would have struck a blow at their dignity.

Since pain was a punishment for sin, and thus a sign of sin and servitude, and therefore degrading, it acquired a positive value only as an instrument of correction, expiation and redemption. This explains the place which was accorded to it in the afterlife, in purgatory, that institution which became more clearly defined at the end of the twelfth century (people were thus left to answer the difficult question: how could a soul which was separated from its body endure physical suffering?). It also explains the prominence of pain in those other instruments of penitence represented by monasteries. The monks scourged their flesh in the same way as they engaged in manual work in order to humble themselves.

Thus the historian of pain will find that the most plentiful evidence he can exploit will be found in texts and images concerning souls in purgatory and those of ascetics. Indeed these are virtually his only source. The literature which provides most information on what today would be classified as medicine – that is to say collections of miracle stories – does not cover physical punishments, except when recounting vengeful miracles performed by outraged saints who took vengeance by tormenting their persecutors. But in healing miracles references to pain are generally absent. In fact these miracles are, for the most part, analogous to those performed by Jesus: they focus on blindness, paralysis and possession, all ailments which are not especially painful. As for chronicles, they certainly describe – and often with complacency – fights and calamities, the vicissitudes of the human body, wounds and horrifying mutilations, but they always do so coldly. Reading these accounts one might think that the victims of these cruelties did not feel any pain. At any rate these men remained impassive. So did the martyrs whose statues were placed at the threshold of the sanctuaries of relics (in the iconography of the twelfth and thirteenth century) – for example, St Sebastian and the decapitated St Denis, cheerfully carrying his head and not trembling at all. It is not that pain was not felt; rather, it was scorned. It was not admitted, except by sinners in their self-critical outpourings.

Nevertheless, this coldness does not appear to have lasted. Restraint in the face of physical pain, the kind of stoicism which repressed any expression of feeling before the suffering of others or before one's own suffering seems to have begun to change very slowly after the end of the twelfth century. One can ask whether this perceptible change affected the feelings themselves and not just the sources from which we learn about them. Indeed, from then onwards not all evidence comes solely from the ecclesiastical elite; the laity also started to express its emotions. This is when there began the long process of secularization and popularization of culture which in the fourteenth and fifteenth centuries gradually showed types of behaviour other than that of pious and chivalric heroes. This process enables us at last to glimpse the common people little by little. Nevertheless it is indisputable that sensibility and the way in which emotions were expressed truly changed at all levels of society; this was essentially the result of the transformation of religious feeling. During the feudal period, which was one of great enthusiasm for the pilgrimage to Jerusalem, piety tended to concentrate increasingly on the person of Jesus, to be sustained by more assiduous meditation on the humanity of the son of God, on his incarnation and thus on his body and what that body had suffered. Christ was the redeemer by virtue of the suffering which he had endured and which was immeasurable, since it was in proportion to his divinity.

This reflection on the text of the Gospels and all the spiritual exercises which accompanied it, and the more widespread dissemination of these attitudes through increasingly effective mass media – the sermons of the great preachers supported by every theatrical artifice – determined the gradual rise in value ascribed to pain in European culture. Christians were called upon to keep alive in their minds the scenes of the Passion, to take their place physically among the players in this great display of collective suffering. In the imitation of Christ, they were invited to identify themselves with the Saviour, and in particular with his bodily suffering.

Two milestones were achieved in the course of this development: at the outset, during the first quarter of the thirteenth century, Francis of Assisi received the stigmata; and at the height of the growth of the *devotio moderna*, in the first quarter of the fifteenth century, there was a rapid dissemination of the two images offered for the contemplation of the faithful, the image of the Man of Sorrows and the image of the *Pietà*. Pain was already being deliberately placed at the forefront of the stage. The attention paid to the suffering body of Jesus was naturally transferred to other suffering bodies, those of the poor, the representatives of Christ amongst men. After the end of the twelfth century, in parallel with the development of a piety which expressed compassion for the punishments of flagellation and crucifixion, there are clear signs that pity was beginning to be shown towards the sick: charitable works were carried out, and hospitals were founded and organized. It was indeed in the continuation of this slow change in attitudes towards pain that science and medical practice began – but still slowly – to concern themselves no longer only with preparing people for a good death, no longer only with curing people, and finally dispensing with the idea that pain, redemptive punishment, was useful for salvation, and acted forcefully and with every means available to suppress it.

14

Memories without Historians

Perhaps it is not as easy as one thinks to talk of memory as a historian, practising a profession which essentially consists of juxtaposing the remains and fragments of memories which are often barely identifiable, and clothing them with the imagination in an attempt to connect them and to reconstruct a picture based on structures, whatever they may be, derived from within oneself; in this manner a picture is built up which often originates less in the past itself than in the historian's own fantasy. What are the underlying reasons for this? The profession of historian is one which aims to 'refresh', as is commonly said – and to what end? – a memory which plunges vertiginously into the depths of the ages. In my case, as a historian of those societies we call feudal, this process involves struggling back over the gulf of nearly a thousand years.

If therefore, I speak of memory and of what is forgotten in summoning back those times, I do not mean the kind of approach to memory – a mere poking in the ashes – favoured by today's specialists in historical discourse; in order to add another floor to it, they scale the verbal edifice which was built by several generations of precursors. I wonder what one can discover about the way the memory of men who lived in the eleventh and twelfth centuries worked. We know very little about this – no doubt because until now, the question has hardly been asked. People are, in fact, beginning to ask this question – I have in mind the research project on the subject which Philippe Joutard has initiated. One of the effects of decolonization was to compel European historians to take greater account of societies without a written tradition – as were, more or less, medieval societies – and to make them discover the role of oral tradition in handing down collective memories, in the construction of a history which is no less substantial than the history whose structure we polish, a history that is no less alive, no less necessary to the organization of social relationships. Nevertheless our lack of knowledge concerning the mechanics of memory in the culture of the Middle Ages stems mainly from the fact that the events are concealed from view – a view which is necessarily filtered through written traces, through texts, and we only ever grasp the memory when it is immobilized by the work of experts whose job was precisely that of seizing it and of imprisoning it in a system of words. When it reaches us, it is always fixed, frozen and dead, and we perceive virtually nothing of the freedom of its movements.

I shall, nevertheless, make a few selective remarks. In feudal societies access to written material was the preserve of a few men who all belonged to the Church, men whose very function – because Christianity is a religion of the book and because its clergy had necessarily to remain in contact with the Scriptures – implied that they had been educated, that they had studied literature and had learnt how to handle skilfully a language (Latin) which was different from the spoken language, and into which all the words used in everyday life had to be translated before being transcribed. All other men, whether or not they were important, managed very well without the written word. Relationships between them were based on memory; in addition, they employed other means to strengthen it, particularly ceremony.

Any social act of importance had to be public and had to take place before a large gathering whose members stored the recollection, and who were expected to bear witness later, perhaps, to what they had heard or seen – words and gestures, confined within a ritual in order better to impress themselves on the memory of the group for recounting at a later date. As they grew old, witnesses felt obliged to pass on to their children what they retained in memory, and that legacy of memories was thus handed down from one generation to the next. In order to prevent the legacy from being too distorted by this process, people had recourse to a number of devices. They took care, for example, to have some very young children present at the gathering, and sometimes to slap them hard at the height of the ceremony, in the hope that the memory of the spectacle would attach itself to the memory of pain and that they would not be so quick to forget the event they had witnessed.

Alternatively they carefully preserved a certain object which, during the rites of investiture, one hand had placed in another hand, in view of the people, to signify the transfer of a right – for example, the branches, knives or stones sometimes still found in the archives attached to a particular piece of parchment or charter which a scribe had nevertheless been called upon to draw up. This, however, did not seem to offer sufficient guarantee, the object appearing a far better memorial than the document, in the eyes of a world which could not read and did not understand Latin.

It was a world which, in order to ensure the ordering of all social relationships, did not rely on texts but on memory, on that collective memory constituted by 'custom', which was a very strict and imperious code, even though it was nowhere recorded. Should people wish to question a particular aspect of this right, they called upon others to recount their memories. The oral inquiry, the periodic questioning, began with the oldest members of the community who possessed the greatest reservoir of memories, which was regarded as more valid because it delved deeper into the past and was one of the major organs of social regulation. A point of great significance was, I believe, the gatherings which at that time were a tradition in eastern France and which on fixed dates brought together all the adult subjects of a lordship so that they could reaffirm customary law and that they could recite the list of obligations which authority enjoined upon them. By the twelfth century the master required the services of men of letters to note down the words of this collective statement. It is then sometimes possible, by comparing several successive records in the same place, to detect shifts in this memory, notably to grasp the manner in which the peasant group resisted seigneurial pressures and expelled from its memory a particular tax or labour service, introducing instead a particular privilege which had been silently won.

Such documents, which are in reality rare, could provide useful material for a systematic study of the mutability of memories. Other documents would also be valuable, for example the verbatim records of depositions at inquisitions (these survive in far greater numbers) when several witnesses were summoned following the appearance of cracks in the social order, after an offence or at a trial. They would reply, one after the other: 'I'm fifty [or sixty or ninety] years old; I remember being there when it happened; I saw this being done at a particular time, I heard such and such...' These accounts are confirmed by one source and contradicted elsewhere: they offer a mine of information, especially to historians of memory, but this has barely been exploited. An enormous amount of information is available, for example, on the tricks of forgetfulness – whether voluntary or involuntary, frank or cunning – in what the people of Montaillou and other places declared, out of fear or spite, before the inquisitor.

I should now like to turn to the subject of genealogical memory. Feudal Christianity is largely, perhaps even wholly, a religion of the dead. Some of the most socially important expressions of popular piety took place near burial places, such as the tombs of saints, which crowds of pilgrims visited, seeking the salvation of their body or their soul; and the tombs of ancestors which were surrounded by periodic ceremonies, gathered together all the living members of a lineage around a monastic team responsible for the celebration. The principal ceremonies took place on the anniversary of a death, and their organization therefore necessitated a calendar being established and special registers being set up where dates and names were noted down – obit lists and necrologies, those books which claimed to be *memoriales* (memorials). Experts at writing, organizers of funeral liturgies, arranged groups of family names there. These collections of words perpetuated the image of kinship. They established in individuals the feeling of belonging to a group, the smaller part of which lived in this world, while the majority lived in the other, requiring respect, care and services – of belonging to that immortal cell, the lineage, which was bound by ties of blood, but far more by a carefully fostered memory which constituted the fundamental framework of this society.

The memory of ancestors was thus preserved through the cult of the dead. It was also kept alive by the need to be fully informed about every degree of relationship in order to observe incest prohibitions. The Church in fact declared all marriages which were beyond the seventh degree of consanguinity illicit, sullied and therefore condemned to be dissolved. When, having gained greater power during the eleventh century, the Church attempted to fight more vigorously for the acceptance of the requirements of an exogamy so immoderately extended as to be impracticable, it multiplied investigations of a particular kind, compelling families to ask questions about their ancestry extending over more than a century and a half, to unravel the dense network of filiations, to count the degrees of consanguinity, to present this report before the ecclesiastical courts and to confirm it under oath. Such procedures further stimulated the genealogical memory which was naturally very keen among the aristocracy where the very concept of nobility was an incentive to take great pride in very ancient ancestors. Other incentives operated at lower levels of the social structure when lords were disputing rights over a particular family of serfs. It was still necessary here, amongst ploughmen and farmhands, to reconstruct genealogies, to list the dead, to name them and to revive their distant memory.

Amongst the most useful written documents in the study of feudal memory are the genealogical accounts which grew in number and richness in France during the twelfth century,[1] at a time when aristocratic society was beginning to perceive what was threatening its privileges and set about consolidating the foundations of its power by every means. Princely dynasties, both large and small, had recourse during that period to the skills of professional scribes, that is, to clerics. They set them the task of exploring and establishing memories, which did not differ substantially from the task which historians nowadays undertake. Writers were urged to manipulate memory, to look for the few remains to which memory was firmly attached, to link them together and to invent in order to complete the picture. I shall use the example of one of these treatises which I am currently studying. It was written at the very end of the twelfth century, by a priest in the service of an aristocratic household – the house of the lords of Ardres – which a recent marriage had joined with the family of the counts of Guînes (both were situated in what today is the *département* of Pas-de-Calais). These masters, who wished to glorify their ancestors' greatness, commissioned him to write the history of the two lineages, tracing them back to their origins. He did this to the best of his ability, bringing to bear all his technical skills, using firstly the Latin language, at which he was adept, and also the available material – charters (but these were very rare; before his time written documents had been largely ignored in the household), obit lists, epitaphs inscribed on tombs (he himself had even written a few since the organization of funeral ceremonies was one of his duties) and, especially, the recollections of relatives. He drew most of his material from living memory, from his patrons, their brothers, cousins and illegitimate children; the aspect of his writing which essentially interests us is the net which he throws over these teeming memories.

The memory of relatives extends over one and a half centuries, going back in fact to the six degrees of kinship which the ecclesiastical injunctions urged people to memorize scrupulously. Beyond that this memory becomes very vague; it barely recalls a few names, solely those of the heads of the family and those of the counts, spanning three-quarters of a century, perhaps even a century. Beyond this threshold memory is completely lost. With such sketchy sources to draw on, the author, anxious to fulfil his task properly, projects his own dream. He imagines heroes, the founders of dynasties, and fantasizes about them. His history becomes a courtly romance, a tale of chivalry, peopled with fictitious characters. Their postures and trappings imitate those of the masters for whom the writer works; their behaviour is modelled on that with which the lords themselves wished to set an example, as were the virtues which they professed as well as their failings of which they were proud, notably generative vigour and the valour which they demonstrated in the games of illicit love. The familial memory whose intricacies this account exhibits thus appeared in all its richness and imperfection. It blended into myth. It projected on to their present-day lives the ideal in which was reflected what the living aspired to be. It shows very little concern for strict chronology.

In the sixty large folio pages that the modern edition of this text runs to, there are no more than fourteen dates, five of which concern events which the narrator witnessed directly as an adult. Eight of them concern ecclesiastical history, learned history: two dates, which are wrong, refer to the launching of the First and Second Crusades (this should not come as a surprise, for the expedition to the Holy Land was uppermost in the minds of the members of this noble family; they all went on Crusades, and the youngest took the cross, although he never actually set off, ten years before this story was written). Six other dates preserved in the charters that the author used refer to the religious institutions founded by the two lineages as necessary annexes to their households. The last six dates concern secular events which relate strictly to the family. The earliest date, which refers to the arrival of the dynasty's founder and is pushed back to the beginning of the tenth century, is quite clearly mythical. The other dates are spread out over the last thirty years, a particularly reliable time span as far as memory is concerned. The two most distant dates are connected with burial places; another date, twenty-five years earlier, refers to the appearance of a bogus ghost: an impostor wanted to pass himself off as the lord of the house who had never returned from overseas; his heirs, quietly exploiting the inheritance, did not wish to see him return; they apparently trembled so much before the unexpected vision of the father that the memory still seemed indelible to the next generation. The penultimate date concerns the young lord of Ardres, heir apparent to the count of Guînes, the narrator's direct employer whose biography received special attention, the man who had commissioned the project, the real hero of the story. This date, Pentecost 1181, is therefore the most important date in his life; it was not the date of his birth or his wedding, but that of his dubbing, the rite of passage which introduced him amongst the knights. Finally the year is carefully recorded when the count of Flanders, dipping into the barrels of silver which the king of England had sent him to finance a war against Philip Augustus, helped the lord of Ardres to pay his debts. Is it a coincidence that, in the minds of these very rich people who, with the sudden arrival of a monetary economy, nevertheless continued to pursue wealth, one of the rare chronological references is connected with a financial episode?

The familial memory, solidified, adulterated and overladen with artificial embellishments, which this text presents to posterity, that is to say principally to the descendants, but also unwittingly to historians, does indeed need to be viewed in its foundations as it becomes identified with the memory of wealth's acquisition.

Indeed, it was through the inheritance, the patrimony, which the eldest of the family for the time being administered, as his ancestors had done before him, each handing on his wealth when he entered the world of the dead, to his eldest son, daughter or brother, and which the eldest son of the present holder waited impatiently to possess, that the clearest and most vivid elements in this fluctuating mass of memories crystallized. They were strongest within the confines of a household, the centre of a network of power, where the dynasty took root, where the head of the lineage resided and where, in the bed which stood at the very heart of this home, in the bed where he himself was born, he conscientiously set about procreating those who were to extend the future of the kinship.

It was a household where his daughters were to remain, jealously protected, until their marriage or their death, where his sons were to spend their childhood, until they reached adolescence, when they would leave to embark on adventures, carrying with them the family name; a household where they would gather on specific dates, where the history of the family was constantly recounted, where sometimes, as was the case here, it was written down. It was, strictly speaking, a domestic story, since it was less the history of a lineage than that of a household, and the manner in which that household had acquired its wealth, how it had defended its rights over the ages, the risks that it had faced and the opportunities that it was able to seize.

Genealogical memory placed a number of effigies on the walls of this house (just as they were fastened to the garden walls enclosing the Rose in the *Roman de la Rose*). Firstly, there were effigies of two living people, the master and his heir. The father and the son were portrayed in poses which befitted them; the old man, the head of the household, wished to be presented as a wise man, but he wanted people to know that he was still capable of making love, whilst the young man is portrayed as an unstable hothead – and the story did not hide the tensions between them.

Then there were the effigies of the dead, placed side by side as in a gallery of ancestors: they were less exact and increasingly obscure as they went further back in time. They were all shown in flattering poses, thereby presenting a model of good behaviour to those who subsequently, with the passing generations, would establish themselves there, to sleep in the bed in their turn, and in their turn to administer the inheritance. For this memory was selective. It retained only the deeds of the living and the dead, whether good or bad, which could be used effectively in an educational account. It taught, and was itself the instrument of an education.

For this reason it imperceptibly manipulated memories, adapted them to the needs of the present and distorted them so that they could fit in with the slow development of a moral code. This is why all these characters I am describing resemble one another. They all wear the same clothing, strut about with the same bearing, figure and behaviour which was deemed fitting, when this narrative was written, by those who commissioned it. In this many-sided mirror they saw their own features reflected, or rather those that they wanted to be seen.

So that they could be completely assured, their faces had to be reflected, stage by stage, backwards into the depths of time. Their vision was therefore directed both towards the house, that stronghold of solidity, that refuge – and towards the ancestors who were born there and who, one after the other, lived there. At the time when the memory of the counts of Guînes and the lords of Ardres was set down in this text that I have taken as an example, another priest, a canon, was also writing not far from there, at Cambrai. He, too, was writing a history, but a more general one, annals in which he attempted to recount everything he had managed to discover about events in the outside world. When he reached the year of his birth in this account he could not resist the pleasure of saying something about himself as well. He allowed his own memory for a moment to fill a gap in his account, an account which was nevertheless very sober, dry and laconic, for in those days people were economical in the way they wrote. What did he talk about? Firstly, he spoke of the house where he was born – it was a paradise of meadows and springs which he described lovingly but awkwardly – with the means available at that time, when writing in Latin, to extol a landscape. Then he described that other haven, that other nest, represented by his family, but hardly said a word about his living relatives, not even the closest, his brothers and sisters, whom he did not even name. He talked about the dead, and in particular about those who were role-models for him, who, like him, but more successfully, had had a career in the Church. He also wrote about military heroes, such as his maternal grandmother's ten brothers who had gloriously perished together in the same battle, one that – and he was very proud of this – 'the songs of the minstrels'[2] still praised in his own day.

During the period of which I am writing, songs were reservoirs of memory which, extending more widely to the people, spread far beyond the enclosure of great households. None the less they were liable to be lost: virtually all these songs have disappeared. However, a few have survived that were recorded in writing. It would be useful, I think, for historians of memory to reread them closely. These songs are a bountiful spring at which they can slake the thirst caused by the arid lands into which – who knows why? – they have wandered and which they are today exploring.

15

Heresies and Societies in Preindustrial Europe between the Eleventh and Eighteenth Centuries

To summarize the conclusions to be drawn from such a fruitful conference[1] is singularly difficult since I intend to express them in the briefest possible way. Indeed, I must be selective and, since I am a historian of neither religions nor heresy, and have concentrated my studies on particular aspects of medieval society, this choice will be as follows.

I shall include very little relating to the doctrinal content of heresies. This represents quite a significant sacrifice because a good bit of important and valuable material was contributed in discussion. Instead I shall attempt to return to the theme that was set for the period of this conference and which was defined by the title that was given to it: 'Heresies and societies'. I shall refer, in particular, to the preliminary questionnaire which was both thought-provoking and very relevant. One of the main subjects it proposed was 'The role of the heretic and his function in society' within a very clearly defined field, that of Latin Christendom between the eleventh and the eighteenth centuries. I need hardly emphasize the value of the contributions which affected areas outside this context, whether they concern the Slavonic fringes which were in the process of being converted to Christianity, and where apostasy seemed like a rejection, or the Byzantine world, Islam and rabbinic Judaism.

Before presenting my views, all of which concern methodology, I would like to make a few general remarks.

I now have a greater awareness of a very important fact in the history of European civilization, namely the permanence and the ubiquity of heresy, which is constantly nipped in the bud and constantly reborn under a variety of guises. Heresy manifests itself like a hydra; it seems nevertheless that this hydra has not always been equally virulent. Firstly, it is essential to show historically its upsurges of vitality, and conversely its periods of relaxation and somnolence. It is, indeed, a matter of observing the heretic 'in the historical process' (to quote the words used in the questionnaire). In other words, chronology is necessary. This work is complete for the most part. Consequently if one refines and compares, one can see very clearly periods when there was an increase in the number of accounts concerning heresy, and other periods when, on the contrary, there were gaps. Thus, over the past few days we have talked on a number of occasions about the seven or eight decades' lull between the spiritual fermentation of the first half of the eleventh century and the very marked upheavals of the twelfth century. Nevertheless if this chronology is examined in its entirety, one is immediately struck by a contrast which I believe to be fundamental.

On the one hand, there is the medieval period, which I would readily call the time of defeated heresies, or rather of suppressed heresies. Heresy, at that time, was firmly established and flourishing; it was endemic, even necessary, and no doubt vital and organic, but it was always crushed. This first period should be split into two successive stages: firstly, the period of short-lived heresies (as has been said, concerning the twelfth century: 'Their life was short, but intense; few heresies survived a second generation'), followed by a stage when heresies became far more deep-rooted and increasingly resistant. After a first period when heresies were stifled, subjugated and gradually reduced, at the beginning of the sixteenth century with the Lutheran break, with that wound which never healed and which contributed towards shattering a hitherto unitarian world, there followed a period of coexistence when the territory was divided, a partition which was tolerated before it was accepted, and was then accepted with increasing indifference.

From then on, the very function of heresy – now established outside society – and even the position of the heretic in relation to himself and others, were radically transformed. This means that the historian of the modern period cannot study heresy in the same way as the historian of medieval history, not only because the documents underwent a complete change, not only because with progress in techniques of expression, the 'weapons' of heresy were no longer the same, but because the general climate changed decisively. Therefore two entirely independent aspects can be distinguished. Indeed we have taken account of them, and the only shortcoming of this conference is that despite several contributions and sometimes very commendable challenges, it has not really given rise to genuine comparisons of methods between the medievalists and the modernists.

In addition, I am now more conscious of the difficulty of defining what a heretic is, and obtaining a clear picture of a heretic from the documents – and this is what matters to historians. We started with a definition that was proposed by a historian and theologian: a heretic is someone who has chosen, who has isolated from the overall truth a partial truth, and who then persists stubbornly in his choice. But we soon realized that our own task as historians scrutinizing the past is to distinguish those who, at a particular time, have been singled out by their contemporaries – at any rate, by some of them – as heretics. Yet during the same period the criteria for this judgement were remarkably different. In a heated discussion an individual could be called a heretic by the person to whom he was speaking, hounded as a heretic by a fanatic from the Inquisition, by people obsessed by heresy or by a political opportunist who would not have been considered as such by a specialist in canon law, or by his confessor. This requires another task which is far more difficult than the chronological ordering which I referred to earlier: to define at each moment what has been described very aptly in these discussions as the 'contour' of the heretical environment. It is a very delicate undertaking and is not really possible since this milieu, which was often concealed, always appears to be very fluid, so fluid that the term 'heretic' eludes definition. I shall return to this in a short while.

Finally, it is worth making one obvious point. All heretics became heretics because of decisions by orthodox authorities. They were first and foremost – and often they always remained – heretics in the eyes of others, or to be more precise, in the eyes of the Church, in the eyes of *one* Church. This is an important consideration, because it shows that the terms 'orthodoxy' and 'heresy' are historically indissoluble. Even so, one should not consider them like two provinces on opposite sides of a river, divided by a definite border. Instead it is more a question of two poles, between which wide margins extend, enormous areas of indifference perhaps, sometimes of neutrality, at any rate undefined and changing fringes. The fact that they were changing can be fruitful for anyone who asks himself questions, not only about the limits of the term 'heretical milieu', but about the stages in the history of heresy, and the actual content of heterodox doctrines.

It is quite clear that, depending on whether Church orthodoxy was more or less demanding at one time or another, a large sector of society was said to be heretical and condemned and harassed as such. Moreover, this is what would make it possible to articulate more vigorously a problem which here has simply been touched upon – that of heresy within a heresy. When a heresy appears at the very heart of heresy, this means that a part of the heretical milieu has established itself as a Church. Perhaps heresy is always a potential Church. Yet it still needs – in order to produce within its centre its own heresies – to become a real Church, that is to say, to start excluding people and condemning them.

Moreover, in considering the different stages, one can see that the periods when virulence seems to have subsided, when accounts about heresy disappear from the sources, are sometimes those when orthodoxy has become less severe and shown itself indulgent and welcoming. This was through laxness – either because the Church was occupied with its own reform and displayed in part the symptoms of a heretic's anxiety – or because it was attempting, on the contrary, in a state of weakness, a measure of reconciliation. The study of heresy, as we have all become aware, leads to the study of tolerance and of its different motivations.

188 Cultures, Values and Society

Finally, the immediate and fundamental role that orthodoxy assumes on the appearance and formation of heresy also affects the very content of heterodox doctrines. In fact it is the sentence of condemnation pronounced by the clergy that isolates a body of belief and names it heretical. By naming this body of belief, it assimilates it (often wrongly, however, through ignorance or through contempt) to dogmas which are already known and classified. Consequently it may well condemn the doctrine to grow at the expense of these old heresies. At any rate it may indeed alter the actual development of the heretical belief.

These brief general remarks should be useful before tackling the main issue, 'Heresies and societies', and examining in what way we are able, at the end of the conference, to modify, adjust and complete the questionnaire which was set at the start.

In my opinion, one of the first contributions of this conference was to highlight the need to carry out historical research very clearly, according to whether it concerns the birth or rather the formation of a heretical doctrine, or its dissemination. To be more precise, I would say that it now appears to be necessary to examine the case of the heresiarch completely separately.

Apart from a few very rare exceptions, the heresiarch belongs to the leading circles of a Church, its inner coteries, schools or small discussion groups – in other words, milieux which the historian can generally penetrate fairly easily because they leave the most documentary evidence. The theological definition of the heretic can be applied to the heresiarch, but to him alone. No doubt, he alone really settles on and proposes the *sententia electa* (the chosen doctrine). In order for there to be *sententia*, there must truly be reasoning, intellectual shaping and consequently, culture. Moreover, this is, most of the time, an individual decision, or at most the decision of a small group. It is therefore permissible for the historian to examine in depth the reactions of the heresiarch to his milieu, to consider the psychology of the heresiarch. This was one of the main questions in our programme: how does the heresiarch come to his decision? By reacting to what he has read? Or by reacting against certain colleagues? These are all questions which it is legitimate to ask in connection with Luther or, as has been shown at this conference, in connection with Wyclif.

As for the heresiarch, depending on the tools which the historian has at his disposal, one can ask one of the suggested questions: Is he a sick man, a neurotic? Does the neurosis arise from anguish, pride, frustration, or from being in a minority? Is he really a 'delinquent'? For we are simply relying on the criteria of people who are confident of being in the right. In addition, because the heresiarch is an 'intellectual' and reacts to a small number of fellow intellectuals who surround him, he appears generally to be a very vulnerable individual who is easy to restrain and bring under control, and he must show true heroism to remain *pertinax* (obstinate in his opinion). There are countless fascinating cases of wavering, self-criticism and repentant return to the bosom of the Mother Church. Finally, consider the strength of the absorptive powers of the orthodox milieu: did the canonization of St Francis merely serve as a means of posthumous neutralization?

The historian's approach must be completely different if he wishes to observe the dissemination of heretical doctrine. He must shift his field of observation in order to arrive at collective attitudes, and he must therefore change his methods. It is useful for him first to consider the instruments of transmission. He must establish a geography of the routes and the places of dispersal; he must also observe the means of propaganda, public and private discourse, documents and images; finally he must track down the agents, the agitators, all the beings who are sometimes individually access- ible to historical observation like the heresiarchs, but who do not have the same psychological attitudes and who, generally speaking, do not come from the same social backgrounds.

Once it is passed on, the doctrine is received. By whom? By people who are dissatisfied, and whose nearest Church has not been able to fulfil their spiritual needs, and who on account of this turn away from it and listen to different messages. The sugges- tion that heresy can sometimes be regarded as a failed devotion, or rather a frustrated devotion, seems to me to be valid. In any case, because of his mental attitude, the heretic also differs from the agitator, and even more so from the heresiarch. More passive and also more negative, his is an attitude of refusal. It is worth noting in passing that there have always been other forms of refusal in so far as religious behaviour is concerned, starting with mystical evasion – dispensing with the priest without, however, attacking the Church – and with the 'flight into the desert', the conversion to the monastic life. Within the time span considered by this history of heresy it might also be fruitful to examine carefully the relationship between the periods of growth of heresies and of religious orders respectively, and to discover whether sometimes they flourished together or whether one replaced the other.

It is not impossible to discover the motives for this refusal, this opposition to discipline and the ecclesiastical authorities; it is worth examining these carefully and listing them. The Church has sometimes been rejected because it was effectively inadequate through a lack of priests (this seems to have been the case in many of the rural areas of Europe during the eleventh century and after the Black Death), or because the most active milieux within the Church did not adapt to the spiritual needs of the people (it is worth reflecting here on St Bernard's failure in the face of the Cathars). But the Church was also repugnant to some people because they considered it to be unworthy; this was a less passive attitude on the part of men who at that time were driven to make moral demands on the priests whom they wished to be purer or poorer. Finally, some churches were rejected because they appeared to be foreign to the nation, or else too visibly allied to detested political or economic powers. Therefore there is clearly the need to carry out – as has been done so admirably here, notably in connection with Hussitism – an economic and social study of heretical circles.

Against this Church which has become so repugnant, a particular doctrine which is propagated seems satisfactory to a group of men who adopt it more or less completely and more or less openly. As we have seen, it is very difficult to obtain information about this group of sectarians. Most of the time history can understand only heresies which have been detected; hidden heresies escape it, as do heresies which prove capable of masking their intent – take, for example, the Waldensians in Italy in the thirteenth century – which they confuse with orthodoxy.

It is at least important to situate accurately – starting with their geographical location – the heresies of those sects which are described fairly clearly in the documents. One of the most urgent tasks, I would suggest, is to work to establish a geography, a cartography of heresy, to pinpoint those areas which were receptive in towns and in the countryside, the places from which their doctrines emanated, the paths which they followed and finally the sanctuaries where the hounded heretics found refuge, such as the valleys of the Alps which for so long protected them. This preliminary research would usefully pave the way for essays on social interpretation, for the efforts to situate groups of followers in relation to the various social strata (rich or poor) and in relation to the different groupings (it may be a heresy which penetrates the framework of families, of trades, of brotherhoods or of other associations such as the *consorterie*).

As I have said, research then becomes complicated. As far as the twelfth century is concerned, we historians have realized just how difficult it is to identify the position of the heretic in the social organization of his time. As regards Jansenism, we have also felt the need for a reliable and accurate analysis of the social classes where a particular heretical doctrine could be propagated. Indeed, I believe that here research often comes up against considerable obstacles. One might question, in particular, how it is possible to grasp the outline of rural heretical circles when it has always been so difficult for historians to gain more than a superficial knowledge of peasant societies.

Finally, on a number of occasions our discussions showed that the doctrines themselves, in being handed down and disseminated, are both debased and renewed. But it also became clear that the documents that might make it possible to observe this debasement and renewal closely are rare and awkward to interpret. This idea of a debasement and of a gradual filtering of the bodies of belief from 'intellectual' milieux to ones with a lower level of culture may enable us to reject the question of erudite heresy versus popular heresy as a non-issue – or at the very least perhaps to ask the question more accurately, or at any rate in a more stimulating manner. For the accepted doctrine always becomes distorted, mainly on account of intermediaries and propagandists – those merchants and crusaders, for example, who brought back from the East a particular notion of Bogomilism[2] or, simply, mothers who from generation to generation handed down secret dogmas.

Heresy is distorted under the influence of the very people who support it since, in the minds of its followers, the doctrine coincides with far simpler and far cruder 'popular' beliefs. Indeed, in milieux

192 Cultures, Values and Society

which appropriate a heresy, there are virtually always latent collective attitudes which create distortion and in addition greatly encourage the reception of the doctrine – those attitudes of anxiety that the Churches call superstitions, but which today we can term instinctive religious attitudes, based on extremely simple representations. It is therefore in the consciousness of the individual that it is worth looking specifically for the roots of prohibitions, of taboos, of the 'means of exclusion and division' which can take very clear-cut forms and which, generally speaking, are dualist in nature. This dualism, whose existence can be perceived at the level of consciousness, forms part of many instinctive drives, notably the feeling of sexual guilt, which explains the frequent requirement within heretical groups of purity, if not in the believer himself, at least in the person responsible for conversion, who is the 'perfect' one.

At this profound level of collective psychologies, it is also possible to discover the very simple themes which lead to 'popular' heresies, the myth of the primitive equality of the children of God, the expectation of the end of time, and finally the ideal of poverty which occasionally emerges but which never ceases to be obscurely desired, as we have seen in heresies between the eleventh and the thirteenth centuries, no doubt because, in certain social circles, this basic idea compensated for a bad conscience caused by ill-gotten gains. At any rate, the gradual merging of the doctrines constructed by heresiarchs with unsophisticated beliefs seems to me to explain the 'resurgences' which clearly stemmed from latent religious attitudes. It also explains certain shifts in heresies from some social spheres which, reaching a higher culture, gradually became hostile towards overly primitive forms, towards other milieux no doubt less advanced. Finally, I will add that these bodies of what we might call 'popular' belief – since they exist in everyone's consciousness, it would be better to regard them as beliefs based on emotion – were themselves susceptible to spontaneous religious ferment, beyond the intervention of any scholarly doctrine. This was, undoubtedly, the period when economic and social stimuli were important. For my part, I do not think that as far as heresy is concerned it is always necessary to scrutinize the economic and social climate. But there are cases when one can truly perceive a dialectical movement. These nearly all correspond to moments in the violent emergence of 'popular' beliefs, such as, for example, the Flagellants who were judged and hounded as heretics by a troubled Church.

I would like to finish by drawing attention to the importance of repression in the history of heresies and heretics. We have seen how orthodoxy gave rise to heresy by condemning it and naming it. One can also see that orthodoxy reabsorbed a great many heresies by subjugating them, by reconciling them and by appropriating them. It is worth adding that, because orthodoxy meted out punishments and hounded heretics, it set up a whole arsenal which then took on a life of its own and which often even survived long after the heresy which it had to combat. The historian must examine very carefully all these institutions responsible for tracking down heretics, and their specialized officers, often former heretics purging themselves. It would clearly be worth carrying out a thorough survey of the psychology of the inquisitor, his training and his handbooks. Orthodoxy, because it punishes and hunts down heretics, also establishes particular mental attitudes – the obsession with heresy, the conviction amongst the orthodox that heresy is hypocrital, that it is covert and that it must therefore be detected at all costs and by all means. Moreover, repression creates, as an instrument of resistance and counter-propaganda, different systems of representations, which continue to work for a very long time. Finally, all this repressive equipment was frequently employed as a useful instrument by the authorities, allied with church orthodoxy. This presents us with a whole range of questions which emerged several times during this conference, but which would require systematic identification, for they are very widely distributed. Let us therefore consider the gradual move of heresy towards politics, something which we noted very clearly when *Frankism*[3] or the English seventeenth century were discussed. Let us also consider, far more simply, the political use of heresy and the heretical group treated as a scapegoat, with all the comprehensive persecution which at the time was thought desirable.

16

Trends in Historical Research in France, 1950–1980

In 1950, at the age of seventy-two, in his office in the VIth Section of the Ecole Pratique des Hautes Etudes, Lucien Febvre was savouring the victory of *Annales*, the review which, twenty-one years earlier, he had founded with Marc Bloch. It had been the weapon of a relentless fight against what remained of positivist traditions which were deeply rooted in powerful institutions; against history as a series of battles; against political history in isolation from other forms of history; against history bereft of ideas. It was first and foremost a fight for economic history and, increasingly, for social history. Finally, the decision to change the name of the review when it started to appear again after the Liberation, replacing *Annales d'histoire économique et sociale* with *Annales. Economies. Sociétés. Civilisations* is very illuminating here: it sought to establish a history that took into account the cultural context, refusing to privilege (within what Michelet referred to as the 'channels', the 'forms' and the 'elements of historical life') those aspects which concern the material dimension of life. It was an attempt to produce a total history, or rather a many-layered history, which moved away from surface details, from the tiny bubbles of 'events', into a broader and deeper exploration: plunging into cycles of long duration, reaching down to those great depths where nothing seems to change, and gazing upon the foundations, the layers of greatest stability, the peasantry.

Thirty years on,[1] this aim remains unaltered: the history that is worthy of study, out of all the subjects which it offers, remains the history of a particular population within the territory it occupies.

However, in 1980 this history is no longer written in the same way as it was written in 1950; fortunately, the approach to history is constantly being renewed, particularly in France.

Recently, there has been talk of 'new history' – too much talk in my opinion. The term is felicitous in so far as it is stimulating and is an incentive to question routine methods. However, the controversial aspect of the term may make it dangerous. It would be regrettable if it were to revive old disputes, restore obsolete restrictions to study or divide the ranks of historians. There are not, in fact, any 'new historians'. There are good historians and less good historians. All are equally spurred on by the inherent shortcomings of an inquiry which, because it is alive, is always shifting its field of study and asking its questions in different forms. The way in which the conditions of historical research in France have changed in a single generation merits close examination.

As each day passes we become increasingly aware of the relativity of our knowledge. 1961 saw the publication, in L'Encyclopédie de la Pléiade, of *L'Histoire et ses méthodes*, an extensive anthology of articles on the spirit and methods of historical research. In part this book took a stand against *Annales*. The editor, Charles Samaran, a member of the Institut, had commissioned a group of excellent former students from the Ecole des Chartes in Paris to present in the best possible light – and this was a very salutary exercise – the admirable monument which positivist history had left and to describe the precise tools which served to collect, conserve and make a critical analysis of historical accounts. This discourse on historical method was, above all, a eulogy of meticulous, rigorous and objective erudition. None the less, in his concern to breathe new life into the study of history and to appropriate everything which he deemed capable of invigorating research, Charles Samaran, after recalling that 'there is no history without erudition', went on to state in his preface that 'history can be total', that it 'is a social science which is indissolubly linked to the other social sciences' (Lucien Febvre would not have expressed himself any differently) and, finally, that 'it knows in advance' that the truth it aims for is 'relative'. The authors included Renouard, Meuvret, Georges Sadoul, Philippe Wolff and Charles Higounet.

Henri Iréné Marrou was asked to write an introduction entitled 'What is History?' and a conclusion, 'How to Understand the Profession of Historian', and it is here, in a paragraph headed 'Objectivity and subjectivity of historical knowledge', that we read:

> As soon as one enters the sphere of strictly human realities, the past can no longer be isolated in its pure state and grasped as it were in isolation: it is reached in an indissoluble whole in which the reality of the past – its objective and true reality – is closely bound up with the present reality of the active thought of the historian seeking to discover the past…History is at once objective and subjective; it is the past, authentically apprehended, but the past as seen by the historian.

Charles Samaran had been anxious to highlight Marrou's assertion that 'history is a spiritual adventure in which the historian's personality becomes entirely involved.'

Nowadays, we no longer need to be convinced of this. Our certainty leads us in the first place to be unassuming. It prevents us from allowing ourselves to be taken in by the mirage of positivism. Without, naturally, relaxing our efforts to 'establish the facts' with the greatest rigour and precision, we have removed the blinkers which stopped us from reflecting with lucidity that this attempt to establish facts is necessarily unsound, that we will only ever gain a derisory knowledge of the past, one which is not always exactly what we wanted, and that the absolute truth is out of reach.

The other discovery is of far greater consequence. We are gauging the influence exerted on our enterprise, on the way in which we articulate questions and in which we seek to find an answer to them, by the history that is described as immediate, that is to say by the turmoils of the present. Our 'active thought' is affected by the repercussions of these upheavals. They modify it, we know, far more than was previously imagined. What is important is that historians have learnt no longer to be so suspicious of these attacks, and to accept them for what they are, as a challenge. Since these are the contradictions of our age, it is our attitude towards them which, to a large extent, contributes to lifting research out of the humdrum routine into which it might otherwise be in danger of sinking. We are therefore less afraid of our likes and dislikes, remaining objective when we evaluate the sources – it is at this stage of the work that subjective preferences are strongest – but accepting these influences when they assert our shortcomings in confronting the problematic and force us constantly to find different approaches in questioning the documents. It is impossible to understand the great strides which history has made before our very eyes without pointing to the increasingly strong feeling that to be a good historian you must be aware of your own age, and that neutral history, the kind written within the confines of the library, is always colourless and cloying.

To take part in the present, to observe what is going on – in a word, to live – means, above all, being aware of the latest findings and changes in the related disciplines of the social sciences. History would be weakened if it were isolated. It needs to play its part fully in a group in which the team members support one another and compete with one another, each one trying to take the lead. It was the distinction of *Annales* (and still is) to have backed this competitive solidarity and to have fought so hard to break down the barriers between subjects. Historians follow developments in other disciplines and endeavour to keep up with the latest research. That is what enables them to transcend the limitations of their subject.

At the height of the success of the *Annales*, the most advanced discipline in France was geography. It influenced everything. I am fond of repeating that, when I was a student, it was my geography teachers who were the first to introduce me to Marc Bloch and Lucien Febvre. What these two scholars themselves owed to the work of French and German geographers is obvious. You have only to look at *La Méditerranée* to realise that the place accorded to the landscape by Fernand Braudel is fundamental. Wind and relief, pastures and orchards, together with migrations, are major elements in the scene which he has superbly depicted; when he sets about analysing the development of nature in history, I wonder whether he does not owe more to the influence of geographers than to that of economists. In other words, this is geo-history, and a body of work like Charles Higounet's reveals the fruitfulness of the alliance.

Reflecting on the contribution of geography it seems to me that the most fruitful and sustained incentive it provided was to make historians far more willing to base their research on regional monographs. They learned to mark out a territory properly; to examine the relationship between all its inhabitants and their environment, that is to say nature which has been influenced at length by history; to link the many different forces which contribute to shaping and changing this population. The study of feudal society that I undertook within the narrow confines of a small region of central France differs little in its aim and approach from the research which geographers such as Allix, Faucher and Juillard had previously carried out in certain parts of the Alps, the Rhône valley or Alsace to compare the structure of a landscape with the structure of the peasantry. In addition, the French school of geography set the example of decentralized syllabuses. Historical research remained centred on Paris, faithful to the long tradition of seeing everything through the eyes of the king in the capital where the seat of state power resided; although opposed to centralization, it responded to the process from the start. In contrast, geographical research, which had long established one of its most active centres at Grenoble, was being pursued at a number of provincial centres, and it was there, locally, that it was achieving success.

I am tempted here to turn to one of the most valuable sources of this new development, namely the recognition of regional history. Indeed, all the perspectives changed. Southern France, which had hitherto been greatly lacking in high-quality historiography, gradually emerged from the background. This challenged certain fundamental propositions. It was thus in the case of feudalism (I shall be using examples from my own field, the Middle Ages). Feudalism developed in the Frankish countries, between the Loire and the Rhine, on the ruins of the Carolingian monarchy. The results of recent surveys, some of which have been carried out in Catalonia and are quite remarkable, now suggest that the Midi did far more than passively receive forms of sociability originating in the north, and that some of the most decisive changes in social relations were no doubt tried out there first. At any rate, certain trends originated on the southern slopes of Gaul and left some of their major features on eleventh-century 'French' culture. I have in mind the movement of the Peace of God, the notion of monastic life as it was practised at Cluny, the so-called Gregorian ecclesiastical reform, and the methods of building and sculpting in stone which are known as Romanesque. This widening of the scope of research was already fully under way thirty years ago. Since then it has been consolidated.

More recently, other challenges have been issued to historians. These have come principally from linguistics and anthropology, the two disciplines which supplanted geography and took over from it in breaking new ground. The work of specialists in linguistics led to structuralism which, as we know, was a success for a while. By encouraging neglect of the changing in favour of the permanent, structuralism denied history. In any event, it marginalized history and provided a spur for historians. It is now clear that structuralism helped to gain an enormous amount of ground. It was an incentive for us to analyse more judiciously what we historians already called 'structures'. Its result was that some of us no longer limited our observations to relatively short periods, and we boldly began to study very long periods, shifting concepts from one period to another in order to distinguish what is constant from what is subject to change. The example of linguistics reinforced the tendency to examine more closely the formal surface of the texts.

In this way the challenge was taken up whilst fashions gradually changed, and in all the social sciences attention was once more focused on the throbbing pulse of society over a short period. From this brief crisis one fact emerges – namely, that no one in recent years has better served historians in determining the field of their investigation than Michel Foucault.

The sole exception is Claude Lévi-Strauss. Anthropology was advancing at the same pace as linguistics. Like the latter, its subject was principally systems, and it readily constructed models and applied itself to demonstrating the permanence of their structures. Furthermore ethnologists were still mainly studying exotic, 'cold' societies, which seem completely removed from history. The success of these studies and the favour which they very quickly won amongst the cultured public, also tended to relegate the work of historians to a subordinate role. Did Lévi-Strauss not urge them to follow a discipline which by then embraced all the others? Referring to Lucien Febvre's book, *Le Problème de l'incroyance au*

XVIème siècle, he observed that 'any good history book is imbued with ethnology' (*Anthropologie structurale*). This is indeed true and it made us very mindful of the methods and discoveries of social anthropology. Moreover, at that time decolonization forced a good number of ethnologists to focus on France, the 'mother country'. They chose the French countryside, and quite soon the towns, as their field of study. A 'French ethnology' developed which appropriated the pioneering role which had for a long time been assumed by human geography.

Over the past ten years the stimulus from these areas has been very strong. The most productive collaboration now appears to have been with the ethnologists. In recent historical research Jacques Le Goff's aim to construct a 'historical anthropology' appears to be the most innovative. However, when challenged in this manner, historians are forced to change their approach. The instruments of historical criticism were, in fact, forged to be applied to coherent descriptions of the vivid dynamic trends of a period. In order to understand properly the slow pace of events and to see what lies beneath the surface, we must use other material and treat the material with which we are familiar differently.

Thus while texts remain our principal source of information and history continues to base the core of its discourse on other discourses, I can perceive two recent changes which tend in opposite directions in the way these documents are treated, sifted through and challenged. In so far as history is interested in structural forms, in fairly small changes which take place over very long periods; in so far as it focuses its attention on the lower echelons of society, on those people who say little and the majority of whose words are lost; and in so far as what is commonplace and banal, whose memory no one dreams of preserving, seems more worthy than what creates a sensation, one must pursue a great many minor details which are barely distinguishable from each other and are scattered amongst archival bundles and registers. Thus, history, which has become a history of substance and of depth – in fact, multidimensional history – must accumulate an enormous quantity of documents of little value, and sift through many dull texts in order to extract a handful of statistical facts. It must count and calculate rates, and trace curves, and to this end arrange in a series a great many similar elements. In the early days of economic history, historians who analysed prices and salaries were soon to use this approach. The example of geographers and, later, specialists in linguistics, as well as the propensity of structural anthropology for mathematical models, led to the increasing use of statistics as a starting point, until a time came when everything was measured and quantified, when machines made these operations both easier and more precise. It was as if tables and graphs were going to play an innovative role in our disciplines in a similar manner to the *papier collé* used in collages in the period around 1910 when painting was in disarray. As positivism was beginning to lose ground, figures and decimal points gave the illusion of precision, that history can, after all, be a science. We now know that not everything is quantifiable, that an overabundance of numerical detail can be misleading. However, it is certain that historical knowledge would never have triumphed so spectacularly in recent times without using the methods of quantitative history.

It was of course historians of the early modern period, the sixteenth, seventeenth and eighteenth centuries, who led the way. The texts dating from this period lend themselves to this approach; there are a great number of them, but not too many, and for the most part they can be counted. At first fluctuations in the value of things, in the money market and in commerce were measured. By applying these methods to records of baptisms, marriages and burials in parish registers, historians soon began to study population movements. Thus demographic history triumphed, spreading the renown of the French school all over the world. Counting the number of engagements or deaths made one question whether such methods could not also help us to understand the non-material aspects of life better. It soon became clear that statistical analysis, no longer of the facts themselves but of the ritual formulas through which they were reported, could be very fruitful. Applying this method to a series of wills, for example, provided some very interesting information on how attitudes to death and the afterlife changed. Thus, quantitative history led to the history of behaviour and attitudes. Because their information is far less dense, and above all is too incomplete, medievalists and historians of antiquity cannot use these procedures in the same way. Nevertheless they realize that computers can become very effective tools for them and that it is useful to process some information by computer, such as data concerning objects discovered in excavations, for which there is no better method of classification, and especially for words. To dissect a vocabulary in this way, to count the instances of words and to evaluate their frequency enables us radically to refine traditional practices in textual criticism, to reveal distortions and interpolations, to specify dates and thus to prepare more accurate editions. In addition, the use of statistics helps us to grasp meaning and to master it better in its depth and its changeability.

It is precisely here that the first current, which I have just described, converges with that other current coming from the opposite direction to effect a transformation of historical method. This second current is a strong tendency to return, after long neglect, to the narrative elements of the written sources, because of the wealth and flavour of what the texts yield. This tendency leads one to reject the chronological approach to history when presented with a series of facts – in other words, to extract from the mass of information the text which is richest in expressive value and in density; and to extract the monumental from the commonplace. However, it is appropriate to read the privileged text in a different light. Historians did not invent these new methods of interpretation. They borrowed them from other social sciences, from social psychology, ethnology and linguistics – all still newcomers to this field. Thereafter language was treated as the raw material, so to speak. The emphasis was not so much on counting its elements as on taking apart its structures and comparing them. Meaning is apprehended from a different perspective, through topology, as it were, surveying its many fields and locating constellations of terms. It is here that history makes its specific contribution by seeking to discern how these sets of terms change in time. But it soon becomes clear that one should not rely on words alone, and that other signs, similarly treated, yield valuable information on the behaviour and mental attitudes of people living in earlier times, as well as on the overall development of a culture and of a social education. Today, historians are concerned with a far broader semiology. They are attempting to revitalize the study of heraldry, iconology, the history of family life and the history of costume by asking challenging questions. They are currently inventing a history of behaviour.

Historians have not remained completely deaf to Lucien Febvre's call, nearly half a century earlier, urging them to refer not solely to words but to the many other signs scattered amongst objects. Historical research in France owes a good deal of its recent success to the rapid growth of archaeology. This is a recent development. However, the sources available to excavators have not been appreciably increased. The success of archaeology is partly due to the vogue which this type of research has enjoyed and which, like the enthusiasm for rural anthropology, popular arts and traditions, and the fashion for second-hand goods, comes from a nostalgia for 'a lost world', which we imagine to be peaceful and ordered – the reassuring world of the countryside.

Its success is mainly due to the fact that its objective is no longer the same. It has ceased to focus solely on what is exceptional. To the aim of saving masterpieces has been added a concern to bring to light, to clean and accurately inventory all traces, even the minutest, of daily life. The project is to reconstruct, as they say in Eastern Europe, 'material culture'. French researchers have simply followed, with considerable delay, in the footsteps of Poland, Romania and Scandinavia. This took place in France almost thirty years ago. Archaeologists began to excavate the sites of fortresses in Normandy and villages in Burgundy, Aquitaine, Provence and Lorraine, sites abandoned after the Black Death or in the modern period. The archaeologists' discoveries contradicted theories which had hitherto been founded entirely on what had been learnt from the texts. This applied to fortified settlements. It had long been recognized that the system of political, economic and social relations which we refer to by the term 'feudalism' had been built around castles. From the archival documents these castles do not appear to be very numerous, yet in all the provinces where archaeological surveys have been carried out, it has emerged that there were a large number of 'mottes' (literally, clumps of earth), those artificial mounds which were built in the eleventh century to serve as foundations for fortifications. Perhaps we should now carefully reread the charters and check whether the place accorded to the knightly class in society is indeed what we have so far imagined it to be.

Another challenge issued by archaeologists resulted from the discovery of great numbers of fragments of pottery among the ruins of a small group of houses near a castle perched on a hilltop in Provence. These appear to have been imported from Italy, Spain and the Barbary coast. This alters our perception of the way currency and foreign goods were introduced into the countryside at the end of the Middle Ages. Finally, by measuring the skeletons exhumed from an old cemetery in the south-west of France it emerges that the peasants of the period had a very different physical constitution from the one that had been attributed to them: they were better fed, more robust, far less susceptible to deficiency diseases and able to live longer – all of which leads us to revise many of our views concerning the circulation of goods, demography, family kinship and, consequently, behaviour and attitudes.

Medieval history has so far benefited most from the contributions of an archaeology which is concerned with the everyday aspects of life. But there is increasing curiosity about the tools, the costumes, the emblems, and all the metaphorical descriptions which, in the past, men and women produced of their material existence and their dreams. These signs naturally increase as one approaches the modern period. They are everywhere, in the towns as well as in the countryside; there are still a great quantity of them, but they are under threat, and we are beginning to realize how fragile they are. Archaeologists have started to collect these remains, to classify and restore them. Industrial archaeology was thus established in the region of Le Creusot, following the example of experiments carried out for some time outside France. Elsewhere, there are collections of postcards showing the layout of villages, the interior of houses and people's physical postures, all revealing a different conception of the world, a value system which still prevailed until only recently, but which we did not realize had already been so utterly forgotten.

What has been modernized in the approach to history, in the manner in which sources of information are chosen and used, is closely linked with the way in which the historian constantly asks new questions. In the history of different societies, which is what we are all striving to produce, the place accorded to economics is relatively limited. At the time when *Annales* was founded, economic history played a major role and social history had a minor place. In the last thirty years the latter has very rapidly become more prominent – but not alone. It has at the same time promoted what Lucien Febvre called the 'history of civilizations.'

What about the history of culture? This expression is not much more helpful. It refers to those factors which are not concerned with the material aspect of life. The historians of antiquity and the historians of the early Middle Ages were largely responsible for the decline in the trend to explain things mainly in terms of economics. Indeed the documents which inform us about these periods provide very few facts which lend themselves to statistical analysis. Scholars of ancient and medieval history were therefore ready to hear Marcel Mauss, Veblen, Polanyi and representatives of the flourishing school of African studies in France. Moreover, they quickly came to see that, in this distant past, money occupied a far smaller position in social relations, that the commercial spirit exerted far less influence on behaviour than customs and beliefs. It soon became apparent that the founders of an economic history of the Middle Ages – historians as talented and as highly successful as Henri Pirenne – had allowed themselves to be drawn into an insidious form of anachronism which was very difficult to avoid: they had projected their vision of the world and their behaviour on to the past in order to interpret its traces. They had momentarily forgotten that things did not occur in exactly the same way in the past as they do today; that, for instance, in Ghent during the twelfth century neither money nor commerce had the same meaning as in the twentieth century; and that theories concerning the setting of prices, as explained by contemporary economists, cannot apply to social groups entrenched in ritualism, which do not, for example, share the same concept of the afterlife. In short, they had forgotten that capitalism belongs to the modern world and that it is not at home in other places and times. Therefore historians of the feudal period were forced to recognize that events had far less deliberate causes than they had imagined. They realized that they might not understand anything about the movement of goods if they failed to recognize that sometimes the pleasure of happily destroying wealth prevailed over the appeal of producing it; that in most societies the values of leisure outweighed by far the values of work; and that largesse, even squandering, is often placed at the top of the scale of virtues. In trade they had to acknowledge the dominance of the gift and the counter-gift over sale and purchase, and that the importance of the symbolical role of the monetary instrument resulted in an entirely new and far more accurate description of the mechanisms of feudal society. The revision of history is a gradual process: today, for example, we are in a better position to understand people's attitude towards property during the eleventh century, when we note that at that time the notions of joint possession and joint and several liability went far beyond the limits of the material sphere, that is to say the visible world.

This is perhaps what led historians to study one of the areas to which anthropology had introduced them, the analysis of kinship structures. The first studies on the history of the family were launched in France some twenty years ago. In no other field was such enormous progress made. Moreover, this research inspired great enthusiasm; the impetus came from the curiosity and concern aroused by the problems which today face our own society.

It is here that one can see, perhaps more clearly than elsewhere, how the preoccupations which trouble the historian may affect his or her choice of subject. It is certainly no coincidence that today, in 1980, there is so much interest in children in the reign of Louis XIV, in courtly love, in prostitution, in female factory workers during the Second Empire, in ladies and peasant women during the feudal period. At any rate, as we learn more about the nature of relationships which developed between a particular man and his forebears, his wife, his brothers, his cousins and his descendants, in (say) the eleventh or the seventeenth century, we come to view political, religious and economic events differently. Associating themselves with the efforts of some Marxist scholars of African studies, medievalists refined the concept of a familial means of production. They attempted to understand the distribution of tasks, profit and authority within this fundamental social unit formed by a kinship which was free to dispose of women as it wished, and which decided who to give them to in marriage; they attempted to measure what the dead were given to eat and drink. In so doing, they gradually uncovered the truth. The vast and overwhelming history of the family naturally forms part of the continuing successes achieved in demographic history. Historians have for a long time concerned themselves with death and marriage. Nowadays they view these events in a different light. They do not content themselves with simply providing statistics on mortality and the marriage rate in order to evaluate their effects on population growth or decline. They are more interested in the aspirations which governed attitudes, in codes, in prohibitions and their transgressions, in the hopes with which people deluded themselves, and in rituals.

Nowadays festivals have become a favourite theme in French historiography. Perhaps this is because it simultaneously discovered the fundamental importance of pleasure for its own sake and the importance of the family, and because ethnology and linguistics led it to observe mainly signs, emblems and behaviour. In the meantime, psychoanalysts required it to devote more and more space to anguish, desire and unconscious impulses. At any rate, we should not be surprised if historiographers scrutinize the ethereal quite so assiduously.

Studying the role of myth, ritual and the imagination in the development of human societies was undoubtedly facilitated once the concept of causality had gradually fallen out of favour. This process was itself hastened by the salutary efforts of the Marxists themselves in the 1950s to produce a critique of 'vulgar' forms of Marxian thought. At the same time factual history was also naturally receding into the background. What caused this event? It is difficult to pinpoint what gave rise to this imperceptible shift in structures. Delving into the depths of history, it becomes clear that the development of a social grouping is determined by countless factors acting in concert. These are themselves acted upon by other factors. How can one say which is the critical factor? It is perhaps futile to ask which one factor is the determining factor 'in the last resort'. Historians have resigned themselves to being able to gain only very incomplete and relative truths, and this conviction has compelled them to be cautious. They have thus persuaded themselves of the indivisible unity of influences. They believe that it serves no purpose whatsoever to struggle to adjust the links in a chain of cause and effect. Their endeavour is to penetrate the finer points of an interplay of correlations, of 'interconnections'; they wish to find logical links between contemporary branches of human activity; their hope is to reconstruct 'coherent and meaningful unities' (Marrou). More narrowly than ever before, their attention is therefore focused on interconnections and the processes which they involve; on how some events coexist, some react against one another and others merge by osmosis, as it were – which leads them to appropriate the concepts used by the exact sciences, the concept of membrane created by biologists, and the concept of interface created by physicists.

Such a shift in the approach adopted by historians in detecting this impalpable reality, the trail of what life was like in times past, has no doubt contributed to the success of a history of attitudes over the past twenty years. Today no historian would fail to acknowledge the need for anyone who wishes to understand a historical event to question what lies in the depths of individual consciousness, beneath active thought; to delve into this chaotic and yet coherent jumble of generally accepted ideas, of codes of conduct, of apparently unclear images whose structures are nevertheless solid enough to force the words to be associated in a particular way. These ideas teach us to behave in a certain manner; an entire vision of the world is based on them. Although they take a long time to change, attitudes are not permanent. It is up to the history of education (a history which is currently flourishing) and of all forms of education – education provided by schools or royal courts, what one learns from one's parish priest or one's grandmother, in the workshop or in the army – to help reveal what brings about changes in attitudes.

The term 'attitude' is undoubtedly an unsatisfactory one. The concept itself is not much more helpful. It needs refining, and this process is now under way. As methods become more precise, it is possible to employ a suitably rigorous approach to study the history of value systems. Research into the history of ideologies has also begun recently. It is fascinating to follow these elusive constructs in their imperceptible shift from century to century and to define their contours amid the scattered signs which make a particular piece of the edifice emerge from what can be deduced. It is a difficult undertaking since one has to extrapolate symbolic expressions from all the traces – irrespective of whether or not they are written traces – of the past. This approach leads historians to discover what interests are served by ideologies, and consequently the milieux which they reinforce and whose actions they justify. It helps them to discern the mediators responsible for their propagation and the devices used to impose them as well as the resistance which these groups arouse. In this way, the researcher moves towards areas where there is an intertwining of the links between what is dreamed and what is experienced, between the reality of material conditions, the idea which one forms of them and the utopian mirages which lead us to change them. In other words, this form of inquiry allows us to renew the statement of a fundamental issue, power, and the methods of political history are thereby updated. But the history of beliefs, fear and poverty which is beginning to be created, and the history of hope which really should be undertaken, may expect equal if not greater profit from the rapid shifts to which the historian's field of inquiry is currently subject. These shifts help to circumscribe the field of religion from age to age with far greater precision. Everything suggests that from this more exact demarcation the history of religions will emerge transformed as radically as economic history is in the process of becoming under the influence of observations on pleasure for pleasure's sake, leisure and the play element – that is to say on one of the aspects of what we refer to as attitudes.

The study of ideologies teaches us that in any moderately complex society there are several ideological systems, and that they are in permanent conflict. Every cultural group is heterogeneous. Historians have now realized this, and they believe that they must study different 'levels of culture' from the past. This metaphor is dangerous: it carries the risk of introducing the image of superimposed layers; it encourages us to compare these layers to the economic stratification of society. The fact is that it underlies a programme of research which can be regarded as the most original of the new French school of thought. I am referring to the attempts to update the old forms of a 'popular culture'.

This project has been under way for a long time. When Jacques Le Goff in 1964, after eloquently outlining the figure of the medieval intellectual, described Western civilization in the Middle Ages in a brilliant work of synthesis, he was firmly distancing himself from history viewed as a series of 'watersheds' and rejecting the cultural artefacts of the elite, the theological treatises, courtly display and cathedrals, in favour of what was buried, obscure and popular. He was one of the first to write prolifically about games, the devil, hunger and the forest, about trades, superstitions, eating habits and the maladies of soul and body. For this reason he became one of the most active supporters of an archaeology of material life and followed ethnology very attentively. He trained enthusiastic disciples who felt committed to a struggle to break away from the past. They wanted to allow the masses to speak, and stood up for them. They exposed the inordinate power which the monopoly of aristocratic learning, writing and all forms of expression capable of surviving down through the ages, gave the producers or proponents of the dominant ideology. It is not difficult to see how the awareness of our civilization's contradictions today goes hand in hand with the various changes which are currently revitalizing the methods of historical research and thus guiding the desire for knowledge.

This convergence of influences could serve as a perfect illustration of the notion of correlation. Indeed, young historians have been attracted by the work of the ethnologists, the close attention which they pay to non-written sources and the position which must be adopted to interpret these. They have followed the reflections on acculturation to which the recent transformations in colonialism have given rise. They have taken an interest in national resistance, imperialism, archaeological findings, the taste for rural life, regionalism and folklore. All these areas have combined to direct young historians towards the barely discernible forms of those cultures which managed to survive secretly despite being overshadowed by the apparatus of power on which attention had hitherto been focused.

A few carefully excavated items have already emerged. They need to be treated with great care; they must be sifted from the dross, their original colour restored, and the separated fragments compared in the hope of reconstructing sets of objects. Anyone who wishes to follow closely the manipulations to which this scant documentary evidence is subject and to get the measure of recent discoveries, should read Jean-Claude Schmitt's *Le Saint Lévrier*, published in 1979. It examines a thirteenth-century autobiographical text written by the Dominican monk Etienne de Bourbon. He recounts that he was preaching in the Dombes region, and peasant women penitents admitted to having sometimes visited the relics of Guignefort, a saint of whom he had never heard. He made inquiries and learned to his amazement that Guignefort was a martyred dog: the animal had fought to protect a baby, and its master, the father of the child, had killed it by mistake. Miracles had taken place at its tomb. Led by an old woman from the village, young mothers would expose their sickly nurslings there, waiting for some mysterious power to make them healthy. Etienne de Bourbon set about razing the site of this shrine in the belief that he was destroying their religious practices. Jean-Claude Schmitt has handled structural analysis with as much brilliance as the best semiologists, explored the site and the surrounding land as archaeologists do, questioned the local people as ethnologists have taught us to do, consulted folklore specialists and recorded their every comment. He has thus succeeded in reconstructing a coherent system of beliefs and rituals; their distorted reflection was handed down through a few Latin sentences written at the height of the campaign against superstition which was spearheaded by the Church authorities. He brought to light the mythical status which feudal power assumed in the minds of country people during the thirteenth century. Finally he traced, right up to the present day, what remains of these attitudes which, he asserted, were perpetuated in the same places despite all attempts at suppression. His work is exemplary – and not only because of what it tells us about ordinary people, which is fundamental. It also reveals to us what the most recent historical research has to offer.

The most visible traces of those ideologies whose rivals triumphed and gradually forced them into the least accessible parts of the cultural and social edifice, date from the period when they were suppressed. For it is the fire of controversy which illuminates them; they are known to us through the proclamations which denounce them, the justifications of their detractors, and the reasons adduced for their sentences. We see them through the eyes of their oppressors. They thus appear to be lacking in depth, as negatives. These ideologies are caricatured and distorted. In the meantime, to detect their existence, it is necessary to read between the lines. In such circumstances the historian, alerted through a careful study of the distortions which censorship today imposes on accounts, can use to best advantage another experience, that gained from the methods employed to analyse the subconscious. Like the psychoanalyst, he must try to discover the truth hidden beneath the unspoken. The demands of this deciphering process therefore call for an adaptation of the traditional methods of historical criticism. This is a necessary adjustment since, when the historian becomes the observer of ideologies, he must reverse the target of his attempts at objectivity. Positivist history tried to establish the truth of events. In this case the events mattered far less than the way they were described, at the time or later. When the evidence is put to the test, it is not a question of separating out what is true from what is untrue in the attempt to be convincing. The evidence puts itself to the test, by what it reveals of the personality of the witness, by what he or she hides or forgets as much as by what it asserts and the way it asserts it.

This rigour in handling information is particularly important when one examines texts which reveal certain aspects of popular culture. Indeed, the expressions of this culture were, until very recently, either objects – the majority of which soon decay – or spoken words which are lost. The voice of ordinary people is rarely heard. Everything we know about them comes through intermediaries who have transcribed what they have learned from hearsay. Their role is of the utmost importance. One must congratulate the organizers of a conference at Aix-en-Provence which recently drew attention to these teachers, preachers and doctors, all of whom were notables from small towns, themselves educated, who set about collecting the details of the lives of less educated men and women. They were the principal channels in the process of acculturation. They were instrumental in disseminating knowledge, customs and fashions which a widespread process of imitation diffused from the upper down to the lower echelons of society. In return, they introduced the 'elites' to those simple ornaments which appealed to the tasteful populism of 'respectable' people. In this second role they provide us with information: we owe everything to the reports which they wrote, to the collections which they built up.

The practice of ethnology puts us on our guard: the process of handing down information over the ages does not take place without the message being more or less distorted. The mediator is never neutral. His own culture influences what he reports, and the traces are even more distorted the more the witness is educated or thinks he is. With the great sense of freedom which he gained from the feeling of dominating from the height of his knowledge, he becomes involved in interpreting the fragile cultural objects which he collects. Because he was partial, it is quite evident that Etienne de Bourbon unconsciously distorted what he had learnt of the cult of St Guignefort from informants who, themselves, had distorted the facts out of fear. But six centuries later, the distortion was no less marked in what was said by the local scholar who was questioned by Jean-Claude Schmitt and who was also partial. Why is he not criticized so punctiliously? Historians of popular culture have perfected the instruments which enable them to obtain and to examine closely the scant information been handed down to them over the centuries. It is worth reminding them that they should be equally, if not more, wary of nineteenth-century folklorists who talked profusely. They should not forget either that everything that it has been possible to gather of the popular arts and traditions dates from the same period, the nineteenth century, and comes not from the villages but from the towns. They should bear in mind that many of these traces have been tampered with, and that it is dangerous to assume that they can inform us reliably about what country people thought and felt one hundred, three hundred, or even nine hundred years previously. Imagining popular culture as unchanging is an affront to ordinary people and treats them as if they were idiots. Their culture is alive and it, too, lasts and is transformed by time.

The final shift which I shall note concerns the attitude of historians towards events. Under the rigorous teachings of the *Annales* 'school' (can one use this expression ? Was it ever really a school?), the habit set in to affect indifference when it came to surface details, to the accidents and epiphenomena which form the spasm-like movement of events. Indeed, Fernand Braudel's work is evidence of this – and no sooner had the great bastions of traditional history been demolished than *Annales* no longer required historians to scorn events. However, it encouraged the current tendency to examine events more closely in order to investigate how they fit into the more stable structures on which they are based, which cause them to erupt and on which their influence rebounds. We should not talk about a rehabilitation of factual history too soon. It is not for its own sake that historians take the event apart and analyse it, but for what it reveals, for the upheaval which it causes, and without which it would remain unnoticed. We are more interested in the repercussions of an event than in the event itself – those ripples which normally elude the historian's observation now come to the surface. Indeed events trigger off a torrent of speech; they recount the unusual; but if one is attentive one can catch some words which reveal underlying structures.

I myself have used the accounts of the Battle of Bouvines to attempt a sort of sociology of medieval war and, measuring the repercussions of the event from generation to generation, both to refine a geography of political awareness and to probe the flexibility of the collective memory. Emmanuel Le Roy Ladurie provides a most illuminating example of this. He is known for his work of measuring the very slow, imperceptible movement of climatic differences, and for his far-reaching studies over that extensive phase of French peasant culture, the period of stability between the fourteenth and eighteenth centuries which makes us regard Restif de la Bretonne as the close cousin of the villagers of Montaillou. In his inaugural lecture at the Collège de France, Le Roy Ladurie defended unchanging history. Nevertheless he chose to study a very short period – the disturbances which marked the carnival festivities in the town of Romans at the end of the sixteenth century – because these disturbances were recounted, and because these more or less truthful accounts provide the means of understanding elusive situations which were, strictly speaking, as old as time itself – such as rivalries between the town and the countryside, or the gestures performed without a thought during the festivals which ritually marked the end of winter. By contrast, François Furet, in a reappraisal of that highly complex event that constituted the French Revolution, invites us in his splendid book to re-examine what we thought we knew about the links between politics and the structures of society.

I have painted the picture of a renewal of French history, in broad outlines. I have emphasized what are, in my opinion, the most significant trends. I am aware that there is much subjectivity in what I say, in the opinions I express and the judgements which I have made. But it must be granted that the results are very positive. Perhaps my readers expect me, before I close, to say something about the shortcomings of historical research and to pinpoint the areas of inertia, the recesses where routine has set in. I could, for example, deplore the fact that biography – which is, in fact, one of the most difficult historical genres – has been so neglected by professional historians over the past thirty years. This is unfortunate since the great man, or the average man, who by chance said a great deal or of whom a great deal has been said, is as revealing as events are. We gain information from all the statements, descriptions and illustrations of which he is unintentionally the subject, and from the consequences of his words and actions. I could say that, compared to the history of the early modern period and the history of the Middle Ages where Lucien Febvre and Marc Bloch, drawing on the natural wealth of documents, were responsible for rigorously promoting the development of the subject (not to mention ancient history which is also flourishing and has some very special links with philology and archaeology), contemporary history in France might seem very much neglected. It is as if research in this field has long been obstructed by the vitality of today's social sciences, by economics, sociology and social psychology; it is as if historians have had to content themselves with what has been rejected, the event alone, the political aspect. But I will immediately add that all this has changed very recently: institutions have been set up and teams of researchers have been assembled, headed by some very talented leaders. They are rapidly making up for lost time.

Finally, I could point to some obstacles which have checked the vitality of our research. I shall indicate two major hindrances. The new research tools represent the first obstacle. It costs time and money to set up an excavation site and to carry out, as is necessary, an expert stratigraphic study; to restore and to classify a collection of objects, to analyse an archive collection using a computer or a particular method of analysis.

Consequently the field of inquiry is narrowed, and the area of study becomes weakened and fragmented. This leads to the kind of short-sightedness which so many history doctorates in America unfortunately display. The exploration of the site of old Rougiers, a town in Provence abandoned since the end of the Middle Ages, has produced splendid results. They are the fruit of a project which has taken nearly twenty years to complete, using as many resources as it was possible to collect. In order to check the results and to disseminate them, it was clearly not feasible to extend the research further and to excavate neighbouring sites, as would have been desirable.

The other obstacle comes from the compartmentalization of research institutions. In French universities, in the Centre National de la Recherche Scientifique, not all the barriers which separate the disciplines have been removed or even lowered. There are still some very specialized, self-contained disciplines where historians of literature, historians of music, philosophy and the sciences continue to closet themselves – some seem reluctant to meet any of their fellow historians. History – and this is where its strength lies today – requires dialogue. It regards a song, a fresco, a poem or the decor of a ballet as documents which are as valuable as a collection of charters or a newspaper editorial. It is still necessary to pursue greater freedom in the circulation of information and ideas. Half a century after the foundation of *Annales*, many confident and determined people are continuing the fight.

Notes

Chapter 1   Marriage in Early Medieval Society

1 *Regula Pastoralis*, III.27, *PL* 77, 102.
2 *Liber II de virtutibus sancti Martini, MGH, SRM*, I.617.
3 'Prius Ecclesiae quam laeserant satisfacerent, sic demum quod prae-cipiant jura legum mundialium exsequi procurarent', *PL*, 126, 26.
4 *Admonitio generalis*, 789, cap. 68; *MGH*, cap. I.59.
5 *Cap. missorum, 802*, cap. 35; *MGH*, cap. I.98.
6 Verneuil Synod, *MGH*, cap. I.36.
7 Bavarian Synod, 743; *MGH Conc.*, II.53.
8 D. Owen Hughes, 'Urban Growth and Family Structure in Medieval Genoa', *Past and Present* (1975).
9 H. Oschinsky, *Der Ritter unterwegs und die Pflege der Gastfreundschaft in alten Frankreich*, unpublished dissertation (Halle, 1900).
10 For the case of Lambert de Wattreloos, see G. Duby, 'Structures de parenté et noblesse dans la France du Nord. XIe – XIIe siècle', *Mélanges J. F. Niermeyer* (Groningen, 1967).
11 *Patrologia Latina* (PL), CLV. 2011.
12 J. -B. Molin and P. Mutembe, *Le Rituel de mariage en France du XIIe au XVIe siècle* (Paris, 1974), p. 50.
13 *PL*, 176, 184.
14 Cap. 149, *MGH, SS*, XXIV.637, 8.
15 *Historia comitum Ghisnensium*, cap. 86; *MGH, SS*, XXIV.601.

Chapter 3   The Matron and the Mismarried Woman

1   *Acta sanctorum*, Aprilis, I, pp. 141–4.

2   He was in actual fact a descendant of the Carolingians through his mother, the granddaughter of Charles of Lorraine. Virtually nothing is known of his father, who was probably an *homme nouveau*.

3   This is how she appears in the genealogies of the counts of Boulogne, excellently edited by L. Génicot (*Etudes sur les principautés lotharingiennes*, Louvain, 1975). The earliest version dates from 1082–7, when her second son, Godfrey, was not yet heir to anything but the name and the ambitions of his grandfather and maternal uncle. Ida is the only female character to merit an individual eulogy in these genealogies.

4   Legends flourished round the person of the first protector of the Holy Sepulchre. 'The story of the swan from which their dynasty is said to have issued' was told about him and his brother as early as 1184: William of Tyre, *Histoire des Croisades*, I, pp. 571–2.

5   D. Baker, 'A Nursery of Saints: Saint Margaret of Scotland reconsidered', in *Mediaeval Women* (Oxford, 1978).

6   *Acta sanctorum*, Julii II, pp. 403ff.

7   Edited by Fr Coens from a Saint-Omer manuscript emanating from the abbey of Clairmarais: *La Vie ancienne de sainte Godelive de Ghistelles par Drogon de Bergues*, ed. M. Coens (*Analecta Bollandiana*, XLIV, 1926).

8   He was the younger son (a cadet and consequently seeking to establish himself by marriage) of a comital officer settled at Bruges. In 1012 the castellan of Bruges was called Bertulf. In 1067 Erembald, the father of a different Bertulf, held the same office. The hero of this story, therefore, probably belonged to the famous clan whose members assassinated Charles the Good in 1127, and not to the family of Conon, lord of Oudenburg and nephew of Radebod II.

9   The expression *justitia christianitatis* appears at the same period in a charter from the Mâconnais in connection with a division of jurisdiction between a count and a bishop: *Cartulaire de Saint-Vincent de Mâcon*, ed. C. Ragut (Mâcon, 1864), no. 589.

10   *Vita Arnulfi*, II.16; *PL*, CLXXIV (Paris, 1854), col. 1413.

11   At a conference held in 1970 on the two texts of the life of Godelive which I have been using some detailed comments were made, notably by H. Platelle. The proceedings were published in *Sacris Erudiri*, 20 (1971). My own interpretation differs somewhat from the majority of views expressed there.

Chapter 4   On Courtly Love

1   [Translator's note] A method of trial in which the guilt or innocence of an accused person was determined by subjecting him to physical danger, especially by fire or water. The outcome was regarded as an indication of divine judgement.

Chapter 6   Towards a History of Women in France and Spain

1   This chapter is the text of a speech delivered at the close of a conference in Madrid in 1985.

Chapter 7   Family Structures in the West during the Middle Ages

1   The best survey of this question in the thirteenth century is L. Génicot, *Le XIIIe Siècle européen* (Paris, 1968), pp. 320–2.
2   K. Schmid, 'Zur Problematik von Familie, Sippe und Geschlecht, Haus und Dynastie, beim mittelalterlichen Adel', *Zeitschrift für die Geschichte des Oberrheins*, 105 (1957); G. Duby, 'Structure de parenté et noblesse dans la France du Nord, XIe–XIIe siècles', *Mélanges J. F. Niermeyer* (Groningen, 1967).
3   G. Duby, *Noblesse, lignage et chevalerie dans le sud de la Bourgogne (Xe–XIe siècle)*.
4   G. Duby, 'Remarques sur la littérature généalogique en France aux XIe et XIIe siècles', *Comptes rendus de l'Académie des inscriptions et belles lettres*, p. 967.
5   R. Fossier, *La Terre et les hommes en Picardie jusqu'à la fin du XIIIe siècle*, Paris and Louvain, 1969, pp. 262–73.
6   H. E. Hallam, 'Some Thirteenth Century Censures', *Economic History Review* (1958).
7   By D. Herlihy and Ch. Klappisch.

Chapter 8   The Relationship between Aristocratic Family and State Structures in Eleventh-Century France

1   K. Schmid, *Studien in Vorarbeiten zur Geschichte des grossfränkischen Adels* (Freiburg–i.–B. 1957); *Zur Problematik von Familie, Sippe und Geschlecht,*

Haus und Dynastie beim mittelalterlichen Adel; 'Adel und Herrschaft im Mittelalter', *Zeitschrift für die Geschichte des Oberrheins*, 105 (1957).

Chapter 9   Philip Augustus's France: Social Changes in Aristocratic Circles

1 W. M. Newman, *Les Seigneurs de Nesle en Picardie, XIIe–XIIIe siècle* (Paris, 1971); E. Bournazel, *Le Gouvernement capétien au XIIe siècle, 1100–1180* (Paris, 1975); T. Evergates, *Feudal Society of the Bailliage of Troyes under the Counts of Champagne, 1152–1284* (Baltimore, 1975); M. Parisse, *La Noblesse lorraine, XIe–XIIe siècle* (Lille, 1976); Y. Sassier, *Recherches sur le pouvoir comtal en Auxerrois du Xe au début du XIIe siècle* (Paris, 1980).

2 V. Cirlot, *El armamento catalan de los siglos XI al XIV*, unpublished thesis presented at the Independent University of Barcelona in 1980.

3 C. Bouchard, 'The Structure of a Twelfth Century French Family, the Lords of Seignelay', *Viator*, 10 (1979).

4 [Translator's note] Division of the inheritance between several brothers who were, however, obliged to retain their share in fief from the eldest brother.

Chapter 10   Problems and Methods in Cultural History

1 Tihany, October 1977.

Chapter 11   The History of Value Systems

1 [Translator's note] Twelfth-century Italian mystic.

2 'In Memoria del Manifesto dei comunisti', *Saggi nel materialismo* (Rome, 1964), p. 34.

Chapter 12   The Renaissance of the Twelfth Century: Audience and Patronage

1 Arnold of Bonneval, *S. Bernardi vita prima*, 2, 5.

2 *Chronica de gestis consulum andegavorum*, ed. L. Halphen and K. Porepar-

din; *Chroniques des comtes d'Anjou et des seigneurs d'Amboise* (Paris, 1913), pp. 140–1.

3 *Historia Gaufredi ducis*, p. 218.
4 *Historia comitum ghisnensium*, MGH, SS, XXIV, pp. 80–1.

Chapter 13   Observations on Physical Pain in the Middle Ages

1 This lecture was delivered in Warsaw in 1985.

Chapter 14   Memories without Historians

1 G. Duby, 'Remarques sur la littérature généalogique en France aux XIe et XIIe siècles', in *Hommes et structures du Moyen Age* (Paris, 1973), pp. 287–98.
2 G. Duby, 'Structures de parenté et noblesse dans la France du Nord aux XIe et XIIe siècles', pp. 267–86.

Chapter 15   Heresies and Societies in Preindustrial Europe between the Eleventh and Eighteenth Centuries

1 Royaumont, 1968.
2 [Translator's note] A Bulgarian sect holding that God had two sons, Satan and Christ, which took root as the dualist Cathar heresy.
3 [Translator's note] Eighteenth-century Judaeo-Christian heresy founded by Julius Frank.

Chapter 16   Trends in Historical Research in France, 1950–1980

1 Written in 1980.

Index

Baldwin, count, erudition of
166–7
Baldwin VI of Hainaut   30–1
Barthélemy, D.   120
béguinages   98
Beguines   53–4
Benedictines   37–8, 43, 45, 131
see also Cluny
benefices, system   107
Beranger of Tours   142
Bernard of Clairvaux, St   143,
155, 157, 164, 190
Bertulf   47–52
bishops   12, 36–7, 45, 50, 52,
55
Bloch, Marc   195, 197, 215
blood ties *see* family structures
body, and soul   27–9
Bologna   84
Bonaventure, St   86, 143
Bouchard, C.   123
Boulogne, counts of   39, 40
see also Ida of Boulogne
bourgeoisie   61, 80, 81, 110–11,
154, 158, 160
Bournazel, E.   120
Bowden, Betsy   58
Braudel, Fernand   197, 213
buildings and architecture   82,
131, 146, 155, 157
see also Cistercians; Clairvaux;
Cluny; Paris, Notre-Dame
Burgundy   108

Cambrai   119, 182
'Capuchon' movement   122
caritas (affection)   23, 25, 27, 59
Carolingian era   12, 16, 66
castellanies   114, 116, 117,
118–19
castles and fortified manors
125, 203
Catharism   17, 90, 190
Champagne, count of   155, 157,
158, 165
Chanson de Roland   162–3

chastity   39–40
children
boys' upbringing   60, 96, 97
and transmission of culture
175–6
chivalric culture *see* knights
Chrétien de Troyes   20, 74, 80,
82
Christianity
as 'popular' religion   86
'bookishness' of   175
and family structures   105
feminized   99–100
and homage to the dead   38,
45, 55, 177–8, 211
new face of   85–7, 90, 143–4
slow spread of   136–7
see also Church
Christine de Pisan   93, 96
Church
cultural monopoly challenged
152
improved administration
154–5
marriage model   10–11,
17–18, 19
motives for opposing the   190
and secular aristocracy   6–7,
11–13, 37, 43–4, 54, 75–6
see also bishops; clergy; heresy;
orthodoxy; popes
Cirlot, V.   121
Cistercians   27, 89, 90, 130–1,
153, 155, 157, 158
civil society, basis   98
Clairvaux   155
see also Bernard
classical authors   10, 22, 62,
67–8, 77, 88, 91, 137, 143,
144, 163
classification, enthusiasm for   87
clergy
attempts to control knights   67
lord enrolled from   164
marriage of   16, 18, 36
see also education; tutors

kings of France   84, 155–6, 165
see also Louis VII; Louis IX;
    Philip I; Philip II
kinship
'horizontal' and 'vertical'
    structures 106–12,
    117–18, 206
see also family structures;
    genealogies
knights
challenged by adventurers
    122
concept and values   73,
    79–80, 152
and courtly love   59, 61
dubbing of   70, 116, 122,
    152, 158, 180
education 68
elevation of   122–3
and learning 158
order of 152
origin 66–7
and pleasure   73, 75–6
see also courtly love; 'youth'
Lambert of Ardres   18, 34–5,
    165–6
see also Guînes, counts of
language 'forms'   131–2
largesse, aristocratic   66–7,
    69–71, 125, 161
laudatio parentum 108
law, historians of   105–6
Le Goff, Jacques   45, 53, 200,
    209–10
Le Roy Ladurie, Emmanuel   214
Lemarignier, Jean-François   114,
    120–1
Lévi-Strauss, Claude   199
L'Histoire et ses méthodes   195–6
Liaisons dangereuses (Laclos)   32
lineages see genealogies
linguistics 199
literature, chivalry and   68
logic, and the truth   142
Lopez, Carmen   96
lords, rural, see seigneurs

Lorraine 121
Louis VII: 157
Louis IX (Saint)   65, 83, 85, 90
clerical and knightly cultures
    under 78
household of 84
love, admissibility in marriage
    20, 32, 79
love and affection see affectio;
    amicitia; amor; caritas; dilectio

Mâcon   117, 118–19, 150
magic and sorcery   52, 54
Manichaeism 91
manners   80, 161
manumission 83
Marchello-Nizia, Christiane   62
Margaret of Scotland, St   42
market economy see trade
marriage
arranging a   8–9, 24
austerity in 98
ceremony   8–9, 11, 18
Church model   10–11, 17–18,
    19
corrupt 44–54
dichotomies   27–8, 31–2
importance of 25
as institution   3–4, 32
'market' 14–15
problems in studying
    medieval 4–6
as sacrament 17
wedding ceremony   9, 11, 13,
    16–19, 26, 60
Marrou, Henri Iréné   196, 208
martyrs   46, 52, 171
Marxism   133, 145–6, 206, 207
Matilda of Boulogne   42
memories see oral tradition
mendicant orders 92
see also Dominicans;
    Franciscans
mercenaries   79, 121–2
middle classes see bourgeoisie